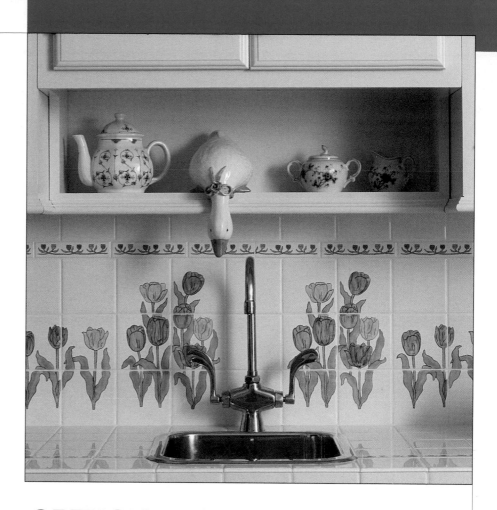

ORTHO'S HOME REPAIR PROBLEM SOLVER
STRUCTURAL EDITION

Created and Designed by the Editorial Staff of Ortho® Books

Writers
Robert J. Beckstrom
Jeff Beneke
Matt Phair
Naomi Wise

Project Editor
Sally W. Smith

Illustration Manager
Cyndie C. H. Wooley

Designers
Barbara Ziller and John Williams, Barbara Ziller Design

ORTHO® BOOKS

Publisher
Robert B. Loperena

Editorial Director
Christine Jordan

Manufacturing Manager
Ernie Tasaki

Managing Editor
Sally W. Smith

Editor
Robert J. Beckstrom

Prepress Supervisor
Linda M. Bouchard

Editorial Assistants
Joni Christiansen
Sally J. French

Editorial Coordinator
Cass Dempsey

Copyeditor
Elizabeth von Radics

Proofreader
David Sweet

Indexer
Frances Bowles

Special Thanks to
Maja Beckstrom
Deborah Cowder
David Van Ness

Photographers
Laurie A. Black, page 5d
Saxon Holt, page 111
Fred Lyon, pages 5e, 153
Ortho Library, page 7
Brent Lindstrom, front cover
Geoffrey Nilsen, pages 13 and 81
Joyce OudkerkPool, page 5a
Kenneth Rice, pages 1, 5b
Sepp Seitz/Woodfin Camp, page 5c

Art Director, Cover
Barbara Ziller

**Design Director,
Special Edition**
Tim Abramowitz

Technical Consultants
Dan Fuller
Michael Hamman
Redwood Kardon

Illustrators
Edith Allgood
William Barrett, William Barrett
    Design
Jonathan Clark, Dart
Wayne S. Clark
Deborah Cowder, Indigo Design
    & Imaging
Tim Graveson, Pandion
    Productions
Dillon Riley
Hal Lewis and Andrew Richards,
    Apple-day
Elizabeth Morales and Jim Roberts
Jenny Page and George Vrana,
    Illustrious, Inc.
Cyndie C.H. Wooley

Address all inquiries to:

Meredith Corporation
Ortho Books
1716 Locust St.
Des Moines, IA 50309–3023

If you would like more information on other Ortho products, call 800/225-2883 or visit: www.ortho.com

Copyright © 1995
The Scotts Company
All rights reserved under international and Pan-American copyright conventions.

1   2   3   4   5   6   7   8   9
95   96   97   98   99   2000

ISBN 0-89721-468-4

ORTHO'S
Home Repair Problem Solver
Structural Edition

Special Edition for
Handyman Club of America

Created and Designed by the editorial staff of ORTHO® Books

Project Editor
Alan Ahlstrand

Writers
Robert J. Beckstrom
John Reed

Handyman Club Library™
Handyman Club of America
Minneapolis, Minnesota

▶ Look up the problem and read how to fix it.

The purpose of this book is to help you solve problems and get on with your life, not do major home improvements. In its four chapters are solutions to more than 700 problems. Each chapter covers an easy-to-recognize area or system of the home. Each unit covers one problem (… has a crack, … won't ring, … leaks). Similar problems are grouped together. If you are not sure in which chapter and category to find your problem, consult the Index (page 172).

After you find the problem and read the solution, you may still want more information. There are four more places to look.

• Descriptions of similar problems are usually within a page or two of the problem you've looked up.

• The Appendix, beginning on page 154, has tables, lists, and other general information that is not covered under specific problems.

• Home Repair Terms, beginning on page 164, provides definitions of terms that may give you new clues about solving your problem.

• The Index, beginning on page 172, makes it easy to look up additional words or terms related to your problem.

▶ Keys to solving any home repair problem.

• Trust your common sense. This book is a useful guide, but you may figure out a better way to do something once you understand the basic principles. There is more than one way to solve most problems.

• Think of a project as a series of small steps. This makes a problem seem less overwhelming, so it's easier to get started.

• Allow plenty of time. Most repairs end up taking longer than you think they will.

• Remember how things are put together as you take them apart. Draw diagrams, make lists, or lay out disassembled parts in an orderly sequence.

• Assume that you will need to make at least one trip to the store. Therefore, don't start a repair late at night or when it will be inconvenient to make the trip.

• Find the right store. A full-range hardware store or home center will supply most needs, but if you can't find what you need there, don't give up. Many people are not aware of specialty outlets or suppliers who deal with the trades. They include appliance service centers, plumbing-supply houses, plumbing contractor showrooms, electrical-supply houses, architectural salvage yards, tile shops, paint and wallpaper dealers, stores for woodworkers and other hobbyists, and specialty lumber yards, such as a hardwood dealer.

• Take the old part to the store with you, or make a diagram of what you think you need, with accurate dimensions.

• Dress appropriately. Put on work clothes before you start, not when it's too late. Wear soft-soled shoes when working on the roof. Have safety goggles, gloves, and a dust mask handy at all times, and use them.

• Get proper permits when required. Many repairs do not require a permit, but any project that involves moving pipes or wires, installing new fixtures, altering walls, building certain outdoor structures, replacing a roof, or exceeding a certain dollar amount ($200 is typical for most communities) may require a permit. Consult the local building-inspection department before proceeding.

• Use the right tool. Some tasks that seem complicated are actually quite simple if you use the correct tool. A basic tool kit (see page 154) is sufficient for most repairs, but if you don't have the right tool, buy, rent, or borrow it. Check the hardware store for variations on common tools. All screwdrivers—or paintbrushes or putty knives or whatever—are not the same; you may think the one you have is fine, but a little investigation may reveal that one of a different size or shape will make the job much easier. See pages 154 and 155 for some ideas on building your own basic (or advanced) tool kit.

• Store your tools where you can find them. Many repairs never get done because it's too much hassle looking for the tools.

• Make time for safety. It takes very little time to secure a ladder, keep the work area clean, turn off a circuit breaker, open a window for ventilation, remove a nail, put on safety glasses, or unplug a power tool while changing blades. Don't think just about getting the job done; think about getting it done safely.

Tip *If your home is under any kind of warranty, do not undertake any repairs without calling a professional first; your repairs may void the warranty.*

Before taking any other steps to make your home comfortable, beautiful, and problem-free, learn what to do in an emergency. In addition to the information and prevention tips presented in this chapter, you will find tips throughout the book for working safely as you make repairs around the home.

▶ *House is on fire.*

Get everyone out fast. Crawl if there is smoke. Call from a neighbor's house (or grab the cordless phone on your way out). Don't go back in; let firefighters handle rescues. Fire spreads through a home astonishingly fast. The biggest danger is smoke asphyxiation.

Evacuating the house

Phoning fire department

▶ *Chimney has fire.*

A chimney fire makes a loud, roaring sound and is incredibly hot (2,000° F or more). It is probably visible from the street. Evacuate the house. After calling fire department from neighbor's house, hose down the roof.

Some experts recommend, if you have time, closing the damper of a woodstove or smothering the fireplace fire with a fire extinguisher or huge amounts of coarse salt; never douse it with water.

Don't use the fireplace or woodstove again until you have the chimney inspected and cleaned.

▶ *Roof is on fire.*

Evacuate everyone and call the fire department.

▶ *Smoke is emerging from around chimney area.*

Extinguish the fireplace fire or close the woodstove damper. Call the fire department. The smoke may be from the fireplace, escaping through cracks in the brick chimney, or it may be from smoldering framing that could erupt into flames. Evacuate if you see flames. Do not reuse the fireplace until the chimney is inspected and repaired.

▶ *Clothes are on fire.*

Drop and roll. Do not run. If possible, smother fire with a blanket.

Dropping and rolling

Using a blanket

▶ *House has small fire.*

Get everyone out of the house. Call fire department. If you can do it safely, return and use a Class-ABC fire extinguisher, aiming toward the base of the fire. Stay between the fire and a safe exit. If you don't extinguish the fire immediately, get out.

Using a fire extinguisher

▶ *Oven has fire.*

Turn off heat. Leave it alone. Don't open the oven door until oven has cooled down. Keep watch.

Tip *With your entire family, plan escape routes ahead of time, especially from bedrooms. Establish a meeting place, usually the front of the home, and designate a person to notify neighbors and call for help.*

Tip *Chief causes of home fires: (1) cooktop flare-ups, (2) falling asleep while smoking, (3) fireplace, woodstove, or kerosene heater, (4) playing with matches, and (5) faulty electrical system or equipment.*

▶ Cooktop has grease fire.

Turn off heat. Smother fire quickly with a large lid, use Class-B fire extinguisher, or throw baking soda or salt on the fire (*never* water, flour, or sugar). Call for help if you don't extinguish the fire immediately.

Smothering a range-top fire

Oven mitt

▶ Electrical appliance or receptacle is smoking, sparking, or on fire.

If it's only sparking or smoking, unplug the appliance or turn off the circuit breaker. Have it repaired before using it again.

If the appliance is on fire, evacuate the house, call fire department, and use Class-C fire extinguisher. *Never* use water—it could conduct electricity to you.

Extinguishing an appliance fire

▶ Fire has damaged house.

Secure the house (board up windows, repair the roof). Remove debris. Store damaged but salvageable items in a safe place. Protect the plumbing system against freezing. Inspect the electrical system before using it. Clean up. Air out carpets and furnishings damaged by water. Take smoke-tainted clothes and fabrics to a dry cleaner with an ozone chamber. Place smoke-tainted books and valuable papers in a freezer until a time when you can have them professionally cared for. Open up walls and other covered areas where water may have caused hidden damage. It's necessary to air them out to prevent rotting. Often, more damage is done by water inside walls than from the fire itself, so make every effort to dry out the house thoroughly, including pumping the basement or crawl space.

Cleaning up after a fire

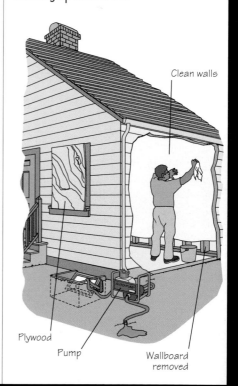

Clean walls

Plywood

Pump

Wallboard removed

Tip *When phoning 9-1-1 or other emergency numbers, don't hang up until told to do so. You may be asked for additional critical information.*

Tip *Do not empty ashtrays into wastebaskets. Use a metal trash can, a container of water, or other nonflammable receptacle for this purpose.*

Fire safety equipment.

■ *Smoke detectors: At least one for each floor. Critical areas are kitchen, rooms with fireplaces, hallway near sleeping rooms, and top of basement stairs. Combination of "hard-wired" and battery-operated types is recommended.*

■ *Extinguishers: Have several (kitchen, basement, shop, smoking areas, each floor). Locate near the room's <u>exit</u>, so you can grab it on your way back <u>into</u> the room after evacuating the house. For all-around use, keep a Class-ABC on hand. For specific uses:*

> *Class-A: paper, wood, cloth, rubber, dry materials*
> *Class-B: oil, grease, gasoline, flammable liquids*
> *Class-C: electrical*

■ *Emergency lights: Place flashlights with fresh batteries by beds, in kitchen, in basement, and in other areas of house. You may also want to get lights that stay plugged into electrical receptacles and which go on only in a power failure.*

■ *Escape ladder (chain ladder that hangs from a windowsill): Locate in any upstairs bedroom that does not have two easy escape routes.*

■ *Sprinklers: Consider them if you are planning a remodeling project, especially if your household includes small children or elderly persons.*

Locating smoke detectors

Avoid this area

3'

4"
4"

Locating a fire extinguisher

Using an escape ladder

Store under bed

Tip *Most fires start at night during sleeping hours. Rooms where most fires start: (1) kitchen, (2) bedrooms, and (3) heater closet or room. Rooms where most deaths occur by fire: (1) living/family room and (2) bedroom. At greatest risk are children under 10 and adults over 65.*

▶ *House has gas odor.*

Very dangerous. Evacuate house immediately, leaving doors open as you go. Call gas company or 9-1-1 from neighbor's house.

If odor is only slight, turn off gas at meter. Open windows and doors. Do not light match, use phone, switch on lights, or do anything that causes sparks or friction. Get out. Call gas company or 9-1-1 from neighbor's house.

If gas is bottled propane (LP), it is heavy and will settle to floor or basement area; things will seem normal at nose level. Do not re-enter house—and especially don't relight pilots—until you are sure the gas has dissipated. Bottled gas ignites more readily than natural gas and is much more explosive.

Turning off natural gas

Turning off liquid gas

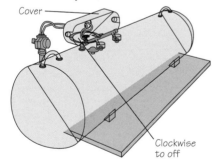

▶ *You smell fumes.*

It's probably improper venting or backdrafting of a gas appliance (in backdrafting, flue gases are forced back down the flue because of unbalanced air pressure, a common occurrence with tightly insulated homes). Although not an immediate problem unless it is highly concentrated in a confined area, this condition is still a serious safety hazard. (The most dangerous component, carbon monoxide, is odorless.) For immediate relief, ventilate the house. Don't operate exhaust fans (such as a kitchen hood or bathroom fan) without opening a window or door first; it will only exacerbate the problem.

For a long-range solution, make sure every gas appliance has a flue to the outdoors and an adequate supply of fresh combustion air. Test by holding a smoking match or incense next to the flue intake while the appliance burner is on; the smoke should be sucked up the flue. If it isn't, have a combustion

Testing for backdrafting

air duct installed to provide a continuous supply of fresh air, even when the house has negative air pressure. Also consider purchasing a carbon monoxide detector.

▶ *House has a sewerlike odor.*

Pinpoint the source—usually a bathroom fixture, laundry sink, or drain. Most likely the water has drained out of the trap of that fixture. Pour water into it and monitor it for several weeks to see if the smell resumes. If so, have a plumber inspect it. If you can't pinpoint the source, inspect under the house for a broken or leaking drainpipe. It could even be underground, so check along the ground above the house sewer line. If you don't know where the line runs, locate the point under the house where the main drain goes under or through the foundation and project a line from that point to the street. A cleanout plug outside the foundation may provide a clue. Dig to expose the suspected source, or call a plumber.

▶ *You smell ammonia or refrigerant.*

This sharp, strong, acrid smell is caused by gases leaking from an air-conditioning compressor, refrigerator, or freezer. It is dangerous. Evacuate the house and then call the fire department from a neighbor's house.

Tip   *If you have bottled gas (LP), have the control valve inspected by a professional. Many defective valves made by various manufacturers have been recalled since 1977. If your local supplier, heating contractor, or plumbing contractor is not aware of particular recalls, contact the Consumer Products Safety Commission (look in the phone book under "U.S. Government" listings).*

▶ Electricity goes off in whole house.

Provide emergency lighting (candles, flashlights, backup lights). You need to check the main disconnect to see if it is tripped. As you approach it, examine the immediate area for loose or dangling power lines. If you see some, call the utility company. If there are no dangling wires, check the disconnect, being careful not to stand on damp ground; wear gloves. If the breaker is tripped, call an electrician. If it is a cartridge fuse or other device besides a breaker, you will need to have an electrician test it for you.

If the breaker is not tripped, see if the power for the rest of the neighborhood is also out. If so, turn on a portable radio for information. If the phone works, report the outage to the utility company. Turn off any large appliances that were on,

so there won't be a heavy demand when electricity is restored. Turn off TVs, computers, and other electronic equipment that could be damaged by a power surge. Don't open the refrigerator or freezer.

In cold weather, if power will be off for more than two or three days, drain the water system and/or put antifreeze in P-traps, appliances connected to the plumbing system (such as washing machines), and plumbing fixtures that have standing water. Steps for draining the water system: (1) turn off main valve, (2) turn off inlet valve (cold water) to water heater, (3) open faucets at the highest point of system, (4) open faucet or disconnect pipe at lowest point, and (5) drain water heater by attaching a hose to the drain valve, running it outdoors, and turning on the valve.

▶ Electricity goes off in part of house.

Blown circuit. Turn off appliances and light switches in those rooms. Reset circuit breaker (or replace fuse). If electricity goes back on, test all the fixtures and receptacles one by one until you discover the one that caused the short. (Turn off each fixture before turning on the next one.) Remove the defective appliance. If none is defective, the problem was probably too many turned on at once. Reduce the load. Eventually, you may have to add a new circuit.

▶ Finding solutions to other emergencies, crises, and household hazards.

Window glass is broken.
    See page 98.
Roof leaks.
    See page 112.
Stair handrail is loose.
    See page 55.
Fireplace fills room with smoke.
    See page 60.
Carpet is torn or burned.
    See page 35.
Door locks aren't heavy enough.
    See page 97.
Fireplace sparks fly onto floor.
    See page 61.
Child is locked in a bathroom.
    See page 97.
Foundation is cracked or sagging.
    See page 65.
Stairs are too steep.
    See page 59.
Animal trapped in window well.
    See page 73.
Windows aren't secure.
    See page 102.
Chimney flashing leaks.
    See page 121.
Floors and carpets are soaked.
    See page 37.
Carpet or upholstery is stained.
    See page 34.

Locating main disconnect

Draining water system

Alternate location inside house

Main circuit breaker

Highest faucet

Intake valve

Water heater

Drain valve

Main valve

Lowest faucet

Tip *The National Fire Protection Association estimates that as many as 33 percent of all residential smoke detectors have missing or dead batteries and are therefore inoperable. Push the test button on your smoke detector to make sure the battery is working.*

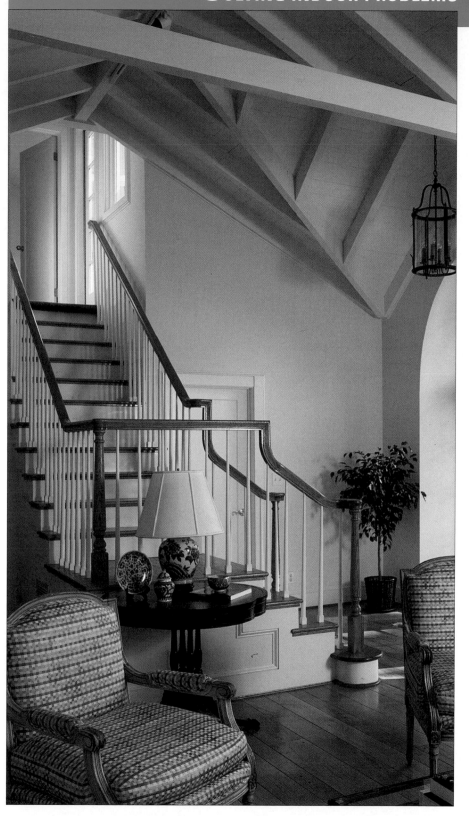

From basement to attic, the inside of a home contains dozens of surfaces and built-in features that are subject to daily wear or constant strain. Even minor problems become nuisances very quickly; other problems, especially those with foundations, basements, and attics, can be more serious. This chapter presents solutions to more than 245 indoor and minor structural problems.

SOLVING INDOOR PROBLEMS

▶ *Ceiling has hairline crack.*

If an otherwise flawless ceiling has one or two hairline cracks, it is worthwhile to repair them. The trick is to blend the repair into the ceiling.

If the crack is fine enough and is not likely to widen, you may be able to hide it with latex paint. Be sure the color matches the ceiling, allowing for fading or discoloration. Scrub the area along the crack with TSP or an all-purpose cleaning agent, to help the paint adhere. After the area dries, paint the crack, using a small roller. Apply a heavy coat and feather the paint away from the crack to avoid a noticeable ridge. Work enough paint into the crack so that it will stretch if the crack opens up again.

If painting doesn't solve the problem, patch the crack with flexible caulk. Choose a color that matches the ceiling or a caulk specified as "paintable." Brush or vacuum away all loose debris from the crack. Cut off the tip of the caulking tube close to the end so the nozzle emits a very fine bead of caulk; run it along the crack. Work the caulk into the crack with an old spoon (not your finger); dampen the spoon in soapy water if it sticks. Clean away excess caulk with a moist rag. Paint according to manufacturer's instructions.

▶ *Plaster ceiling has narrow crack.*

Fill with a nonshrinking spackling compound, and sand flush with the surrounding area. Various spackling and patching compounds, some lightweight, are especially designed for this purpose. Avoid those that shrink; they will require two layers.

Start by widening the crack with a lever-type can opener, linoleum knife, or improvised scraping tool, such as the tang end of a machinist's file or a tack puller. Widen the crack to ⅛ inch or so. Brush or vacuum out the crack and apply the filler according to manufacturer's instructions. If two layers of compound are required, scratch the first layer after applying it so it provides better adhesion for the second layer. Smooth the compound with a 3-inch taping knife (broad knife), feathering the edges. After the filler dries, sand it flush with the surrounding ceiling. If the ceiling is textured, match it by applying spackling compound with a putty knife or wet sponge (see page 21). After it dries, prime and paint the area.

Widening crack

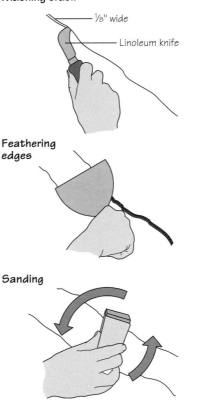

Feathering edges

Sanding

▶ *Plaster ceiling has wide crack.*

For cracks that seem to follow a stress joint in the house structure, apply fiberglass-mesh tape to prevent the crack from reopening. Prepare the crack, as described for a narrow crack, widening it to ¼ inch and undercutting (angling) the sides. Fill the crack with compound and let it harden overnight. Cover the crack with the self-sticking mesh tape along its entire length, making sure the tape bridges the crack. Cover the tape with a layer of compound and smooth it with a 6-inch taping knife. Let it dry, sand it, and repeat with a 10-inch knife. Then sand, texture, prime, and paint as described for a narrow crack. *Note:* Some products should not be sanded; follow manufacturer's instructions.

Embedding tape

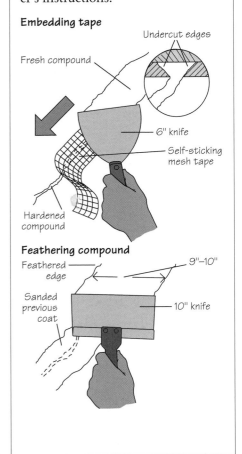

Feathering compound

Tip *The tape and compound applied to a crack will form a ridge over the crack. To minimize this problem, feather the compound 12 inches or more from the crack. You can eliminate the problem altogether if you scrape away enough plaster on both sides of the crack to embed the tape below the surface of the surrounding plaster, then cover it with patching compound.*

Tip *Always wear safety goggles when doing ceiling work. In addition, wear a dust mask when sanding or scraping.*

▶ *Ceiling has small hole.*

To patch a small hole (up to 3 inches), cut three or four strips of fiberglass-mesh tape and stretch them over the hole in crisscross fashion, or apply a large patch of reinforcing mesh. Apply patching compound over the mesh tape with a 6-inch taping knife. Holding the fabric taut, work the compound into the mesh so it will grip when it hardens. Spread the compound 3 or 4 inches beyond the hole, feathering it at the perimeter. After this coat dries, sand it lightly and apply a second coat, feathering it about 12 to 18 inches beyond the first layer. Let it dry, sand it smooth, texture the area as needed, prime it, and paint it.

Applying tape

Fiberglass-mesh tape

Applying compound

▶ *Ceiling has large hole.*

For large holes (wider than 3 inches), add backing behind the hole before applying fiberglass-mesh tape. Use a wad of newspaper or scrap of plywood or wallboard.

Secure it with paneling adhesive or with screws driven up through the ceiling. Then apply mesh tape over the hole and finish patching, as described at left.

Adding backing

Scrap of wallboard

Wallboard screws

Additional scrap

Applying tape

Fiberglass-mesh tape

▶ *Cracks open up between ceiling and walls.*

In newer homes that have roof trusses, cracks can occur between the ceiling and interior walls because the lumber in the trusses shrinks and causes them to rise. Thin cracks can be sealed with flexible caulk. Conceal larger cracks by installing crown molding around the room. Nail it to the ceiling, not the walls, so a new gap will not open up should the trusses (and ceiling) rise more (see page 31). Poor attic ventilation and unsealed openings between the home and

attic, although not totally responsible for this problem, contribute to it and should be taken care of. If severe gaps develop (1 inch or more), seek advice from an experienced professional.

▶ *Plaster is sagging.*

Gently probe the area where the plaster is coming loose from the lath. If it is loose, crumbly, or weak, the ceiling is a safety hazard and should be recovered with new wallboard. If the plaster remains firm and doesn't break up, you can secure it back to the lath with 1½-inch wallboard screws and plaster washers. With a power screwdriver, drive several screws, with washer attached, into the weakened area. Try to hit joists wherever possible; otherwise, wood lath. Space screws 6 to 8 inches apart. Drive them deep enough to embed the washer into the plaster slightly. Cover the washers with spackling compound. Sand, prime, and paint the patches when dry.

Reattaching plaster

Joists

Lath

Sagging plaster

Plaster washer

Wallboard screw

Tip *Don't dump leftover plaster or patching compound into the sink or sewer—it will clog drains.*

▶ Plaster is missing from a small area.

Replace missing plaster with two to three coats of new plaster. First secure the old plaster around the hole with wallboard screws and washers, as described on page 15. (If the lath is also missing, screw new wood or metal lath to the studs.) Undercut the edges of the plaster around the hole, as described on page 14. Then mix enough patching compound for the first coat, according to manufacturer's instructions. Brush a coat of latex bonding agent onto the exposed edges of the old plaster and wet the lath. Trowel a layer of plaster onto the lath thick enough to fill the hole almost flush with the surrounding surface. Score hatch marks on the wet plaster with a nail. After the plaster hardens, wet it and trowel on the second layer slightly below the original plaster surface. After it hardens, add a final coat of compound and then sand, prime, and paint the area.

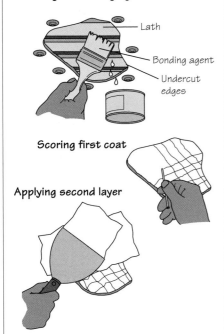

Brushing on bonding agent

Lath

Bonding agent

Undercut edges

Scoring first coat

Applying second layer

▶ Ceiling has extensive cracks and unevenness.

A badly damaged plaster ceiling is not worth trying to patch. Cover it with ½-inch wallboard. First look for areas of sagging plaster. Remove the plaster or, if it's stable, secure it with wallboard screws and washers, as described on page 15. Where plaster is missing, patch the hole with ⅜- or ½-inch wallboard (no need to tape joints). Remove all molding and light fixtures from the ceiling. Add box extenders to electrical boxes. Install the wallboard with the long sides at right angles to the joists; use 12-foot sheets, if possible. If you are doing the job yourself or with only one or two helpers, rent a wallboard jack for the day. It will lift the sheets and hold them in place while you secure them with 2¼-inch wallboard screws driven into the joists, 8 to 10 inches apart.

Install, tape, texture, and paint the new wallboard as you would any new ceiling. If the ceiling is uneven, screw 1x4 furring strips (strapping) across it, at right angles to the joists and 16 inches on center, with a vapor barrier between the ceiling and the strapping. Attach the strapping with two 2½-inch screws at each joist. Bring the strapping into level alignment by inserting shims between the vapor barrier and furring strips where necessary. Then attach new ½-inch sheets of wallboard to the strapping.

Note: Check the size of joists and measure the spans before covering a ceiling with new wallboard. Consult a professional to be sure they will support the extra load (½-inch wallboard weighs 1.9 pounds per square foot, 60 pounds per 4x8 sheet).

Covering a damaged ceiling

Joists

Damaged ceiling

Vapor barrier

Shim

1x3 strapping at 16" OC

New wallboard

Using a wallboard jack

Wallboard jack

Tip *Traditional plaster consisted of two coats: a "scratch coat" or "brown coat" of thick plaster applied to the lath; and a layer of white plaster, made from gauging plaster and lime, for a thin, hard, finish coat.*

Tip *To ensure a strong bond between old and new plaster, brush some latex bonding agent onto the old surface before applying new plaster.*

▶ Ceiling wallboard sags.

Major job. The causes might be: improper nailing; moisture in the attic; ceiling joists spaced too far apart for the thickness of wallboard used (joists must be no more than 16 inches apart, on center, to support ½-inch wallboard); the wrong type of wallboard (moisture-resistant wallboard is not intended for ceilings); or wallboard with the long sides installed in line with the joists rather than across them.

If the problem is only improper nailing, the wallboard will move upward when you push on it. You can reattach it to the joists with 1½-inch wallboard screws, spaced 6 inches apart along panel edges, 12 inches elsewhere. Use T-braces to force the sagging panels up and support them while you attach the screws. If sagging has deformed the wallboard so much that it won't flatten easily, force the panels up and hold them in place with long 1x4s screwed to the ceiling joists. After a few weeks, screw the wallboard to the joists, as explained above, and remove the 1x4s. Spackle and sand the holes and nail depressions, then touch up with primer and matching paint.

If the sagging results from any other cause, you will need to remove the existing wallboard and install the proper type (½ inch for joists 16 inches on center; ⅝ inch for wider joist spacings). First check for moisture problems and correct them (see right). If removing the old wallboard is too difficult (because of blown-in attic insulation, for instance), leave it in place and follow the procedures described on opposite page.

▶ Ceiling has moisture.

If the wallboard is soggy or an attic inspection reveals water stains above the ceiling, check for a leaky roof (or leaky water pipe in the attic) and fix it. If there's no leak, the moisture probably comes from condensation in the attic formed from water vapor that originates inside the house and penetrates the ceiling, a situation most prevalent in climates with freezing winters. This not only dampens the ceiling, which is a minor problem, but can lead to serious structural rot in the attic, which is a major problem. The best prevention is adequate ventilation in the attic and a vapor barrier (4 mil plastic sheeting) installed between the ceiling and ceiling joists. First try to improve attic ventilation, because installing a vapor barrier requires that you remove, or at least re-cover, the ceiling (see page 74).

Preventing moisture above ceiling

Condensed vapor

Moisture patch on ceiling

Plastic vapor barrier

▶ Ceiling framing sags.

Major job. The problem could be undersized ceiling joists, too much weight in the attic, or moisture problems in the attic. The solution is structural reinforcement. Consult a competent contractor, architect, or structural engineer.

▶ Ceiling has water stains.

Water stains seem innocuous, but are devilish to deal with. You can't just paint over them, because the stain will bleed through most paint.

First make sure the source of the stain (leaky pipe, roof leak, upstairs spill) has been fixed. Then cover the stain with an impermeable sealer such as white-pigmented shellac with a high (65 percent) titanium dioxide content. Apply the sealer in two or three light coats rather than one heavy coat. Let dry, then prime and paint.

If acoustic ceiling tiles are stained, spray a solution of 1 cup household bleach in 1 gallon water onto the stains, experimenting on a small area first. Wear protective clothing and eye protection.

▶ "Popcorn" ceiling needs painting.

If an acoustic texture (sometimes called a "popcorn" or "cottage cheese") ceiling was installed after 1978, there is no danger of releasing asbestos fibers, and it can safely be painted with a roller. However, test the ceiling first by lightly rolling a dry roller over it to make sure the acoustic texture won't come loose during painting. Use a roller with ½-inch or longer nap. If the texture material comes loose, or the ceiling predates 1978, use a paint sprayer to avoid disturbing the texture material.

Tip For speedy touch-up work, you can use quick-drying primers that are ready to paint in as little as half an hour.

Tip Although acoustic texture applied before 1978 most likely contains asbestos fibers, patching materials currently on the market do not. If you don't disturb the existing material during the patching process, there should be no danger of releasing harmful asbestos fibers.

▶ "Popcorn" ceiling needs patching.

Patch small areas of acoustic texture with appropriate patching materials that are widely available. Some are applied with a putty knife or trowel, some with a paint roller, and some with a disposable sprayer included with the kit. The patching materials are available in two shades of white, to match both new and older, discolored ceilings.

Patching a popcorn ceiling

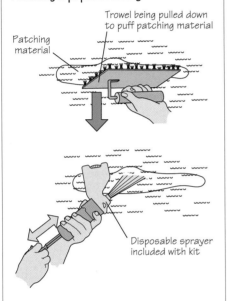

Patching material

Trowel being pulled down to puff patching material

Disposable sprayer included with kit

▶ "Popcorn" ceiling needs removing.

If the acoustic texture on the ceiling was applied before 1978, it most likely contains asbestos fibers. Consult an asbestos abatement company before deciding to remove the material. It is usually easier to leave the ceiling alone, or to cover it with wallboard, than to go through the expense and inconvenience of having the texture professionally removed.

Note: This applies only to acoustic texture, not normal wallboard texture. Acoustic texture is puffy and lumpy, like cottage cheese or popcorn.

▶ Ceiling tiles are damaged or missing.

With a utility knife score all four joints around the damaged tile and carefully pry it out of the ceiling. Remove any loose pieces, staples, glue, or other debris from the cavity. With the knife and a straightedge, cut off the tongue from one side of the replacement tile. Apply adhesive, according to manufacturer's instructions, and press the tile into place. Secure it with a long brace until the adhesive dries.

Replacing a ceiling tile

Damaged ceiling tile

Utility knife

Straightedge

Tongue

Old staples removed from furring strip

Adhesive

Tongue slips into groove of next tile

▶ Exposed beams have cracks.

It is normal for beams and timbers to crack, or check, as they age, especially those cut from the center portion of the log (so the end grain resembles a target with a bull's-eye). In severe cases the beam will also twist and warp. If it is severely deformed, it must be replaced; consult a professional. Otherwise, the cracks can be ignored. However, if their appearance is not pleasing, you can have the beams sandblasted. This accentuates the grain pattern and makes cracks seem more "at home" in the rustic beam. Another approach is to stain the beams a dark color to camouflage the cracks. Or, if only one or two cracks are objectionable, fill them with wood putty mixed with sawdust or stain pigment to match the beam color (experiment with wood scraps first).

▶ Water leaks along beams from outside.

If the ceiling beams slope upward toward the exterior wall, as is the case in homes with clerestory windows, rainwater may collect on the outdoor section of the beams and seep back toward the windows and possibly into the room. Cut a shallow groove along the bottom and both sides of each beam at a point well protected by the overhang. This drip groove stops water from traveling farther along the beam.

Cutting a drip groove

Drip groove

Tip *Finding replacement tiles may be the hardest part of repairing a ceiling with damaged tiles. If you can't find exact replacements at a local supplier, use existing tiles from a closet or back bedroom and replace them with whatever you can find at the store.*

▶ Wall studs are hard to find.

One technique for finding studs is to knock along the wall with your knuckles or a wood tool handle for 3 or 4 feet, listening for changes in sound. The predominant hollow thunking sound indicates stud cavities; a sharper rapping sound indicates studs. Also look for visual clues. Electrical receptacles almost always have a stud on one side or the other. Many wallboard installations have telltale nail depressions or joint outlines along studs; shining a light from the side accentuates their faint outlines. Nails along the upper edges of a baseboard go into the studs.

The most reliable way to locate studs is by probing. One technique is to drill a ⅛-inch-diameter hole into the wall, angled toward one side, and probe through the hole with a piece of stiff wire. When the wire hits a stud, mark the wire where it enters the wall by holding your thumb against it, slide the wire out, hold the wire against the outside of the wall in the same position, and note where the end of the wire falls. You can also find studs by drilling a series of small holes along the wall, spaced 1 inch apart, until you hit a stud, or by driving a 6d finishing nail into the wall at 1-inch intervals. All of these probing techniques leave holes that you'll have to fill with spackling compound when you are finished.

You can also locate studs with stud sensors. Magnetic stud finders work best on old lath-and-plaster walls, where lots of nails were used to fasten the lath to studs. A density gauge works better for wallboard walls; it uses sound waves to locate solid objects behind the wall surface.

Finally, you may be able to pinpoint the location of a stud if you already know where a nearby

stud is located. The walls of most homes built since the 1940s have studs centered every 16 inches, although studs next to windows, doors, and corners may not fall into the 16-inch pattern.

Locating studs

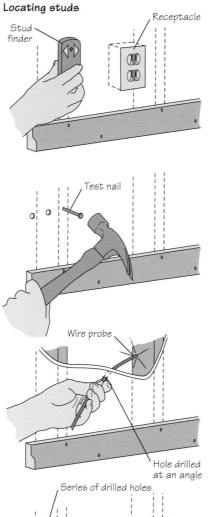

Stud finder

Receptacle

Test nail

Wire probe

Series of drilled holes

Hole drilled at an angle

▶ Wall needs fasteners for hanging objects.

If the object you are hanging is light (1 to 2 pounds), any fastener is adequate, whether secured to a stud or not. An ordinary 1-inch screw will handle most needs. Don't be afraid to put a hole in the wall—it's easy to patch.

For medium loads (2 to 7 pounds), your choice of fastener will depend on whether you are attaching it to a stud. The easiest fastener for attaching to studs is an ordinary screw or nail. It should penetrate the stud at least ¾ inch. To hang something on a wall between studs, use a hollow-wall fastener. Expansion bolts and plastic, drive-in, and screw-in anchors leave a device in the wall that can be reused a number of times. A toggle bolt is the strongest fastener for hollow walls, but you must thread the bolt through the object to be hung, or through a hanger, before inserting the bolt and toggle into the wall—you cannot take the bolt out of the wall without losing the toggle.

Heavy loads should always be attached directly to studs, usually with lag screws.

For masonry walls use a fastener designed for masonry. When you drill into the brick or concrete, use a masonry bit of the same diameter as the outside of the fastener.

▶ Hanger comes out of wall.

The original hole might have been too large for the hanger, or the wall covering may be too soft. Do not return the hanger to the same hole. Replace it with a type that spreads out wider on the backside of the wall, such as an expansion bolt or toggle bolt.

Tip Framing for a standard 8-foot-high wall consists of a 2x4 soleplate resting on the floor, 94¼-inch studs nailed to the plate every 16 inches, and a double top plate consisting of two 2x4s nailed to the tops of the studs. Walls sometimes have 2x4 blocking, called fire blocking, between the studs halfway up the wall. Windows, doors, and other openings have a header, or beam, across the top that carries any loads above the opening. Each end of the header rests on short trimmer studs, which are nailed to full-length king studs that flank both ends of the header.

▶ Object seems too heavy to hang.

Use several hangers, all attached to studs. If the object is too narrow to span at least two studs, use several expansion bolts, or attach a 1x2 furring strip to the wall, bolting it into studs, and hang the heavy object from it.

▶ Hanger leaves mark or hole in wall.

Patch the hole with spackling compound and, if necessary, sand it smooth. Touch it up with paint to blend in with the wall.

▶ Plaster wall has cracks.

Widen the crack, undercutting the edges. Fill it with patching compound, smooth the compound with a 3-inch knife, and let it harden. Cover the crack and compound with self-sticking fiberglass-mesh tape. Apply compound over the tape with a 6-inch knife, let it harden, sand it smooth, and apply a thin top coat with a 10-inch knife, feathering the edges. Let it dry, sand it, and texture the patch to match the rest of the wall; then paint. *Note:* Some commercial patching kits require different techniques (for example, applying mesh first, then compound). Follow manufacturer's instructions. (For additional information, see page 14.)

▶ Plaster wall has hole.

For a small hole (less than 3 inches in diameter), first remove all the debris. Then wet the lath and surrounding plaster and fill the hole with patching compound or plaster of paris (mix according to instructions) to just below the level of the wall surface. Let it harden. Cover with fiberglass-mesh tape, then more patching compound, and texture the surface.

For a larger area (3 to 12 inches), you will need two coats of patching compound. Chip out weak plaster and clean out the area to expose the original lath. If necessary, secure the surrounding plaster with perforated plaster washers and 1⅝-inch wallboard screws. Apply a bonding agent (or mix of 2 parts water to 1 part white glue) to the edges of the old plaster. Moisten the lath. Apply the first coat of patching compound, scratch to texturize, and let dry. Then apply the finish coat. (See also page 15.)

For a huge hole or for extensively cracked areas, patch with wallboard. Cut out a large patch of ⅜-inch wallboard, sized so its edges will center over studs or other framing members. Use it to trace a cut line on the wall. Carefully cut out old plaster, using a saw or hammer and cold chisel; avoid jarring the plaster loose. Wear a dust mask. Screw the wallboard patch to the framing and lath. Tape joints with fiberglass-mesh tape; cover joints with compound. Texture the patch to match the surrounding area, then prime and paint.

Repairing a large hole in a plaster wall

Lath
Plaster washers
Cold chisel
Studs
Wallboard patch

▶ Plaster wall is a mess.

Walls with extensive cracks or multiple layers of paint or wallpaper are not worth patching. Cover the area with canvas underliner material, and paint or paper over it, according to manufacturer's recommendation. Install the underliner with vertical seams slightly out of plumb, so wallpaper seams won't align over them. Or, for a smoother surface, forgo the underliner and cover the wall with wallboard. Be warned, however, that this is a big project that involves extending electrical boxes and door and window jambs, removing trim, lugging large sheets of wallboard, taping seams, and texturing. (See page 16.)

Applying underliner

Seams slightly out of plumb, or applied horizontally
Adhesive rolled onto wall
Underliner
Filled holes
Second coat of adhesive applied over fabric

Tip *Although patching is quite simple, practice on closet walls and back bedrooms before taking on living room and dining room walls.*

Tip *Hairline cracks are inevitable. Patching other kinds of cracks is futile if you don't find out the cause and eliminate it. Moisture damage, indicated by water stains, must be fixed at the source. Stress cracks, usually around windows and doors, may be caused by house settling, or seasonal expanding and contracting of lumber. If the cracks are severe or continue to widen, consult a professional. Other cracks can be stabilized by patching with self-sticking fiberglass-mesh tape, as described above.*

▶ Wallboard has hole.

Small: Make sure the wall is free of dust, grease, and loose paint. Cover the hole with wallboard tape (or cloth soaked in thinned compound) and compound, using a knife wide enough to bridge the entire hole—otherwise, the corner of the knife will push the tape into the hole. (See also page 15.)

Medium: First cut the hole into a square shape. Install a small scrap of wallboard or plywood behind the hole, attaching it with wallboard screws driven through the wall. Cut a wallboard patch to fit into the square hole, attach it to

the backing with one or two wallboard screws, tape the joints, and finish the patch and screw depressions to match the surrounding wall surface.

Large: Enlarge the hole by cutting the damaged area back to the framing, then install a new piece to fit the enlarged hole. Tape the joints and finish the patch to match the surrounding area. If you aren't confident about your taping skills, try to plan the cutout so that joints will be hidden behind furniture or cabinets, or locate joints at floor, ceiling, or corners.

▶ Wallboard joint tape is coming loose.

If the peeling tape is in only a small area, remove the loose section in a boat-shaped cutout. Fill the cutout with joint compound and smooth it with a 3-inch taping knife. If the tape is peeling in a large area, remove the tape (slice carefully with a sharp knife) and redo the area with new tape and compound.

▶ Texture of new patch doesn't match wall.

You probably won't be able to match the original texture perfectly because techniques, materials, and individual skill vary so much. However, before calling in a professional plasterer, experiment with the following techniques on some scraps of wallboard. To achieve a coarse, lumpy texture, apply slightly thinned finishing compound with a sponge and mold contours into it. For a uniformly bumpy texture, apply thinned compound with a large-nap roller. For a texture with variable bumps, use rollers with different nap sizes. For an orange-peel texture, use a small-nap roller or, with a texture sprayer, spray a mixture of thin compound and extrafine sand onto the area. To produce a random pattern of raised flat spots, spray or trowel thinned compound onto the surface and lightly flatten the high spots with a wide (24- to 36-inch) trowel. Stippling fresh compound with a stiff brush, fine broom, or crumpled newspaper also creates textured effects, all of which can be further enhanced by flattening high spots with a wide trowel.

Patching a medium hole / **Patching a large hole**

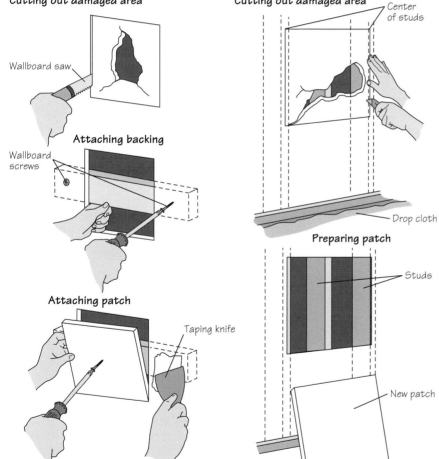

Tip *Wear eye protection and a dust mask when sanding or chipping.*

Tip *Can't tell if wall is plaster or wallboard? Wallboard has a layer of thick paper just beneath the paint or wallcovering; probe with a knife or nail. Other telltale signs of wallboard are faint nail depressions along studs and joint tape over seams. Plaster has a hard surface over a crumbly brown coat.*

▶ Wallboard nails are popping out.

Just hammering the nails back in won't work. Pull out the nail and replace it with a 1⅝-inch wallboard screw, or hammer the popped nail back in and secure it with a second nail driven close enough so its head overlaps the first. Be careful not to drive the screw or nail in so far that it breaks the paper facing on the wallboard. If this happens, remove the fastener altogether and drive a new one 2 inches away. Cover the dent and tear with compound and then spot-paint the area.

Removing popped nail

Replacement screw

Securing popped nail with new nail

Old nail
New nail

▶ Wallboard panels don't join evenly.

When installing large patches (or full panels) of wallboard, sometimes you can't avoid butting the beveled edge of one panel against a full (unbeveled) edge of another, creating a discrepancy in thicknesses. A twisted stud may also cause an uneven joint. Before taping the joint, build up the low side. Use the type of joint compound, sometimes called "hot mud," that hardens by chemical reaction (hydration) rather than

evaporation (which causes shrinking). Hot mud is available in 30-, 60-, and 90-minute setting times; use 90-minute to allow adequate working time. Apply it on the low side only, feathering it out from the joint 10 to 12 inches. After the compound hardens, lay a long straightedge (such as a 4-foot level) across the joint to see if the low side is built up evenly; if not, build up the low spots with another layer. After it hardens, tape the joint like any other: Apply a coat of compound and embed wallboard tape into it. After it dries, sand the joint smooth and apply two to three light coats of compound, sanding each coat after it dries before applying the next. Coats should be successively wider—for example, 6, 12, and then 18 inches wide. Prime and paint to match.

▶ Wall feels cold to the touch.

If the exterior walls in a heated home feel uncomfortably cold, they do not have enough insulation. New insulation can be blown in, or you can remove siding and install rigid insulation under the new siding (which is a big job). As a simple alternative, try baseboard heaters set at a low temperature.

▶ Wall feels damp to the touch.

This problem is caused by a combination of humidity, cool wall surface, and lack of ventilation. Try to control all three by warming the room and providing increased air circulation. A baseboard heater along the wall should provide sufficient heat and create convective air currents, but it may be too expensive to operate for extended periods of time. If operating it for short periods doesn't control dampness, supplement with a small fan set at a low speed and run it continuously, or as long as necessary.

▶ Wall is discolored and smells musty.

The problem is mildew. Eradicate with mildew remover, either a commercial preparation or a home-made solution: ½ cup vinegar, ½ cup borax, and 3 gallons of water; or 1 teaspoon washing soda and ½ cup chlorine bleach in 1 gallon of water. Wash with a sponge, then rinse with a sponge and warm water. If you need to repaint, have the dealer add mildewcide to the paint. In any case, eliminate the source of the problem: lack of ventilation and high humidity.

▶ Walls are not soundproof.

There is a progression of steps you can take to soundproof walls, each involving a more complicated process. Start by plugging up or muffling all areas where air (and sound) can get through the wall. First remove covers from electrical fixtures and receptacles (on both sides) and seal cracks around the boxes with spray insulating foam. Seal holes inside the boxes as well. (Be sure to deaden each outlet first by turning off the circuit breaker.) Next install sound-deadening liners inside heating ducts shared by two rooms. Look for cracks along the floor and ceiling and seal them. Add weather stripping around doors, and a door sweep on both sides of each door. Replace hollow-core doors with solid-core doors. If sound persists, install resilient channels horizontally along one side of the wall, 16 inches on center, and attach new wallboard to the channels. Sound-deadening board is an alternative to the channels; you can install either over the old wallboard, but you may prefer to remove it to reduce wall thickness. Adding insulation between

Tip *The secrets to successful patching of holes and cracks are as follows. (1) Multiple layers. Don't try to build up a deep crack or hole in one layer; use several. Let each layer dry, then sand, and apply a new layer. (2) Feathering. To make sure that the patch won't show, finish with a loose skim coat of topping compound feathered 2 to 3 feet beyond the crack or hole. (3) Spot-prime before painting.*

the studs is not an adequate deter-rent by itself; it is effective only when used with sound-deadening board or resilient channels.

Sealing openings

Installing resilient channel

▶ **Bathroom walls and ceiling have colored spots.**

If not mildew (see opposite page), the problem is condensation that leaves an accumulating residue of dissolved pigments and dirt. Common in bathrooms, condensation is more likely with latex-based

paint than with alkyd-based. It can be removed by wiping down the walls and ceiling with a damp cloth, using a mild cleaning solution, if necessary. Try to improve ventilation in the bathroom.

▶ **Fingerprints and smudges show on walls.**

Enamel paints (glossy, hard) and flat paints (dull, rubbery) require different cleaning techniques.

Enamel paint: Clean with a sponge and a solution of 1 gallon lukewarm water mixed with 1 teaspoon washing soda. Wear rubber gloves. Do not use ammonia or all-purpose cleaners with ammonia—they can dull and etch the paint. For fingerprints and nongreasy stains, increase the amount of washing soda to ¼ cup, *or* use TSP or an all-purpose cleaner that does not contain ammonia. Rinse with a damp sponge. For greasy stains rub lightly from the center of the stain

outward, using a cloth dipped in alcohol and a dry cloth to blot as you go until the stain is gone.

Flat paint: Clean with a solution of 1 gallon lukewarm water mixed with 2 tablespoons washing soda, *or* use TSP. Wear rubber gloves. Rinse with plain water. Overlap sections to avoid streaks. Use only a white cloth because colored sponges may leave a dye. Don't scrub—it will leave marks. For greasy stains first blot with a crumpled paper towel, then cover the spot with two or three clean pieces of paper towel and go over it with a warm iron. Repeat until the stain is almost gone, changing the paper towel each time. Then blot with a commercial wall-cleaning paste, or make your own by mixing a cleaning fluid, such as liquid laundry detergent, with fuller's earth (for dark surfaces) or with cornstarch or whiting (for light surfaces). Apply the paste to the stain, let it dry thoroughly, then brush it off.

▶ **New paint doesn't cover old paint or new patch.**

The following chart shows which primer and paint to use over what surface. Problems often result from omitting primer over enamel, trying to cover red colors with one coat, not washing the walls first, using low-quality paint (not enough pigment and resins), and rolling out the paint too thinly.

Surface	Primer	Paint
Latexed walls and ceilings	Spot-prime spackled and patched areas; seal stains and smoke marks; if using different color, cover with tinted primer.	Latex flat
Bathroom/kitchen walls and ceilings	PVA primer for new wallboard; tinted oil-based or latex for painted surfaces.	Oil-based latex gloss, or latex eggshell
Enameled trim	Enamel primer	Oil-based or latex gloss
Masonry (concrete/brick)	Latex flat masonry paint	Latex flat

Tip *High-gloss paint and light colors accentuate wall bumps. Flat paint in neutral or dark tones minimizes imperfections.*

▶ New paint doesn't cover stains.

If scrubbing the stain with a solution of water and TSP doesn't remove it completely, seal it with white-pigmented shellac containing at least 65 percent titanium dioxide. Prime and paint after the shellac dries.

▶ Old paint layers make wall uneven.

Remove all loose paint with a putty knife. Wash the walls with TSP for proper adhesion. Skim-coat a thin layer of joint compound over the entire wall with a wide (24- to 36-inch) putty knife to fill in the depressions. After it dries, sand lightly; repeat if necessary. Seal/prime the wall with PVA sealer, then paint. Apply an undercoat primer if you plan to wallpaper. See also page 26.

▶ Textured paint needs removing.

The technique you use will depend on whether the textured paint is latex-based or oil-based. (You may not be able to tell until you try; assume [hope] it's latex. Test on an inconspicuous area.) For latex paint, buy a paint stripper specifically designed to remove textured paint and follow the instructions. For oil-based paint, try a home-made solution of 1 gallon water, 2 cups liquid fabric softener, 1 cup white vinegar, and proper ratio of enzyme-based wallpaper remover, according to label instructions. (The typical bottle size is 16 to 22 ounces.) With a clean garden sprayer, apply the solution to one small area at a time. Wet the area, wait five minutes, wet it a second time, wait five minutes, spray it a final time, and wait five minutes more. Then scrape the area with a 6-inch

putty knife. Clean the smoothed wall with a solution of 1 gallon water and ¼ cup white vinegar. After it dries, seal the walls with white-pigmented shellac.

If strippers don't work, your options are to skim-coat the wall to install new wallboard, or to apply wallpaper liner and wallpaper (see page 20).

▶ You want to paint over wallpaper.

It is never advisable to paint or wallpaper over an old wallcovering. The paper may not be adhering well to the wall. Paint wets the wall-covering, and it may pull away. Also dyes in the underlying wallpaper may bleed through the paint, and some wallcoverings include flocks or foils to which paint will not adhere. Finally, paint will exaggerate any seams, blisters, tears, or other imperfections in the wall-paper. If at all possible, remove the old wallpaper before you paint the walls (see opposite page).

▶ Wallpaper is dirty and needs cleaning.

Washable wallpaper: Clean with a solution of mild soap and cool water. Rinse with cold water and blot the paper dry with a clean cloth. Remove fingerprints and nongreasy stains with an art-gum eraser. For greasy stains first blot with crumpled paper towels, then hold several clean towels over the spot and press with a warm iron. Repeat until the grease is absorbed. Remove mildew with a light application of commercial mildew remover, or sponge with a cloth dampened in alcohol.

Nonwashable wallpaper: Clean with a solvent, because the wall-covering is vulnerable to water. Dampen several terry cloth towels with kerosene. Allow them to air-

dry. Wrap one of the towels around the head of a broom or mop, securing it with tape. Wipe the walls from the ceiling down, overlapping the strips as you move around the room. Turn or change the towels as they become grimy.

▶ Wallpaper seams are loose or curling.

With a razor or utility knife, cut slits above and below the loose area, starting at the seam and slicing away from it diagonally for 2 to 3 inches. Carefully peel back the loose section of wallpaper and apply wallpaper paste onto the exposed back. Press the paper into place to spread the paste onto the wall, then peel the paper away again. Let the paste dry slightly until it's tacky. Then carefully press the paper into place again. Gently apply pressure with a damp sponge, and use the sponge to remove any paste that oozes out of the seams. If a long section of seam has curled, do this process in short segments of 4 to 6 inches each.

Pasting a loose seam

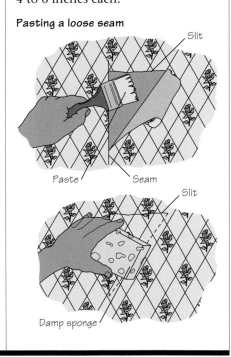

Slit

Paste   Seam

Slit

Damp sponge

Tip *If you paint with a roller, "prime" the roller first by dipping it into the paint and running it over some newspapers or cardboard a few times to eliminate air bubbles and to saturate the fibers. After painting a section of wall or ceiling, always stand back and look for "holidays"—spots you missed—and touch them up while the paint is fresh.*

▶ *Wallpaper has blisters or bubbles.*

If the blister is small, slit it and inject acrylic wallpaper adhesive under the blister with a glue syringe (available from a wallcovering store). Smooth the paper with a damp sponge. If the blister is larger than a quarter, cut an *x* over the blister with a razor or utility knife and peel back the wallpaper in four sections. Apply paste to the exposed back of each section. Press the sections into place, peel them away again, and let the paste dry until tacky. Then press the sections back into place, using a damp sponge to apply gentle pressure and to mop away any excess paste.

Repairing a small blister

Small slit

Syringe with acrylic adhesive

Repairing a large blister

Blister

Cut "x"

Wallpaper paste

▶ *Wallpaper has hole or tear.*

The wallpaper has to be patched. Start by taping a scrap of wallpaper over the hole or tear, matching the wallpaper pattern; use masking tape or other tape that won't damage

paper. With a utility knife and straightedge, cut a clean-edged shape through both the scrap material and the installed wallpaper. With hot water and a putty knife, remove the damaged section of wallpaper from the wall and discard it. Apply paste to the back of the patch, press it into place, remove it to let the paste dry until tacky, then press the patch into place again. Smooth the patch and clean up with a damp sponge.

Cutting scrap and damaged wallpaper

Straightedge

Utility knife

Removing damaged wallpaper

Putty knife

Pasting patch in place

▶ *Wallpaper is peeling off in large sections.*

The wall wasn't prepared properly before wallcovering was applied. Strip off the paper and start over (see below).

▶ *Wallpaper needs removing.*

Remove old paper first. If it's a strippable type, you should be able to lift up a corner and peel strips right off the wall. Remove paste residue with hot water and a scraper. If it's a solid vinyl type, the vinyl will peel off but the backing paper needs to be stripped. To remove the backing paper or non-strippable wallpaper, start by scoring the surface with a wire brush or a spurlike perforation tool designed for this purpose. Don't press too hard or you will damage the wall. Then mix a solution of 3 gallons very hot water, ¼ cup liquid fabric softener, 2 tablespoons baking soda, and the appropriate proportion of enzyme-based wallpaper remover, according to label instructions. Observe all instructions printed on the product labels. Pour 1 gallon of the solution into a clean garden sprayer. Working from floor to ceiling, one section at a time, spray the walls with a fine mist. Immediately repeat the process two more times, then wait 15 minutes. Then, section by section in the same order you sprayed, scrape the wall-covering with a 6-inch taping knife, and peel off, working from the bottom up. Remove residue with a sponge soaked in the remover solution. Then rinse the walls with 1 cup white vinegar in 1 gallon water. Clean up. Now you're ready to prep the walls for the new paint or wall-covering. Wash walls with a mild household cleaner, patch holes and

Tip *If you don't know whether you'll be painting or wallpapering the wall, apply undercoater. You can have it tinted, so it will look like painted walls if you decide not to install wallpaper. Use two coats.*

gouges, smooth the wall surface (skim coat or underliner—see right), dust, and finally prime with acrylic primer designated as wallcovering undercoater.

Removing strippable wallcoverings

Removing nonstrippable wallcoverings

Perforations

Pump sprayer

Residue

Scraper

Sponge or barbecue grill brush

▶ Wall is too uneven for new wallpaper.

Textured or cracked walls and walls with many years' accumulation of paint and wallcoverings are poor surfaces for new wallcoverings. Removing them and installing new wallboard is sensible only if extensive wiring, insulating, plumbing, or structural changes make it necessary to expose the wall cavities. Installing thin wallboard over the walls is only slightly easier, as it requires altering electrical boxes and molding, and taping all the joints. The better do-it-yourself options are to apply a canvas underliner, or to skim-coat the walls.

Canvas underliner is available from wallcovering outlets. Apply according to manufacturer's instructions.

To skim-coat (or "float") a wall, start by scraping off loose and peeling paint (not textured surfaces). Then sand the walls with 40-grit sandpaper (wear a respirator); clean up by damp-mopping. Seal the walls with two coats of white-pigmented shellac, according to label instructions.

Mix a batch of joint compound, thinned with water to the consistency of stiff cake batter. Apply it to the walls with a 10-inch taping knife, working up from the base of the wall in 4-foot-square sections. Let dry overnight, then sand with 120-grit sandpaper and apply a second coat. Let dry, sand again, then seal the walls with one application of oil-based undercoater.

▶ New wallpaper won't stick to wall.

The wall probably was not primed correctly. For brand-new wallboard or plaster walls, use PVA primer. For walls painted with latex paint, use latex undercoater. For walls painted with oil-based paint, use acrylic undercoater.

▶ Paneling is worn and dirty.

If the paneling has a factory-applied lacquer or plastic finish, you can clean it with warm soapy water and a sponge; then wax it, if desired. If the paneling has a wax finish (one you can scratch with a fingernail), restore it by rubbing with a beeswax- or carnauba-based paste wax. If the paneling has an oil finish (which has a soft sheen, rather than shiny, and feels oiled), clean by rubbing with boiled linseed oil or lemon oil (light finishes) or Danish oil (darker finishes); remove any excess to avoid leaving a dust-attracting film. Do not use furniture polishes containing silicone for factory-finished paneling; it may break down the finish. Instead, spot-clean and dust, using lemon oil on a cloth, or follow paneling manufacturer's recommendation.

▶ Paneling has scratch or nick.

Apply furniture paste wax (for wax finishes) or furniture oil (for oil finishes) to the blemish and rub it in. If that doesn't work, dab it with a putty stick that matches the color of the paneling. Remove excess putty with a cloth. You may also be able to match the color with a felt-tipped pen, shoe polish, or wood stain (experimenting first in an obscured corner).

Tip *How can you tell if paint on a wall is latex or oil-based? A flat (not shiny) surface is latex; a glossy surface could be latex or oil-based. Hold a wet sponge to the wall for a few minutes. If the paint bubbles or dissolves, it's latex; if it stays intact, it's oil-based.*

▶ Paneling has darkened with age.

Some solid-wood paneling, especially pine, may have darkened with age. If cleaning with warm soapy water does not lighten it enough, try to renew the finish by rubbing it with fine steel wool (#4/0) dipped in mineral spirits; experiment in an inconspicuous area. If this doesn't work, you will have to strip off the old finish completely. Use a paste furniture stripper and apply according to instructions. Finish the bare wood with a urethane or oil finish, staining or bleaching the wood first, if desired.

▶ Paneling has stains.

Clean stains on lacquered, waxed, or plastic-coated paneling with warm soapy water or by rubbing with paste wax. If this doesn't work, use a commercial furniture-restorer product (available at home centers), following label instructions. Clean oiled wood by gently rubbing lemon oil into the stain with fine steel wool. Reoil, then wipe off excess. If the stain was caused by moisture, be sure that the source of the problem has been located and eliminated.

▶ Edge of paneling has come loose.

With a flat pry bar and a padded woodblock for a fulcrum, carefully pry the entire loose edge away from the wall, inserting wood spacer blocks between the wall and the panel edge as you work your way down. With the seam completely opened, apply a generous bead of paneling adhesive to the exposed bearing surfaces (such as wallboard or furring strips). Wait for the adhesive to get tacky but not hard, then remove the spacer blocks and press the panel edge into place.

Slide the padded block along the seam, tapping it with a hammer to ensure a tight bond. Clean off any adhesive residue with a clean cloth dipped in mineral spirits. For additional strength, add paneling nails (grooved finishing brads) along the seam. *Note:* If there's a chance that the seam will leave a slight crack between panels, first paint the wall behind the seam black, so the crack will be dark and less visible. Let the paint dry before applying the adhesive.

Opening the seam

Loose panel   Sound panel

Pry bar   Padded woodblock

Applying adhesive

Panel adhesive

Background painted black

Padded woodblock

Closing the joint

Tip   *Traditional paneling in most period homes consists of wide boards, or panels, with flat trim applied around each panel. This arrangement, called frame-and-panel, is capped by a continuous ledge built up of molding pieces. An alternative type of paneling consists of tongue-and-groove boards with beaded edges, of random or uniform width, installed vertically and capped by a continuous band of molding.*

▶ *Paneling is damaged or coming loose from wall.*

Remove the panel. (You may need to remove the baseboard first; see right.) If it is secured by nails, pry around the edges with a pry bar and padded fulcrum. Pull the panel away from the wall, and use pliers to pull out any nails left in the wall. If the panel is glued in place, start by chiseling through the panel along a line 2 to 3 inches in from one of the edges. Remove the larger section, breaking the adhesive bond by prying with a wrecking bar or flat shovel. Work carefully along any seams with other panels. Then gingerly remove the smaller strip of paneling remaining along the original seam; break the adhesive bond by hammering lightly on a taping knife or putty knife. Scrape off adhesive residue in the same way.

Inspect the wall for moisture or other damage and eliminate the cause of the problem. Replace loose plaster or wallboard, patch holes, scrape off flaking paint, and seal the wall with primer.

To install the new panel, apply adhesive to the furring strips, stud faces, or wall surface (around the edges of the opening and down the center every 16 inches in a zigzag pattern). Press the new panel into place and immediately secure the top with four finishing nails. Pull the bottom of the panel about 10 inches away from the wall, so the adhesive breaks full contact, and insert blocks every 10 inches to hold it for 10 minutes. When the adhesive gets tacky, remove the blocks and press the panel into place. Secure the bottom and edges with finishing nails, setting the heads and filling the holes with putty colored to match the paneling.

Scoring the edge

Split
2"–3"
Sound panel
Edge of damaged panel

Removing panel

Sound panel
Groove cut with chisel

Installing new panel

Finishing nails
New panel
10" spacer
Adhesive

▶ *Baseboard needs removing.*

When replacing an entire panel, you probably have to remove baseboard and other molding strips to get full access to the panel. Pry them loose with a flat pry bar. Use two pry bars in stubborn areas, applying gentle pressure on one, then the other. After removing the molding, pull out any nails left in the wall. Remove any nails left in the molding by pulling them through from the back with pliers or nippers. If the face has any nail holes, touch them up with a putty stick after you install the new panel and nail the molding strips back in place.

▶ *Paneling has crack or hole.*

If the paneling is solid wood, not sheet, you will need to replace the entire damaged board (see left). If the paneling is sheet, you can patch it as follows: From a scrap of identical paneling, cut a rectangular patch slightly larger than the damaged area. Plan the patch so that the grain pattern will align with the pattern in the wall around the hole. Cut out the patch with a sharp utility knife and straightedge, rather than a saw, to ensure straight, clean edges. (Practice elsewhere on the scrap first.) Next tape the patch over the damaged area with masking tape, aligning the grain patterns. Carefully trace the outline of the patch with the knife, then set the patch aside. With the utility knife, cut through the paneling along the scored outline. Make several passes with the blade, cutting deeper each time. Then remove the damaged piece, gently prying it away from the wall, if necessary,

Tip   Always scrub walls and woodwork before painting them. They accumulate an invisible greasy film over the years that prevents paint from adhering properly. If warm soapy water does not remove the film, mix a solution of 1 gallon water, ½ cup low-phosphate TSP substitute, and 2 tablespoons liquid fabric softener. Apply it with a clean garden sprayer, let stand for five minutes, then scrub with a damp sponge (wear latex gloves). Rinse with a solution of ¼ cup white vinegar in 1 gallon water.

with a putty knife or pry bar. If the paneling is applied over furring strips, center 1x3 cleats under the edges of the cutout. Attach them with paneling adhesive and, if possible, nails. Apply paneling adhesive to the back of the patch, wait for the adhesive to get tacky, then press it into place. Over cleats, attach the patch with paneling nails (grooved finishing brads) as well.

Cutting the patch

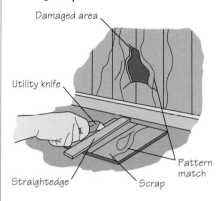

Damaged area

Utility knife

Straightedge

Scrap

Pattern match

Cutting out damaged area

Utility knife

Patch

Tape

Adhering the patch to cleats

Adhesive

Patch

▶ *You want to paint paneling.*

First scrub the walls with warm soapy water and a sponge. Let dry. Fill cracks and holes with patching compound, let it dry, then sand it flush with the wall surface. Roughen the paneling surface with 150-grit sandpaper so the primer will adhere. Brush or vacuum away the residue and wipe the paneling with a damp cloth. Spot-prime all knots with a shellac-based sealer, then apply a base coat of latex or alkyd primer. Finish with two coats of latex paint—flat or semigloss, depending on your preference.

▶ *Solid-board paneling is damaged.*

Replace the entire damaged board. First remove the baseboard. Next, using a circular saw with the blade depth set to the thickness of the paneling, rip the board in half along its entire length. (Finish the ends of the cut, where the saw won't reach because of the floor or ceiling, with a chisel.) Pry both halves of the board away from the wall, starting with the half that has the groove edge. Be careful not to break the tongue of the adjacent board. The half of the damaged board with the tongue edge may be blind-nailed, so don't force it because the sudden release of the blind nails may cause the adjacent board to split. Instead pry under it enough to lift both the damaged board and adjacent board away from the wall, then change the direction of pressure so you are prying the damaged board away from the neighboring board as well as from the wall.

Prepare the replacement board. Cut it to the same length as the damaged board. Then, with a chisel or a circular saw with the blade set at a shallow depth, remove the back flange along the groove edge of the board (the groove is formed by two

flanges—one in front, that always shows, and one in back, that is always hidden).

To install the new board, fit the tongue into the corresponding groove of the adjacent board and snug it into place by hammering on a padded woodblock along the entire length of the board. Nail it with 8d finishing nails, set the heads, fill the holes with putty, then finish the board to match the rest of the paneling. Replace the baseboard.

Sawing damaged board

Damaged board

Removing cut sections

Groove

Tongue

Trimming new board

Face

Installing new board

Tongue

Tip *To dull a finished wood surface for painting, you can sand it, or, wearing latex gloves and eye protection, you can apply a liquid deglosser, following manufacturer's instructions.*

Tip *If you are painting frame-and-panel paneling, paint the recessed panels first. Drag the paint out from the corners and edges toward the center of the panel, then finish with vertical strokes in the direction of the wood grain.*

▶ *Insects are behind paneling.*

Paneling that has been installed over old walls without protection from external moisture provides a natural haven for insects, especially termites and wood-boring pests. Look for small piles of fine sawdust, tunnels, or holes near the bottom of the paneling. If you suspect insects, call a qualified exterminator to conduct an inspection and recommend treatment.

▶ *You can't tell whether wall is a bearing wall.*

All exterior walls are considered bearing walls. For interior walls, look for clues in the attic or basement. In the attic note the direction of ceiling joists; if they run perpendicular to the wall, it is probably bearing, especially if the joists are overlapped or spliced. In the basement or crawl space, look for the main girders; walls located directly over them are probably bearing. Also doubled-up floor joists probably support bearing walls. Posts and footings within the perimeter of the foundation usually support bearing walls as well.

   If a central hallway runs the length of the house, only one wall is the bearing wall. Look in the attic to see where the ceiling joists overlap. Short walls running perpendicular to ceiling joists, such as closet walls, are probably not bearing, especially if parallel walls are close by.

▶ *Mitered joints of casings have opened up.*

Miter joints will open up as the wood expands and contracts with changes in humidity. The wider the casing, the greater the problem. (This is one reason why wide casings in Victorian homes always have butt joints or block joints, not mitered joints.) This problem can

be minimized by priming every side and edge of each board before installing the casings. If a joint has opened up, lock-nail the joint from both directions and fill the gap with caulk, which works better than spackling compound because it's flexible. Be sure the caulk label specifies "paintable." If the casings are stained and not painted, use a wood filler—not caulk—that can be stained to match them.

Lock-nailing

Filling gap

▶ *Molding piece is missing or damaged.*

Replacing most molding pieces is a matter of cutting a new piece to the right length and nailing it into place. There are some tricks of the trade, however, that will ensure precise, tight-fitting joints.

• When butting two pieces end-to-end, cut the ends at matching 45-degree bevels (rather than 90-degree straight cuts) so if the joint opens up it won't create a gap.

• When cutting miter joints for door and window casings (picture-frame joints), don't automatically cut two 45-degree angles—the corner may not be a perfect 90 degrees. Instead cut the first piece at 45 degrees and nail it in place. Then lay the second piece of stock in place, overlapping the first piece, and mark where the two ends of the miter angle of the first piece intersect its edges. Join the marks and cut along the line.

• Lock-nail all miter joints, using glue and 4d finishing nails (drill pilot holes first).

Joining pieces end-to-end

Marking for a miter joint

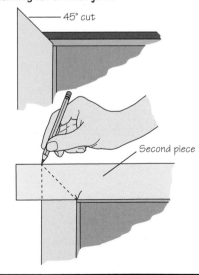

Tip   *The corner joint at the top of a door or window, where side casings meet the head casing, can be a mitered joint (each piece of casing cut at a diagonal angle), butt joint (side casings butt against the bottom of the head casing, which is cut long enough to extend slightly beyond the side casings), or butt joint with corner block (both the side and head casings abut a square block placed at the intersection).*

SOLVING INDOOR PROBLEMS

▶ *Replacing molding requires coped cut.*

When joining baseboard or similar molding at an inside corner, use a coped joint. Square-cut the first piece of molding to butt against the wall. The second piece of molding abuts the first, but because molding has irregular profiles the end of the second piece must be shaped to fit tightly to the face of the first piece. Create this shape with a coped cut. First cut a 45-degree bevel on the *face* side of the board. Then, with a coping saw, follow the irregular outline created by the bevel cut, angling the saw backward slightly. Test how well the coped cut fits against the first molding and make adjustments. Then, at the opposite end, cut the second piece of molding to length (add 1/16 inch), and nail into place.

Cutting molding at 45°

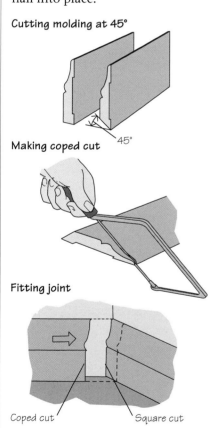

Making coped cut

Fitting joint

Coped cut   Square cut

▶ *You can't find replacement molding to match original.*

Look for a lumberyard that has been in business for a long time. If they don't have the material, they may be able to make a piece if they still have cutter blades to match your pattern. Other places to look are cabinet shops and hardwood dealers who do their own milling. Look for contractors who specialize in restoration work, and ask where they get hard-to-find moldings. Another place to look is a recycling center that specializes in used building materials or "architectural salvage." Finally, look in closets or back bedrooms of your own house (or even a willing neighbor's) and use an existing piece that you can replace with something reasonably close to it.

▶ *Crown molding is missing.*

Crown molding is the most difficult to cut and fit because it is installed at an awkward angle, plus you must also compensate if the walls and ceiling are not square or the ceiling isn't level. Install the corner pieces first. They require compound bevel cuts (the end of the board is cut with 45-degree angles going in two different directions), so once they are in place it will be easier to get the lengths right on pieces requiring less complicated cuts. Make corner cuts at a textbook-perfect 45-degree angle first, then make gradual adjustments by testing the pieces in place and shaving the cuts as needed. (A power miter saw makes precise trimming easy.) Cut the piece to length only after the corner cut is completed. Install crown molding by nailing into the "flats" along both the ceiling and the wall edges. Gaps due to irregularities in the wall or ceiling surface may be filled with spackling compound.

Fitting a compound bevel cut

Both pieces cut at compound bevel

90°   45°

Cutting with compound miter saw

45°

45°

Work held vertically against fence

Cutting with ordinary power miter saw

Clamp

Wall edge of molding

Ceiling edge of molding

45°

Tip *Types of moldings used to trim a room: Casings, which are the trim around windows and doors that resembles a picture frame; baseboards, which may be a single piece or may be built up with a base cap and base shoe; chair rail, which is a continuous strip of molding around the room at the height of a chair back; picture rail, which is a continuous strip of molding around the room approximately 1 foot below the ceiling; and crown molding, which covers the joint between walls and ceiling.*

▶ *Floor squeaks.*

Squeaks are annoying but rarely indicate major problems. They occur when a board rubs against a nail or another board. No movement, no squeak. First pinpoint the squeak by observing the floor closely while a helper walks, stands, and moves on the floor. The problem may be with finish floor boards that you can see, or it may be with boards hidden from view.

If you can see surface boards rubbing together, sprinkle talcum powder or squirt WD-40® into the joint for a temporary fix. For a permanent solution, secure the boards by driving wallboard screws up into them through the subfloor. Have your helper stand on the floor to force the board down, or predrill screw holes through the subfloor (but not through the finish floor); screws should penetrate only halfway into the finish floor. Use washers if the subfloor is soft or spongy. If there is no access from below, or if the finish floor is face-nailed, secure the board from the top with 6d (for 5⁄16-inch flooring) or 8d (for 3⁄4-inch) annular-ring finishing nails (or 16d finishing nails if you can nail directly into a joist). Predrill pilot holes to prevent splitting; set the nail heads and fill the holes with wood putty. If the flooring was installed directly over joists with no subfloor, screw 2x2 cleats to the sides of the joists and secure the squeaking floorboards to them by driving long wallboard screws up through the cleats (predrilling first), or secure from the top, as described above.

If the squeak is hidden from view, the movement could be subfloor boards or it could be finish boards covered by carpet or other floor covering. Make observations from below the floor while your helper squeaks the board from above. If the subfloor or joists don't move, the problem is in the finish floor, hidden between the subfloor and floor covering. Secure the suspect board(s) by driving wallboard screws from below, or nails from above (through the carpet), as previously described. If you detect movement of the subfloor boards or joists, secure the boards in one of the following ways: (1) insert (don't force) shims into gaps between the joist and moving subfloor boards (dab construction adhesive on both sides of the shim first); (2) screw a 2x2 cleat into the side of the joist; or, if you don't have a 2x2, (3) snug (don't force) a 2x4 cleat up against the creaking subfloor next to a joist, and screw it securely to the joist (apply construction adhesive to the top and side of the cleat first).

Securing loose boards to subfloor with nail or screw

Securing subfloor with shim or cleat

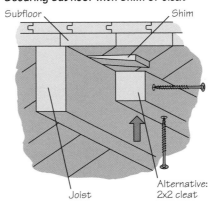

▶ *Floor sags or bounces.*

If the problem occurs in a small area, inspect under the floor for a cracked joist or missing bracing between joists. If you have a cracked joist, temporarily shore it up on both sides with joist material; splices should extend 12 to 18 inches beyond the crack in both directions. Apply construction adhesive to the splice pieces first, then secure them to the joist with 16d common nails or 2¾-inch decking screws, spaced 12 inches apart along the tops and bottoms of the splices and randomly across the middle. Replace missing braces with solid blocking cut from lumber the same dimension as the joists (for example, 2x8, 2x12, and so on).

If the problem exists across the entire floor, the joists are undersized or poorly supported and need reinforcement. Consult a remodeling contractor, architect, or structural engineer.

Splicing a floor joist

Replacing blocking or bridging

Tip *Anatomy of a floor system. Most residential floors have three layers: a finish floor of wood, carpet, resilient sheet material, or other floor covering; a subfloor of plywood, 1-by boards, or other material that provides a structural membrane; and a supporting framework of joists that rest directly on foundation sills, girders, or bearing walls. The joists, which are 2-by lumber set on edge, are stabilized by blocking that is placed between them at the ends and at the midpoint of long spans.*

▶ Subfloor has hole or rot.

If the subfloor has a moisture problem, eliminate the source first. Then cut out the damaged area of subfloor. The cutout should be rectangular, it should extend at least 12 inches beyond any rotted wood, and its edges should be centered over floor joists. Use a circular saw with the blade set to the depth of subflooring. Next saw a replacement patch out of plywood of the same thickness as the subfloor, cutting it ¹⁄₁₆ to ⅛ inch smaller around the edges to allow for expansion. Glue and nail 2x4 cleats between the joists so all four edges of the patch will be supported. Apply a bead of construction adhesive to the exposed tops of the cleats and joists, set the patch in place, and nail it with 8d annular-ring finishing nails. In some cases you may have to make a second patch for a layer of underlayment over the subfloor. If the rotted area is around a closet flange (toilet drain), cut the patches in two, as shown.

If rot has damaged a floor joist, support the joist at both ends of the rotted section with temporary shoring and cut the section out. Then install a new joist next to the truncated joist. The new joist should be long enough to rest on the girders or other bearing members. If this is not possible, it should at least extend 4 feet beyond the cutout section in each direction. Nail the two joists together with 12d or 16d common nails along the top and bottom edges.

Cutting out damaged area

Damaged area

Cut lines centered over joists

Installing patch

Plywood patch

2x4 cleats

Joists

Variation for closet flange

Underlayment patch

Subfloor patch

2x4 cleats

▶ Floor over unheated crawl space is cold.

Carefully fit R-19 fiberglass insulation batts between the floor joists, vapor barrier facing up. Use wire insulation supports to hold the batts in place. Be sure insulation fits against the rim, or band, joists but does not cover the foundation vents. In colder climates insulate the inside face of the foundation and kneewalls as well. First cover the bare dirt with a vapor barrier of 6 mil polyethylene sheeting. Bring it up the wall 6 inches, lap all joints at least 6 inches, tape them securely, and weight them down with stones. Then hang R-19 fiberglass batts against the foundation or kneewall, securing them by nailing wood lath along the top, into the foundation sill or rim joist. Each batt should extend down the wall and out onto the plastic vapor barrier 2 feet or more. Batts should butt together snugly. Insulate the rim joist. Lay lengths of 2x6 on the batts to prevent movement.

Insulating a crawl space

Mudsill

Lath

Joist

Insulation
Subfloor

Stones

2' 2x6 Tape

Tape

Foundation

Vapor barrier

Tip *The areas most likely to have moisture problems are around the tub and toilet.*

Tip *When reinforcing a joist by nailing another one next to it, use 12d or 16d common nails spaced no farther than 12 inches apart along the top and bottom edges and 16 inches apart in the middle area. Drive the nails at opposing angles to keep the boards from separating. As you drive each nail, be sure the boards are clinched together; if necessary, use clamps to draw them together before nailing.*

▶ *Floor over basement or garage is cold.*

Install carpeting over insulating panels of high-density hardboard. These panels, designed for this purpose, are ½ inch thick and 4 feet square. Do not install them in bathrooms, over concrete, or on other surfaces where moisture may be present. Following manufacturer's recommendations, nail them to the floor, then install the pad and carpet.

▶ *Concrete slab is cold.*

Install carpet over a thick, dense urethane foam pad. Consult a local carpet dealer for additional recommendations. If you prefer a different floor covering, it is possible to install a false wood floor over 2-by sleepers with rigid foam insulation between the sleepers. Consult an experienced builder or floor specialist for specific details; moisture must be controlled or the wood will warp and eventually rot.

▶ *Carpet is dirty.*

If you want your carpet cleaned professionally, look for a reputable, bonded, and insured company that is willing to guarantee its work. Ask what methods they employ—the most common are steam/extraction, shampooing, and absorbent (dry) cleaning—and whether any chemicals they use might be irritating to crawling babies, pets, or other family members. If they use a steam/ extraction method, ask what percentage of the water and chemicals will be removed; it should be 85 to 95 percent. If they use water, ask how long it will take for the carpet to dry completely. If they use a dry compound or solution that dries to a powder, ask if they remove all of it; any residue will quickly attract dirt.

If you are cleaning carpets yourself, the best approach is to rent a heavy-duty deep-cleaning machine: steam/extraction, shampooing, or absorbent cleaning. All are effective, but each has distinct disadvantages with certain types of carpet. Steam uses water, which must be removed almost completely to prevent mildew and quick resoiling. It is risky to use on wool carpets and may take the twist out of some other fibers. Shampooing machines have a rotary action that may damage plush, shag, cut-and-loop, or frieze (twist) carpets. Dry cleaning requires a very strong vacuum cleaner to remove the absorbent cleaning material afterward, which would otherwise attract dirt quickly after cleaning. Get complete instructions from the rental agent. Also be sure that you vacuum your carpets thoroughly before cleaning them.

▶ *Carpet has spilled liquid.*

Spills happen. Be calm. With most spills the trick is to act quickly, before they dry and become stains. Blot the spot gently with white paper towels or a soft, clean cloth. (For nongreasy liquids you could also use a large, moist sponge). Do not rub! It only loosens the nap and makes the carpet yarn better able to absorb stains. Change towels or rinse out the sponge and repeat several times. When the towel or sponge no longer absorbs any liquid from the carpet, pour some cold water on the spot to dilute any colored residue. Blot to remove as much water as possible. To be sure all the color from the spill is out of the carpet, blot (don't rub) the wet spot with a white cloth or paper towel. If a stain does emerge, see right. Otherwise, cover

the spot with a stack of white paper towels, weight them down, and leave them for four to six hours.

▶ *Carpet has spilled mess.*

Scrape up as much material as possible and follow procedure for liquids. To reduce odors apply a solution of 1 tablespoon ammonia in ¾ cup water; blot it up. Wash the area with a detergent-and-vinegar solution (see below); then blot, rinse with cold water, and blot dry.

▶ *Carpet has mud tracks.*

Use none of the procedures for other kinds of damage. Rather, let the mud dry and vacuum it up. If stains are left, see below.

▶ *Carpet has candle wax.*

Uh-oh. Try placing a cardboard blotter or small stack of paper towels over the wax, then use an iron or hair dryer to heat the wax so it will melt into the blotter. Watch the temperature carefully to avoid overheating or even burning the carpet fibers.

▶ *Carpet has chewing gum.*

Freeze the gum—several ice cubes in a plastic bag work well. When the gum is frozen, break it into pieces and lift them away from the carpet.

▶ *Carpet has stains.*

Determine the cause. Water-soluble stains can be washed out with a mild solution of 1 teaspoon white vinegar, 1 teaspoon powdered (or equivalent liquid) detergent, and 1 quart warm water. Pour some over the spot and scrub gently with a soft brush. After scrubbing, blot up as much liquid as possible (see

Tip *Vacuum your carpets at least once a week (some experts recommend daily). The best types of vacuums have a beater bar, not just straight suction. Take six or seven strokes over each section of carpet—long, slow strokes if the vacuum has a beater bar, short strokes if not. Once or twice a year move heavy furniture and vacuum under it.*

opposite page). Rinse with cold water and blot again.

Greasy stains, including lipstick and crayon, require solvents or stronger cleaners. An all-purpose household cleaner may work; read the label and follow directions. For a stronger cleaner, try trichloro-ethylene. Ready-made carpet solvents also work but are risky to use because they can dissolve the latex backing glue. In all cases test the product first on an inconspicuous section of the carpet. Wipe it up with a damp sponge.

Urine, vomit, and pet messes leave very persistent stains. If they are not cleaned up immediately before they dry, try treating the stain with ammonia. Apply a solution of 1 tablespoon ammonia in ¾ cup water; blot it up. Follow with a solution of 1 part vinegar in 2 parts water. Then rinse with cold water and blot dry. If you have several such stains, it is best to have the carpet professionally cleaned.

▶ Carpet has burn spot.

If the burn is superficial, you may be able to trim off the charred fiber tips with scissors and clean the area with liquid detergent. Follow up by cleaning again with a solution of 1 part white vinegar in 2 parts water.

If a small area is badly burned, use a sharp knife to cut away the tuft of charred fibers by carefully slicing it off flush with the backing material. Cut a replacement tuft from a scrap or hidden section of identical carpet. Glue it in place with hot-melt or all-purpose glue. Then carefully trim the top of the replacement to match the height of surrounding fibers.

Replace larger burns with a patch (see right).

▶ Carpet has damaged area.

Replace the damaged area with a patch. First, with a sharp utility knife and framing square, cut out the damaged section in a rectangular shape, parting the nap first so it will be easier to slice through the carpet backing without shredding yarn unnecessarily (the more threads intact, the better the seam). Cut a replacement patch from a carpet scrap or the back of a closet, using the damaged section as a pattern. Cut the patch with the pile leaning the same direction as the original. Check for fit.

The easiest (but not strongest) way to seam the patch is with double-faced carpet tape. Stick the tape to the floor or pad, centering it under the edges. Peel off the protective paper and press the patch into place. You can strengthen the bond by applying carpet-seam cement to the edges of the backing before setting the patch in place. You can also seam with needle and thread or, for the strongest and cleanest seam, heat-bond tape. See page 36.

For small areas obtain a circular cutting tool from a carpet supplier, plus a few adhesive disks. The tool works like a cookie cutter and ensures that the cutout and patch are identical. Cut out the damaged area, then cut out a patch. Adhere the adhesive disk, sticky side up, to the bottom of the hole and press the patch into place.

Cutting out damaged area

Parted nap

Checking pile

Cutout piece

Carpet scrap

Cutting out patch

Damaged piece

Parted nap

Carpet scrap

Seaming patch

Patch

Backing

Double-faced carpet tape

Tip *Some stains are very difficult to remove, especially those with pigments (paint, stain), dyes (ink, nail polish), or tannins (grape juice, red wine). Use only a stain removal method recommended for that stain, or call a professional.*

▶ Carpet has large faded or worn areas.

Try a new furniture arrangement or cover the areas with accent rugs. If you have a large scrap of identical carpet, you can probably have the worn area patched, although a perfect color match may not be possible due to fading and wear. Consult a professional installer.

▶ Carpet has tear or loose seam.

Sew up the rip with a heavy curved needle and linen carpet thread or fishing line. Thread the needle with about 5 feet of thread, double the thread, and knot it. Starting at one end of the tear, push the needle into one edge of the seam and pull it up through the opposite edge. Pliers will help you push and pull the needle through the tough carpet backing. Work along the length of the tear, using a basic loop stitch. The carpet nap should cover the seam; be sure to keep the nap out of the stitches. Tie off the thread and groom the seam with small scissors.

For long rips and seams, use heat-bond tape, available through carpet suppliers. You will also need to rent a carpet-seaming iron, or use an old iron (steam is not necessary). First tidy up the tear so the two edges can be pressed together with no debris or carpet nap between them. Then cut a strip of tape slightly longer than the tear. Tuck it under the seam so it lies on the carpet pad, glue side up, with the seam centered over it. Heat the iron to 250° F and, starting at one end, separate the carpet so you can set the hot iron directly on the tape; then slowly glide the iron along the tape. As you do this, reach back with your other hand and pinch the carpet seam together,

pressing it down onto the heated glue of the tape. Have a helper set heavy objects on the bonded seam as you press it together. When you reach the end of the seam, pull the iron away from the tape carefully to avoid getting hot glue all over the carpet. Quickly set it down on a board (placed in position ahead of time) and finish pressing the seam together and setting weights on it. Remove all the weights after 5 to 10 minutes and groom the seam with small scissors.

Sewing carpet

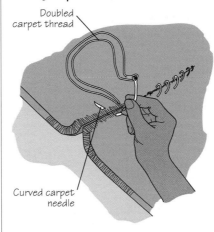

Doubled carpet thread

Curved carpet needle

Heat-bond tape

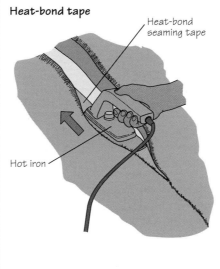

Heat-bond seaming tape

Hot iron

▶ Carpet is loose.

If a small area is wrinkled or loose, have a helper assist in pulling a section of carpet loose from the nearest edge. Then stretch the carpet tightly back to the wall and force it down on the tack strip. You may be able to rent a knee kicker to make this easier. With a putty knife or other wide, blunt tool, tuck the carpet edge in between the wall and nailing strip, making sure that the tucking operation does not force the carpet off the pins of the tack strip. If there are several loose areas, or the carpet is too stiff to stretch, rent a knee kicker. Pull a short section of carpet up along the edge, as described above, but use the kicker to force it back onto the tack strip instead of doing it by hand. If the entire carpet is loose, call an installer.

Stretching carpet by hand

Putty knife

Using a knee kicker

Knee kicker

Knob adjusts bite

Tip   To brighten dull-looking carpet, liberally sprinkle cornstarch over it and leave it alone for about an hour, then vacuum.

▶ Padding is bunched up under carpet.

If the problem is extensive or is near the center of the room, call a carpet installer. Either the pad was not installed properly or it is disintegrating. If the problem is small and located near a corner, pull back just enough carpet to expose the problem area. Straighten out the pad and staple or tack it securely to the floor. If the problem was a loose seam between two pieces of pad, place duct tape over the seam. Then flop the carpet back in position and stretch it onto the tack strip (see opposite page).

▶ Carpet has depressions from heavy furniture.

The bent and compressed fibers should straighten out with the help of moisture. Place an ice cube on each depression. The gradual release of moisture will help the fibers to expand slowly as the moisture evaporates from them. If this does not work, periodically direct steam onto the dents from a steam iron or humidifier without soaking the carpet. Gently coaxing the carpet strands with a soft brush may also help.

▶ Carpet causes static electricity.

This is a common problem with older nylon carpets (but not with newer generations of nylon). For short-term relief, apply antistatic spray to the carpet, according to directions on the label. Be careful—oil-based sprays might attract dirt. A longer-lasting solution is to use a humidifier.

▶ Carpet is wet from flooding or leaks.

Synthetic carpets (such as nylon, polyester, and acrylics) will not mildew, but their jute backings will. Therefore, pull up the wet sections of the carpet and turn them over, exposing the backs to air circulation. For best results get them off the floor so air can also circulate underneath. Improvise a drying frame with chairs, sawhorses, or boards. A portable heater or heat lamp also helps; keep it from direct contact with carpet or other materials.

Carpets of organic fibers, such as wool or cotton, mildew easily. They should be dried more quickly. Use a clothesline, large dryer, or professional cleaner, depending on the type and value of the carpet.

A wet pad should also be pulled up in order to ventilate the floor itself. Rubber and foam pads can be dried out and saved, although they are inexpensive to replace and may not be worth the effort. Jute and horsehair pads are very difficult to dry out and are probably not worth the effort.

▶ Glued-down carpet needs removing.

If you're removing a cushion-backed carpet and not replacing it, there will probably be scraps of backing and adhesive residue left after the carpet is pulled up, which can be difficult to remove. Be sure the floor is worth preserving before you go through all the effort to restore it (it may be easier to lay down a new subfloor and floor covering).

First try scraping off the scraps with a flat shovel or floor scraper. If that doesn't work, rent an industrial floor buffer with a fiber pad. Get instructions for using the buffer

from the rental agent. Have a helper vacuum the floor as you buff it, to eliminate flying dust. After buffing, you may still need to rent a floor sander to remove the adhesive residue or stains. (See page 43.)

Removing residue of glued-down carpet

Heavy scraper

Scraps of backing stuck to floor

▶ New carpet has strong odor.

The odor is caused by chemical emissions from the adhesives and other components used to manufacture the carpet. Most, if not all, manufacturers subscribe to strict industry standards to ensure that these emissions remain at safe levels, although they may be obnoxious. To remove the odor as quickly as possible after installation, ventilate the room for 48 to 72 hours. Leave doors and windows open, if

Tip   *The most common type of carpet padding used today is rebonded foam rubber, which looks like bits of rubber floating around in a blue, gray, or green soup. Quality varies with the density and weight of the material.*

possible, and increase the flow of fresh air by placing a fan where it will exhaust room air through a window. If your home has a ventilating system that exhausts air to the outside (rather than circulating it within the house), run that too.

If the new carpet has not been installed yet, vacuum the old carpet just before removal; then vacuum the floor immediately after the carpet and pad are removed. Open windows and run exhaust fans during installation. If you or someone else in the house is unusually sensitive to the emissions, request that the dealer or installer unroll the carpet in a well-ventilated area for a day or two prior to installation, and make arrangements to be away from the house during installation and for a day or two after installation, if recommended.

▶ Resilient flooring looks dirty or dull.

If dust mopping or damp mopping with clear water doesn't spruce up the floor enough, apply a coat of water-based vinyl floor wax (unless the flooring is no-wax vinyl, which should be polished with a no-wax finish). Do not use a paste wax or other solvent-based finish on a vinyl floor. If the floor still looks dull, you will have to strip off all the old layers of wax or polish and start over. Apply a solution of 1 gallon warm water, 1 cup ammonia, and ½ cup TSP to the floor. Let it soak into the wax for a few minutes, then scrub with a brush or floor polisher. Wipe up the solution with a sponge mop, or squeegee it into a dustpan. Rinse the floor with clean water and let it dry thoroughly before rewaxing.

▶ Resilient flooring is scratched.

You can "erase" a small scratch by rubbing over it lightly with the edge of a coin. Fill deeper scratches and gouges (on unpatterned floors) with a homemade paste. Grate or scrape flakes from an identical scrap of flooring, grind or chop them into a fine powder, and mix the powder with white glue (clear nail polish, acetone, shellac, or polyurethane might also work). Protect the area around the gouge with masking tape and, with a putty knife, smooth the paste into the crevice. When dry, sand smooth with fine steel wool. Restore the shine with clear nail polish or floor wax. Acceptable substitutes for the paste are tub-and-tile caulk (mixed with latex paint to match color) or epoxy glue mixed with acrylic paint.

Making paste for repairing resilient flooring

Matching scrap

Flakes

White glue

Filling resilient flooring

Gouge

Putty knife

▶ Resilient flooring has stains.

Try your usual floor polish, following its instructions. Ammonia, vinegar, or undiluted liquid laundry detergent might also work. Other stain removers include charcoal lighter fluid, liquid bleach, paint thinner, and rubbing alcohol. Test the cleaner in an inconspicuous place before using it. Wipe it up quickly to avoid damaging the floor finish.

▶ Resilient flooring has chewing gum or paint.

Scrape up as much as possible with a putty knife or spatula. Remove what remains with a small amount of dry-cleaning fluid or paint thinner (except on rubber tile—try buffing lightly with fine sandpaper).

▶ Resilient flooring has blister.

Blisters or bubbles are sometimes caused by poor installation, but more often by moisture wicking up through the subfloor. First inspect under the floor for a moisture source and, if you find one, eliminate it. To repair a small bubble, poke a tiny hole in the center with a large sewing needle or sharp wire to let out trapped air; allow any moisture to evaporate. Then lay a towel or aluminum foil over the area and press it with a warm iron to soften and flatten the bubble. The heat will also soften the old adhesive. Place wax paper on the area and weight it down for a few hours to get the area to adhere. If the old adhesive doesn't stick, inject glue through the hole with a glue syringe, place wax paper over the area, and replace the weights.

To repair large blisters, place a towel or foil over the area and press it with a warm iron to soften the flooring. With a sharp blade, slice across the blister and ½ inch beyond on each side; allow any

Tip When trying any cleaning or repairing technique, experiment in a hidden corner first to see how it affects the floor material.

Tip If the old floor looks dated and replacing it is too expensive, get creative. Resilient sheet flooring and tile lend themselves to patchwork. Buy a small remnant of sheet flooring or a few bright tiles and inlay a border, an accent strip, or some brightly colored squares to liven up a dull, monotonous floor.

moisture to evaporate. Scrape and vacuum away any specks of debris, then dab some adhesive into the cavity with a putty knife. Press down on the blister and remove adhesive residue with lacquer thinner. Cover the repair with wax paper and weight it down. After 24 hours remove the weights and apply seam sealer to the slit.

Repairing small blister

Repairing large blister

▶ Resilient flooring is torn, burned, or damaged.

Repair damaged area with a replacement patch. Lay a scrap of identical flooring over the damaged area, with patterns aligned, and tape it to the floor. With a sharp utility knife and straightedge, cut through both layers of flooring at the same time. Where possible, align cut lines with pattern lines. Set the patch aside. Remove the remaining scrap and the damaged cutout, carefully scrape away the adhesive residue, and vacuum away all debris. With a notched trowel, spread flooring adhesive onto the underlayment, then press the patch into place. Clean off excess adhesive with recommended solvent, then, following label instructions, carefully apply seam sealer to seams.

Cutting patch

Installing patch

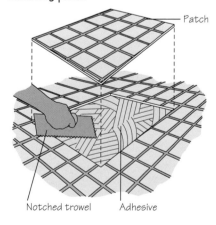

▶ Resilient flooring telegraphs bumps or cracks.

Because they're thin, resilient flooring materials easily "telegraph" subsurface imperfections to the surface. Cracks between underlayment panels, nail heads, even specks of grit create grooves, dimples, and bumps on the floor surface. There is no way to smooth them out because they are trapped under the flooring material. All you can do is wait until you install new flooring to create a perfectly smooth underlayment. Until then, try to minimize their effect by balancing or changing light sources (shading windows, changing location of lamps, adding new lights).

▶ Edge of resilient flooring is coming loose.

First check for moisture problems, especially around bathtubs and sinks, and fix the source of the problem. Then carefully clean out any old caulk or other debris from under the flap and press it down gently. Some materials are supple enough that you can simply staple or tack down the edge and cover it with baseboard. If the edge is too stiff to force down easily, you will have to heat it first. Use a warm iron over aluminum foil, a heat gun, or a hair dryer. Soften the flooring enough to press down; then tack it with HDG annular-ring nails, or, if the material is flexible enough, with adhesive instead of nails. Recaulk the joint if the flooring abuts a bathtub.

▶ Resilient tile is loose, damaged, or missing.

To remove a damaged tile, cover it with a clean towel and heat with a hair dryer, heat gun, or hot iron. Pop the tile up with a putty knife. Scrape off adhesive residue from the

Tip *Flooring materials have varying tolerances for cleaning agents. If the flooring is vinyl or vinyl-asbestos, do not use nail polish remover. If the flooring is asphalt or rubber tile, do not use nail polish remover, turpentine, or lighter fluid. If the flooring is cork, do not use chlorine bleach. Avoid using abrasive scouring powder on any resilient flooring.*

underlayment and vacuum up all debris. With a notched trowel, spread the adhesive recommended for the replacement tile; set the new tile in place. If you don't have a replacement tile that matches, remove one from a closet or hidden corner (under the refrigerator, perhaps).

▶ Resilient flooring needs removing.

Old flooring may contain asbestos fibers; to be safe, assume it does (today's products do not). These fibers are classified as "encapsulated," not "friable," which means that they are locked into the flooring material and present no danger of becoming airborne so long as the flooring is not cut, torn, abraded, or broken up. For this reason it is preferable to install new flooring over old, rather than run the risk of releasing the asbestos fibers. However, if removal is necessary, there are certain precautions you must follow. The following work practices include recommendations by the Resilient Floor Covering Institute; check local regulations for additional requirements.

• Never work with asbestos-containing materials without wearing a MSHA-NIOSH–approved respirator for asbestos.

• Seal off interior doorways with plastic sheeting. Transfer the debris directly to the outdoors as you remove it.

• Never sand or abrade the flooring surface or backing.

• Never remove flooring, backing, or residual adhesives dry. Before pulling up or scraping an area, cut it into strips with a utility knife, then moisten the backing with a solution of 1 ounce liquid dishwashing detergent in 1 gallon water, applied by sprayer. The detergent must contain anionic, nonionic, and amphoteric surfactants. Check the label.

• Never sweep up debris; use a tank-type wet/dry vacuum cleaner (shop vac) with a disposable dust bag, a metal floor attachment (no brush), and a HEPA filter. Position the vacuum so the outtake air blows away from your work area, preferably out a window. If you absolutely must sweep, wet the floor area with the detergent solution first.

• Place all debris in heavy-duty polyethylene bags (6 mil), seal the bags tightly, label them clearly as containing asbestos, and dispose of them at an approved site.

• Wear gloves at all times when handling the material. When finished, remove and shake out your work clothes out of doors and shower immediately.

Wetting resilient backing

Flooring cut into strips
Scraper
Residue
Detergent solution

Cleaning with a vacuum

Exhaust facing away
Vacuum with HEPA filter

Disposing of debris

Tape
Label
CAUTION CONTAINS ASBESTOS
Heavy-duty plastic bags

▶ Old adhesive remains on the floor.

If adhesive residue remains on a finish floor after you remove the old flooring, try eradicating it with an adhesive remover available from flooring dealers. Follow all directions on the label, especially regarding ventilation, protective clothing, and flammability.

▶ Old wood floor is dull and worn-looking.

If routine waxing does not renew the luster of an old wood floor and you are considering sanding and refinishing it, you may be able to restore it by removing all the layers of old wax and grime. To check, rub a small (hidden) area with steel wool dipped in alcohol until all layers of wax are removed. Then damp-mop the bare wood and apply a paste wax. If the results are satisfactory, clean the entire floor with a commercial wax stripper made for wood floors, or a solution of 1 gallon warm water, 1 cup denatured alcohol or ammonia, and ½ cup TSP. Test the solution in a small area first. Apply the solution to the floor and let it soak in for a few minutes, then scrub with a brush or floor polisher. Wipe up the solution with a sponge or sponge mop. Rinse with clean water, or vacuum with a wet/dry shop vac. Allow to dry thoroughly, then apply a paste wax. *Note:* Floors that have a urethane finish should not be waxed.

▶ Waxed wood floor has marks or stains.

For water or alcohol marks try buffing with a damp cloth and mixture of 1 part toothpaste and 1 part baking soda; or rub the spot with fine steel wool and floor polish or wax. If the mark persists, rub

Tip *Routine care to keep your wood floors looking new: (1) Dust-mop frequently with an unoiled mop (unless your floors are oiled instead of waxed; then use an oiled mop). (2) Remove spots, marks, or stains as soon as they happen. (3) Wax periodically (one to six times per year, as necessary), but only in high-traffic areas to avoid waxy buildup over entire floor. Buff the entire floor. <u>Note:</u> Floors that have a urethane finish should not be waxed.*

with steel wool and odorless mineral spirits. Wash and rewax.

For black heel marks rub with fine steel wool and floor polish or wax.

For minor burns sand lightly, wash, dry, and rewax.

For chewing gum, wax, crayon, or tar, cover with ice cubes in a plastic bag. Scrape up the frozen material with a putty knife or spatula. Rub any residue with fine steel wool and odorless mineral spirits. Rewax.

For dark stains remove the wax or polish with TSP or a commercial wax stripper. Wash with vinegar and allow to soak in; then wipe dry. Repeat, if necessary. If the spot still remains, apply 1 tablespoon oxalic-acid crystals (read the label carefully for cautions and directions) dissolved in 1 cup water. Allow to soak until spot disappears; then wipe up with a damp cloth and rinse well. To see if the wood is still sealed, sprinkle with a few drops of water. If it beads up, the sealer is undamaged. If the drops soak into the wood, reseal with a wood sealer, then refinish with the appropriate wood stain. Rewax.

For grease or oil spills, wipe up immediately. Sponge with undiluted liquid dishwashing detergent. Sprinkle with baking soda and leave overnight. Wash with a general household cleaner containing ammonia. Rewax.

▶ Wood floor has scratches or gouges.

For superficial scratches try a putty crayon that matches the color of the floor. Deep scratches and gouges can be filled with wood filler matched to the color of the floor. (You can also make a paste of wood glue mixed with sawdust from a spare floorboard.) Clean the area to remove all the wax or oil.

With a putty knife, fill the gouge; after the filler sets, sand it smooth, and wax.

▶ Nails are protruding from wood floor.

Pull them out and replace them with annular-ring nails, matching the existing nailing pattern (see illustration below), and set the nail heads. Fill the holes with quick-drying wood filler stained to match the floor, or use a putty crayon of matching color.

Attaching solid wood flooring

¾" tongue-and-groove

Blind-nailed

¾" tongue-and-groove

Screwed and plugged

⁵⁄₁₆" strip flooring

Facenailed

Attaching laminated wood flooring

Plywood core — Hardwood veneer

Blind-nailed — Subfloor

▶ Decorative plugs are missing from wood floor.

You may be able to obtain replacement plugs from a flooring dealer who specializes in wood floors. Otherwise, make plugs from hardwood dowels of the same diameter as the hole. Cut each plug slightly long, spread a thin layer of glue around the base, and tap it into place; wipe away excess glue immediately. After the glue sets, make the plug flush with the floor by sanding or by shaving it with a sharp chisel or a fine-toothed saw. (A hacksaw blade is flexible enough to bend, so you avoid scraping the floor around the plug; protect the floor with a piece of thin sheet metal.) Sand the plug smooth, stain it to match other plugs, and wax the area.

Replacing missing plug

Plug cut from dowel

Cutting off excess plug

Sharp chisel

Finishing replacement plug

Tip *How to wax a wood floor: (1) Move furniture out of the room or out of the high-traffic area you are waxing. (2) With a large cloth, rag mop, or wax applicator, spread the wax on 3-foot sections at a time. If using paste wax, apply a second coat to heavy traffic areas. Apply only one coat under large area rugs to reduce danger of slipping. (3) Buff by hand or with a buffing machine, following the grain of the wood. Labels generally advise that you allow paste wax to dry completely before buffing, but recommend you buff liquid waxes while they are still damp.*

▶ *Floorboard is damaged and needs replacing.*

If the damaged board is short, you can remove the entire board. Carefully split it and remove sections with a chisel and pry bar. If it is tongue-and-groove, remove the tongue with a sharp knife and pry up the entire board. If it is face-nailed square-edge (strip) flooring, simply drive the nails through the board with a nail set to release it.

If the damaged section is in a long board, mark a cut line square to the long edges of the board and bore large holes across the board inside the line (do not drill into the subfloor). Split out pieces of the damaged board and remove them, being careful not to damage adjacent boards. Carefully trim the board to the cut line with a sharp chisel. Sweep and vacuum away the debris. Cut a replacement board to the same length as the cavity and, if the flooring is tongue-and-groove, remove the bottom flange of the groove side of the replacement board. Set the board into place and check the fit. If the floor has been sanded and refinished in the past, the new board will be thicker than adjacent boards. Sand it down to match the level of adjacent boards before installing it. Predrill pilot holes for flooring nails or finishing nails at both ends of the new board, following the existing pattern. Nail, set the nail heads, and cover them with stainable putty (or with color-matched putty after finishing). Stain and finish the new board to match the old flooring, testing stains first on scrap pieces of wood, especially if the replacement board is a different species of wood from the original floor (red oak versus white oak, for example).

If adjacent boards are damaged, stagger the cut lines so the replacement boards won't look like an obvious patch.

Removing a short board

Scrap

Tongue removed first

Removing damaged section of a long board

Spade bit

Cut lines

Pieces split with chisel

End trimmed with chisel

Fitting replacement board

New board

Bottom flange removed

Ends staggered

▶ *Large area is damaged and needs replacing.*

The best-looking repair is to cut out and replace each board individually (see left), so you can stagger the joints to avoid a patched look. A quicker fix is to cut out and replace the entire section as a rectangular patch of new boards. Use a framing square to mark the cut lines. If the floor is blind-nailed (tongue-and-groove boards), mark the cut lines slightly inside the board joints to avoid sawing into nails. Set the saw blade just deep enough to cut through the flooring but not into the subfloor. Cut carefully to avoid running the saw blade past the corners. You'll have to chisel out the parts of boards that the blade does not cut through.

After removing the damaged boards and cleaning out the debris, cut new floorboards to length and install them. If the boards are tongue-and-groove, remove the bottom flange (groove side) of the last board before installing it.

Cutting out damaged area

Saw depth adjusted to thickness of flooring

1x board

Cut line inside joint to avoid nails

Installing new boards

New boards

Square

Flange removed from last board

Tip *If removing floorboards reveals rot or damage to the subfloor, repair it before patching the finish floor.*

▶ Wood floorboard is cupped or warped.

Remove wax or finish and lay a damp towel over the board; keep it damp for 48 hours to moisten the wood and make it supple. Then force the board down with heavy weights and secure it to the subfloor with screws. Screws can be driven into the flooring from below (see page 32) or from above (drill pilot holes and countersink the screws). Drive the screw as far as is possible without straining the board, then tighten it a half turn or so each day until the board is flat. Use enough screws to flatten the board, spacing them approximately 3 to 8 inches apart, then cover them with plugs or wood filler to match the flooring.

If two adjacent tongue-and-groove boards are warped enough that the joint has buckled, it may be impossible to realign the tongue into the groove. Instead, with a hooked knife or a saw set to a shallow depth, remove the tongue from the moistened board and pull the resulting wood strip out of the joint. Then insert screws as just described.

Moistening floorboards

Damp towel

Warped board

Subfloor

Screwing down floorboards

Countersunk screw

Moist board

Subfloor

Alternative: Screw from below

Predrilled hole

Fixing warped tongue-and-groove floorboards

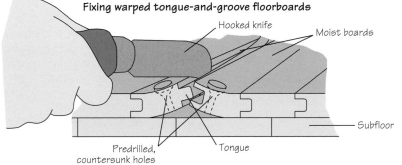

Hooked knife

Moist boards

Subfloor

Predrilled, countersunk holes

Tongue

▶ Wood floor needs sanding and refinishing.

Sanding and refinishing a wood floor is a major undertaking, best done when the house is vacant or during a major renovation.

You will need a drum sander and a floor edger. Both machines are heavy-duty and require some strength to operate. Have the rental agent show you how; machines are not all alike. Pay attention to procedures for changing the sandpaper, lowering the drum, and emptying dust bags. You will need several grades of sandpaper in both sheets and disks. Take home plenty—you won't be charged for what you return unused.

Before sanding make sure the flooring is at least ¼ inch thick by inspecting the board ends at a floor register or by pulling up an inconspicuous board. Then remove all furnishings, including curtains. Cover built-in units and doorways with plastic sheeting secured with masking tape. Remove baseboards. Fill deep holes, replace damaged boards, and set protruding nail heads. Make sure you have a dust mask and shoes with clean soles (not black rubber). You may also wish to wear ear protectors.

Strip floor: Start with a drum sander and the coarsest sandpaper (medium grade for new floors). Always sand with the grain. Because the drum is constantly rotating, never let it engage the floor unless you are rolling the machine forward. Start near the center of one wall and a few inches away from it, standing with your side to the wall. Proceed toward the wall you are facing and stop just before you reach it. Disengage the sanding drum and roll the machine back so the next pass will overlap the previous one by half the width of the drum. Continue, always starting at the

Tip *Estimated time for sanding and refinishing the floor of an average-sized room: Day 1 (two to five hours): Remove furniture, remove baseboards, make repairs, seal off room from the rest of the house, and rent equipment. Day 2 (three to four hours): Sand floor, return sanding equipment, vacuum, wipe floor with tack cloth, and apply stain or sealer. Day 3 (two hours): Rent floor buffer, buff floor, vacuum, wipe with tack cloth, and apply first coat of finish. Day 4 (one hour): Buff finish and apply final coat(s).*

Preparing the floor

Base shoe or baseboard removed

Holes filled

Nail heads set

Drum sanding

Where to stop

Centerline of room

Sanding with an edger

Sanding around corner

Buffing between coats

Buffer with steel-wool pad or screen

midpoint and overlapping passes until you have finished half the room. Turn to face the opposite direction and complete the other half in the same way. Sand the border separately—with the grain— after you finish the main area.

After sanding the entire floor, repeat with the next finer grade sandpaper. Replace the paper when you no longer see any results; the finer paper wears out more quickly. When this second sanding is done, fill any remaining open cracks or nail holes with wood filler. When it dries, sand the entire floor with the fine-grit sandpaper.

Use an edge sander to sand along walls and in tight spaces. This rotary sander uses sandpaper disks, is faster than the drum sander, and is more prone to gouging. It also sands across the grain. Start out in closets or other hidden spaces until you get the feel of it. Using a scallop motion of small semicircles rather than a straight back-and-forth motion helps to avoid gouging. In corners where the border joins at right angles, turn the edger to go with the grain, and go back and forth around that turn several times. Again, sand first with the coarsest paper, then with medium, filling cracks and nail holes before the final sanding with fine-grit paper. Use a hand scraper and sanding block to get into awkward corners that the edger misses.

Parquet floors: Using coarse paper, sand the entire floor diagonally in one direction. Then sand diagonally at a right angle to the first direction with medium paper (thus forming an *x*). Finish with a fine grit, sanding parallel to one set of walls. Sand twice (make two passes) with each grit, always in the

Tip *Fine sanding dust, most floor finishes, and finish fumes are all flammable. Keep the room ventilated, extinguish pilot lights, and do not smoke while working. Empty dust bags and dispose of rags according to instructions from the rental agency or on the product labels.*

same direction. Use the edger as for strip floors. A parquet floor is likely to need a lot of filler, so buy a 1-gallon can and goop it on liberally before the final sanding.

All floors: Seal or stain the floor the same day that you finish sanding to prevent it from absorbing moisture from the air. Vacuum the floor and all horizontal surfaces in the room thoroughly, then wipe the floor with a tack cloth. Apply the sealer or stain with a sheepskin applicator, wiping away all excess after 10 or 15 minutes.

After the stain dries, buff the room with fine steel wool (#2/0)—unless the finish is water-based, in which case use window screening or very fine sandpaper; steel wool leaves particles that rust. Then vacuum and dust with a tack cloth. Apply the finish, according to instructions. Oil-based finishes require two coats, with 24 hours of drying time between coats; water-based finishes dry more quickly but require more coats. Lightly buff between coats.

▶ Heat registers don't match wood floor.

Warm-air heating systems often have vents, or registers, located in prominent places. If the appearance of an ordinary metal grille is not acceptable, you can obtain handsome wood grilles from flooring dealers or installers. They come in a variety of sizes and wood species. You can stain the unfinished wood to match your flooring, or choose a contrasting color. The grille fits flush with the surface of the floor, so you may have to trim the floor opening if the edges are ragged. The edges of the grille can also be trimmed to fit. Decorative brass grilles are also available, but usually only in standard dimensions.

▶ *Wood floor on concrete slab is warped.*

Wood floors installed over concrete slabs, especially in basements, are often exposed to moisture and unstable conditions that cause the wood to expand and contract, leading to warping, splits, and other problems. Solid-wood flooring is particularly sensitive to these conditions and may continue to be so even if you replace individual warped boards.

The best solution, if you want a permanently durable wood floor, is to install prefinished, laminated (veneer) wood flooring in place of the solid-wood floor. Because it is thinner (⅜ inch) than most solid-wood flooring and because the veneers (plies) are oriented in different directions, this type of flooring does not expand and contract easily. Tongue-and-groove joints on the edges and on the ends, consistent dimensions, and adhesive bonding make this flooring easy to install. Some types may be attached directly to the

concrete slab with a recommended adhesive (so long as the concrete is structurally sound and free of moisture problems). Where there is any danger at all of dampness coming through the basement floor, install the wood floor by "floating" it on a ⅛-inch-thick foam pad laid over 6 mil plastic sheeting. The boards are glued together at their edges, but not to the floor—hence, a "floating" floor. Install according to manufacturer's instructions.

A second way to install a wood floor if there's danger of dampness is to install a wood subfloor over the concrete: Lay down a moisture barrier of 6 mil polyethylene sheeting; attach 2x4 pressure-treated sleepers to the floor with a nailing gun; nail ¾-inch plywood to the sleepers (leave ¹⁄₁₆- to ⅛-inch expansion gaps around the panels). If the floor needs insulation, install foam panels between the sleepers.

Installing a wood floor on a concrete slab

Tongue-and-groove on edges and ends

Adhesive applied directly to dry slab

Edges glued together

"Floating" a wood floor on a concrete slab

Expansion gap

⅛" foam

Concrete

6 mil polyethylene sheeting

Installing a subfloor on a concrete slab

Finish flooring

Adhesive

Plywood subfloor

4"

Asphalt mastic

Maximum 48"

Polyethylene sheeting

12"

Tip   *The most popular wood-floor finishes are polyurethane, which are available in oil-based or water-based forms. The water-based ones emit fewer volatile organic compounds (VOCs) and are easier to touch up or recoat, but they are harder to spread and require more coats. Follow label directions carefully and, to ensure compatibility, use sealers, stains, and finishes from the same manufacturer.*

► **Wood floor has carpet adhesive on it.**

See page 37.

► **Slate floor needs cleaning.**

For routine cleaning, vacuum thoroughly and wash with a mild solution of water and washing soda or laundry detergent. Do not scour with abrasive pads and powders. If the floor is dull from waxy buildup, remove the old wax with a commercial floor wax remover. Experiment in a hidden area first. If it doesn't work, TSP or a water-based paint stripper may work; test first. After scrubbing the floor and letting it dry, apply a penetrating tile-and-brick sealer. If you prefer a softer sheen, apply a paste wax instead; use one with carnauba (test first; some stone is not porous enough to hold the wax and it will just come off on people's shoes). However, you will have to renew it every few months and remove the wax buildup when it becomes dull and dingy.

Clean stains with phosphoric acid diluted in water, following label directions.

► **Quarry tiles need cleaning.**

Use the same techniques as for a slate floor (see above).

► **Ceramic-tile floor is old and needs replacing.**

Before you tear it out and replace it, consider painting the tiles or installing new tiles directly over them. The present floor must be free of cracks and the subfloor structurally sound.

For painting, the surface must be roughened, usually by sanding (which you can do yourself), or by

acid etching (which requires a professional). Then you can paint the floor with epoxy paint.

If the present installation is sound and the new tiles will not create a height or weight problem, install new tiles over old with epoxy adhesives. Roughen the old tiles, as described above, and remove the dust with a damp sponge. Fill in grout depressions with new adhesive. Install the new tiles.

► **Floor tile is cracked and needs replacing.**

See page 48.

► **Baseboard doesn't touch flooring.**

Unless the gap is more than ⅛ inch, this condition is desirable. It prevents the baseboard from interfering with the normal expansion and contraction of resilient or wood flooring materials. If the gap exceeds ⅛ inch, nail a base shoe into the baseboard—not the floor. Place cardboard shims under the shoe while nailing it, so there will still be a ⅛-inch gap.

► **Corner joint of baseboard has gap.**

Corner joints may open up as the house settles or the baseboards shrink. Outside corners, which are mitered, are more prone to reveal a gap than inside corners, which are usually coped. If a miter joint gap is small, fill it with plastic wood filler, or, if the board is painted, nonshrinking spackling compound. Work the patching material into the crack and roughly contour it with a putty knife or your finger. After it sets, sand it to the same shape as the baseboard profile and finish it to match the baseboard. Larger gaps may require replacing

one or both sections of baseboard. See page 31 for instructions on making corners.

► **Baseboard is damaged.**

See page 30.

► **Baseboard is too plain.**

If the baseboards are a modern style with simple lines and you want something more traditional and ornate, you may not have to replace the baseboards completely. You may be able to add molding strips to the existing baseboards to create a more elaborate profile. Obtain samples of small molding strips, such as base shoe, chair rail, picture molding, or fluted bead, and experiment with various arrangements to see if they can be combined with existing baseboard to create a more appropriate style. If so, install them using techniques described on page 30. Be sure to nail all the pieces into the baseboard or wall, not the floor.

Adding molding to baseboard

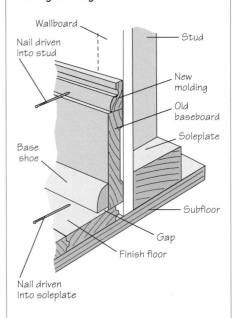

- Wallboard
- Nail driven into stud
- Base shoe
- Nail driven into soleplate
- Stud
- New molding
- Old baseboard
- Soleplate
- Subfloor
- Gap
- Finish floor

Tip *When painting baseboards that have carpet installed against them, use a paint shield (or thin sheet of metal or stiff plastic; a spare slat from miniblinds works well) to hold the carpet tufts away from the baseboard as you paint it. Wipe off the shield every time you move it.*

▶ Tile is dirty, stained, or mildewed.

For general cleaning of glazed tile, use a commercial scrubbing foam, a mild detergent, or a solution of ½ gallon water and ¼ cup ammonia. For stains caused by mineral deposits, wipe with vinegar or a solution of equal parts ammonia and water; then rinse. For other stains, mix TSP or washing soda with just enough water to make a paste. Apply it to the stain, holding it in place with tape if it won't stick. Leave it for several hours, rewetting when necessary. Remove the cleaner by rubbing it with vinegar. For stubborn stains, use oxalic acid, following label directions carefully. For mildew, spray with commercial mildew cleaner or a chlorine bleach solution, as recommended on the bleach label. Then wipe with a solution of baking soda and water to remove the chlorine odor. Most of these treatments involve agents that contain acids or alkalines, which can break down the portland cements used in grout, so use them sparingly. Use mild detergents or tile cleaners for routine cleaning. For unglazed tiles, such as quarry tile, always use mild detergent. Avoid acid-based cleaners.

▶ Marble or other stone tiles are dirty or stained.

Clean with a mild solution of soap flakes or marble cleaner. Rinse well with water and let dry. Do not use ammonia, vinegar, or any cleaners with acids or alkalines.

To remove stains from marble, make a paste of soap flakes and hydrogen peroxide. Spread it on the stain; rub in the direction of the grain. Rinse well with water and let dry. Repolish, if necessary, with whiting powder (calcium carbonate).

▶ Grout is dirty or stained.

To clean stubborn dirt from grout, use a stiff brush (a grout brush or old toothbrush works well) with scouring powder that does not contain bleach. Test the cleaner in a concealed area to make sure it doesn't discolor the grout. For stubborn stains use a mild solution of water and phosphoric acid, according to label directions; increase the concentration of acid, if necessary. Wear rubber gloves and avoid spilling the acid solution on glass shower doors; it may etch them (but not your skin—this type of acid shouldn't irritate any but the most sensitive skin, if you follow all label precautions).

▶ Grout is deteriorating or missing.

For small touch-up work, replace missing areas of grout with color-matched caulk. To replace large areas of damaged or missing grout, first remove all remnants of the old grout with a grout saw. This is a tedious job; there is no shortcut. Work it back and forth along each grout line. After removing the grout, vacuum out the cracks. Look for loose tiles, deteriorating subsurface, or other damage that may have caused the grout to fail; fix before proceeding.

Remove soap scum and other residue from the tile surface by washing it with phosphoric acid and water, mixed according to label directions (see above). Wait until the area dries completely to mix the grout.

Grout comes in many colors, so you should be able to match the existing grout by checking samples at a tile shop. For installations with wide grout lines, use sanded grout. For wet installations (showers, tubs, countertops), mix the grout powder with a latex or vinyl additive instead of water. For kitchen countertops use epoxy worktop grout; it's waterproof and resists dirt, bacteria, and stains.

Apply grout with a rubber float, spreading it diagonally in both directions across the joint lines and packing it firmly into the cracks. Remove the excess with a damp sponge. After about 30 minutes shape the joints with the damp sponge to match the original grout. Wait another hour, then polish the tile with a soft cloth. After the grout sets (usually 24 to 48 hours), apply a grout sealer according to label directions.

Removing old grout

Grout saw

Applying new grout

45°

Rubber float

Sealing new grout

Tip *Ammonia or cleaners containing acid should never be mixed with chlorine; it makes a poisonous gas. Never mix chlorinated laundry bleach with other cleaning products.*

Tip *Extend grout life by applying a grout sealer once or twice a year, according to label directions. Use silicone-based sealers in tubs and showers, but not on kitchen surfaces where food is prepared. Use natural lemon oil instead. For most sealers, the grout must be completely dry before sealing and must not be wet for a certain time after sealing, which will prevent use of the shower or tub. For greatest convenience, do only one bathroom at a time, or plan this procedure around vacations.*

► Grout around bathtub is missing or damaged.

The joint around a bathtub where the wall meets the tub is an important moisture seal and must be maintained to prevent structural damage. It should be sealed with caulk, not grout. (The vertical corners above a bathtub or shower floor, where tiled walls join at an angle, should also be sealed with caulk.) To renew a joint, scrape out all of the old grout (or caulk) with a grout saw, screwdriver, or similar tool. Then vacuum away the debris and clean the area thoroughly with vinegar or a phosphoric acid solution of 1 part acid in 10 parts water. Let it dry. Apply a bead of tub-and-tile caulk (specified as 100 percent silicone) to the joint. Smooth the caulk with a moistened finger or old spoon dipped in soapy water. Wipe away excess with a rag. While you are at it, recaulk any gaps around faucet handles, spouts, and showerheads. Moisture that leaks into these gaps can cause serious problems.

Removing old grout or caulk

Corner joint

Applying caulk

Caulking gun

► Grout color is unappealing.

The most reliable way to change the color of grout is to replace it , but you may be able to stain grout if it has not been sealed. Choose an acceptable stain color and experiment in a hidden area. Using a nylon-bristled brush, clean the grout with scouring powder or a mild solution of phosphoric acid and water. Let it dry. With a small artist's brush, apply the stain to the grout. Keep lines straight and avoid getting stain on the tile surface. After the stain dries thoroughly, apply a penetrating sealer that can be used over colored grout, following label directions.

► Tile is cracked or loose.

Remove the old tile. If it's loose, you should be able to pop it up with a screwdriver (don't wedge the screwdriver against adjacent tiles). If not, you'll have to break the old tile and chip out the pieces. Wear heavy gloves and eye protection—broken tile is very sharp. Cover any drains and protect surrounding surfaces with newspaper or cardboard. First remove the grout around the damaged tile (see page 47) so hammer blows won't jar adjacent tiles. Then break up the tile with short, sharp hammer blows; chip away the pieces with the hammer and a cold chisel. Carefully chisel away all adhesive residue and any leftover grout. Don't use chemical removers to clean off the old adhesive; it will weaken the bond of the new and surrounding adhesive. Fill depressions in the backing with patching compound and paint it with latex primer.

Dry-fit the replacement tile to make sure that it doesn't protrude above the surrounding tiles. Attach it with the same type of adhesive as the original (thin-set resembles

cement mortar; organic mastic resembles hardened rubber). Apply adhesive to the back of the tile with a notched trowel to within ½ inch of each edge. Twist the tile slightly as you position it. Use a rubber mallet or a hammer and woodblock to tap the tile firmly into place. Remove excess adhesive, especially from inside the joint crack. To keep the tile aligned as the adhesive sets, place matchsticks, shims, or tile spacers in the joints; on vertical surfaces, secure the tile with tape. After the adhesive sets (24 to 48 hours), remove the shims and grout the joints (see page 47).

Removing broken tile

Grout removed

Removing old adhesive and applying new

Adhesive stops ½" from edges

Depressions filled

Aligning tile

Vinyl tile spacer

Toothpick or matchstick

Cardboard

Tip *If you can't find an exact replacement for a missing tile, create an accent by buying a decorative tile or a tile of a contrasting color. Replace several tiles, if necessary, to establish a pattern or to create a small mosaic. You may be able to match bathroom tiles by removing some from behind the toilet tank and replacing them with something else. This is a last resort, as you'll have to remove the toilet tank, remove all grout around the tiles, and then take your chances trying to pop them off without breaking them by striking a broad chisel under the edge of each tile.*

▶ Tile is chipped.

If it's only slightly nicked and not in a conspicuous place, try covering the nick with appliance touch-up paint. It adheres well and dries very hard. If you have trouble matching the color (only white and almond can be tinted with paint), try acrylic or epoxy paint. If painting doesn't work, replace the tile.

▶ Trim pieces are falling off of counter edge.

The procedure is the same as for replacing a missing tile (see opposite page), except that you'll have to improvise a way to hold the trim piece in place while the adhesive sets (masking tape works well). If several pieces have fallen, it's probably because they didn't have enough support. Remove the rest of the trim pieces and attach a wood strip to the edge of the countertop substrate with glue and screws. It should be just thick enough for the L-shaped trim pieces to clear. Prime or seal the wood strip, let the sealer dry, and reinstall the trim pieces over it.

Supporting trim pieces

Trim pieces
Tape
Adhesive
Support strip
Substrate

▶ Tile surface has adhesive stuck to it.

Old adhesive bonds so tightly to tile that it is almost impossible to remove. You may be able to chip it off carefully, but pieces of glazing and tile will probably come off with it. Muriatic acid may work, if the adhesive is a cement-based compound, such as thin-set. Combine 1 part acid with 10 parts water and apply a tiny amount directly to the adhesive, following label directions. Wear rubber gloves and eye protection and protect nearby surfaces; the acid will eat into grout. If this doesn't work, replace the tile or paint the adhesive to match the tile.

▶ Tile color is unappealing.

Tile can be painted with epoxy paint that is designed for this purpose. Consult a tile supplier and follow label directions. Roughen the tile surface with 120-grit sandpaper, then clean thoroughly before painting. Plan to paint the grout lines as well, unless you have great patience and a steady hand (and the grout is worth leaving exposed).

▶ You want to install new tile over old.

If the old tile is sound and the new tile won't create a thickness or weight problem, install it directly over the old. Otherwise, remove the old tile and prepare a new underlayment. Several adhesives are suitable for installing tile over tile; consult a dealer and check product labels. Before installing the new tile, roughen the old tile with a masonry rubbing stone and level the grout joints with adhesive.

▶ You want to install tile over laminate countertop.

Look for delaminated edges or other loose places and glue them down. Clean the plastic laminate thoroughly with TSP or a similar all-purpose cleaner that will remove grease and other residue. Roughen the surface with sandpaper and wipe clean with a damp sponge. Fill cracks or gaps with epoxy adhesive. Use epoxy adhesive to install the tiles, using the same setting method as for any new tile installation.

▶ You want to drill a hole through tile.

Use a variable-speed drill with a glass- or tile-drilling bit. Some bits are shaped like traditional twist drills; others have spear points. Either type should have a tungsten carbide-hardened tip. To keep the bit on target as you start drilling, scratch a small *x* into the tile surface with a glass cutter, machinist's file, or other hardened steel tool. Run the drill at a very slow speed and lubricate the bore with antifreeze as you drill. After you drill through the tile, change the bit if you want to extend the bore into wood.

Drilling hole in tile

Straw
Antifreeze
Spear-point tile bit

Tip   *Update an old countertop by replacing the trim pieces around the edge. This is much easier than replacing the entire countertop.*

Tip   *If paint is stuck to the surface of tile, apply a water-based commercial paint remover, leave it on for an hour, then scrape off the softened paint with a putty knife or razor blade. Do not use steel wool; it scratches the surface and leaves steel fragments in the grout that may rust later.*

▶ *Cabinet drawer is tight or stuck.*

If a drawer sticks all of the time, sand or plane down the high spots on each side of the drawer. These spots will look worn and smooth, or can be located by rubbing chalk all along the drawer edges and seeing where it wears off first. Do not sand or plane too much wood or the drawer may wobble.

If the drawer has mechanical guide rails on the side or center, clean out any dust or grease that might cause sluggish movement. Lubricate the guides with a non-sticking lubricant, such as graphite. If the guides are badly worn or bent, replace them with identical hardware. If the guides are wood, check for a loose guide that binds the drawer and secure it with screws (predrill pilot holes).

If the drawer sticks only during wet or humid weather, it is swelling temporarily but will shrink back to normal size. For temporary relief rub a bar of soap, a candle, or a silicone grease stick along the drawer edges and runners. Then, during dry weather when the drawer works normally, paint or seal the sides (all faces and edges) to stop them from absorbing moisture.

▶ *Drawer is loose and wobbly.*

Remove it and check to see if the center guide is broken or out of alignment. If so, reattach it to the cabinet frame with screws or, if it's broken, replace it with a new one. Use a framing square to install the guide perpendicular to the cabinet face. If there is no center guide, check to see if the support rails inside the cabinet have channels for keeping the drawer aligned. If not, attach a strip of wood to each rail, just outside the path made by the bottom edge of the drawer side. Tack it in place after

sliding the drawer in and out to make sure the strip will guide the drawer properly. Then glue and nail or screw the strips in place. In addition check for excessive wear on the bottom of the drawer and on rails inside the cabinet. Replace worn parts, or cut away the worn sections of wood, cut new strips of wood to replace them (hardwood is best), and attach the strips with carpenter's wood glue and short paneling nails (grooved finishing brads); predrill to prevent splitting. An alternative to cutting new strips of wood is to build up the worn area with self-sticking (or iron-on) veneer strips used for edging plywood or particleboard.

Attaching center guide

Attaching guide strips

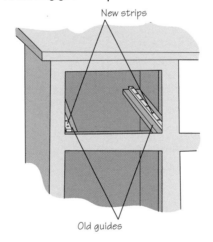

New strips

Old guides

▶ *Drawer won't stop and falls out.*

Remove the drawer. Screw a scrap of wood or metal to the inside of the drawer back. The scrap should protrude about 1 inch above the top of the back—high enough to bump against the front rail of the cabinet frame when the drawer is pulled open, but not high enough to scrape against the bottom of the countertop or drawer above.

▶ *Drawer bottom is loose; contents fall out.*

Remove and empty the drawer and inspect it. Most drawer bottoms are held in place by grooves cut into the drawer sides and front, with tacks holding the drawer bottom to the bottom of the drawer back. The tacks may have come loose, allowing the drawer bottom to sag and pull free from the grooves in the drawer sides. To reattach the bottom, slide it out of the grooves and turn it upside down (or replace it with a new bottom cut from plywood). Then nail it to the bottom of the drawer back with paneling nails (grooved finishing brads).

If the bottom fell out because the drawer sides have separated from the drawer back and spread apart, disassemble the drawer by knocking the loose joints apart with a rubber mallet or hammer and woodblock. Glue the sides and back together with carpenter's wood glue, clamp the drawer together (or use string and tape as shown on opposite page), and let the glue dry overnight. Then slide the drawer bottom into the grooves and tack it in place with paneling nails.

If the bottom fell out because part of a side split away (the part below the groove), remove all of the remaining drawer side below the groove with a plane or fine-toothed saw. Cut a new strip of

Tip   *Some drawer problems may be a simple matter of the wrong drawer in the slot. Before starting a repair, switch around drawers of identical size to see if they'll work better.*

wood to replace the old runner (straight-grained hardwood works best), and attach it with glue and paneling nails (drill pilot holes for the nails; the sides are probably brittle).

Tacking bottom

Drawer front
Bottom
Side
Drawer back
Paneling nail

Clamping drawer

Woodblock
Woodblock
Plastic sheeting

Alternative

Cardboard
Pencil or dowel
Strong twine
Tape

Attaching a new runner

Hardwood strip
Bottom

▶ *Handle has pulled off.*

The threads in the handle have probably been stripped, so the bolt or screw that holds it to the drawer face can no longer get a grip. If you can't find a replacement handle, try squirting some adhesive or silicone caulk into the threaded hole of the pull; then reassemble and wait 24 hours before testing it. If the handle is plastic, you could also replace the screw with a slightly larger sheet-metal screw.

▶ *Drawer and door handles need changing.*

Buying new drawer and door pulls is an easy and inexpensive way to upgrade kitchen cabinets. Although looks should be your main consideration in choosing new handles, also consider the alignment of screw holes—the job is much easier if the screw holes for the new handles line up with the holes in the cabinet faces. If not, try to use at least one of the holes in the cabinet face, then drill a new one for the second handle screw. If you're left with a blank screw hole in the cabinet face, fill it with wood filler stained to match the cabinets, or use a putty stick that already matches. Some handle designs include a face plate that will cover unused screw holes in the door or drawer front.

Replacing cabinet handles

New hole
New pull
Old pull
Stove bolt

▶ *Cabinet doors don't align.*

Cabinets built recently should have adjustable hinges for fine-tuning the alignment of the door. Just by rotating one or more adjusting screws, or loosening and tightening a sliding setscrew, you can tilt the door from side-to-side or front-to-back. While you make adjustments, count the number of screw rotations for each setting you try, in case you need to go back to a previous setting.

If the hinges don't have adjusting screws, you can still make adjustments by loosening screws and inserting cardboard shims behind a hinge leaf. To tilt the door from side-to-side, place shims behind leaves attached to the cabinet frame; to tilt it front-to-back, place shims behind leaves attached to the back of the door.

Aligning doors with adjustable hinges

Shimming nonadjustable hinges

Cardboard shim

Tip *Avoid scouring pads or abrasive powders on laminated plastic finishes.*

▶ Cabinets have fingerprints and smudges around handles.

Apply mechanic's hand cleaner to a rag and scrub lightly (heavy-duty bar soap specified for hands also works). For stubborn buildup, use mineral spirits or paint thinner. Restore the finish with furniture oil or paste wax.

▶ Cabinet door sticks.

Note the exact places where the door edge sticks to the frame; look for worn spots. Hold a straightedge against these areas, first on the door edge and then on the corresponding area of door frame, to see which side has the high spots. Smooth down the high spots with a plane or, if dust will not be a problem, a belt sander. Finish with fine sandpaper and touch up with paint or stain to match the cabinets.

▶ Cabinets don't provide enough accessible storage space.

There are dozens of space-saving organizers that you can install in, on, or near existing cabinets to increase storage capacity and access. Install heavy-duty lazy susans or half-susans (semicircular shelves attached to the door) in lower corner cabinets, and multitiered lazy susans in upper corner cabinets. Mount shallow spice racks on the inside of doors, or store spices in a drawer (in a spice tray) to free up cabinet space. Convert the front panel of a sink cabinet to a tilt-out tray. Equip drawers with two-tiered utensil trays. Install pullout shelves or baskets in lower cabinets to make the contents more accessible. Utilize space under the sink by installing slide-out baskets, trash containers, or shelves; or attach storage trays, a trash container, or a towel rack to the inside of the sink cabinet doors. Free up cabinet space for pots and pans by installing a pot rack on the wall or ceiling near the range. Hang stemware from racks mounted below the wall cabinets.

If organizers aren't enough, look for places to install new cabinets that match existing ones. Consider a deep cabinet above the refrigerator, a pantry unit on a blank wall, a tall pantry unit to replace narrow upper and lower cabinets at the end of a counter, or an appliance garage on a corner of the countertop or recessed into the wall behind a straight section of countertop. Consider a portable kitchen island with a cutting-board top and storage shelves.

▶ Upper cabinets are cold in the winter.

Probably, the soffit above the upper cabinets opens directly into the attic and is not insulated. From the attic, install ½-inch wallboard over the soffit cavity (use screws to avoid pounding and raising dust). Cover the wallboard with insulation batts equal to the thickness required in your area (typically 8 to 12 inches).

▶ Stained wood cabinets need painting.

Remove the doors and drawers. With TSP or a similar cleaning product, wash the doors, drawer fronts, and cabinet frames thoroughly and let dry. Roughen the surfaces with 120-grit sandpaper, vacuum them, and wipe them with a tack cloth. Prime all surfaces with a high-quality white-pigmented shellac, following label directions carefully. Use a high-quality oil-based enamel for the finish coats. Make sure the room is well ventilated and free of dust.

Sand between coats with 220-grit sandpaper; remove dust with a thorough vacuuming and then a tack cloth. Doors and drawer fronts should be horizontal when you paint them, to eliminate sags and droops. Spray painting gives the smoothest finish, then foam rollers, then brushes, then conventional rollers. *Note:* If the cabinets are oak or other porous wood, the grain will show through the paint. To get a smoother finish, use 150-grit sandpaper when roughening the surface and let the dust fill the pores—don't vacuum or wipe it all out. Then seal it with two coats of primer.

▶ Wood cabinets need bleaching or pickling.

Remove the doors and drawers and strip all cabinet surfaces to bare wood by removing the finish with a solvent-based or water-based stripper. Follow label directions carefully, including safety precautions, working times, disposal instructions, and specifications for the types of scouring pads to use. If there are still traces of the old finish, apply two coats of wood bleach. After stripping off the old finish, clean the surfaces as specified on the product label and, when dry, sand them with 120-grit sandpaper. Then apply a white pickling stain over the bare wood, according to label directions.

▶ Plastic laminate cabinets need painting.

Plastic laminate surfaces can be painted using epoxy paints, but it should be done professionally. Consult a local painting contractor who has experience painting this type of cabinet.

Tip *When painting, stripping, or staining cabinets, test a small section first to make sure you will be satisfied with the results before you take on the entire kitchen.*

▶ Cabinets are too plain.

If changing the handles or painting the cabinets isn't enough, you can try dressing up the fronts of cabinet doors and drawers with decorative moldings. Buy samples of several different sizes and profiles, then experiment with various combinations to create borders and designs. Try duplicating cabinet fronts that you've seen before and liked. Don't make a final selection until you've mocked up a sample of a complete door (one of the actual doors or a plywood substitute), painted it, and looked at it in the kitchen over the course of several days.

Another option is to have all of the cabinets refaced. Most areas have local contractors that specialize in this process.

▶ Solid-surface countertop has scratches, burns, or stains.

"Erase" the mark by scouring it lightly with household cleaner and a damp cloth, or with very fine (600-grit) wet/dry sandpaper dampened slightly. Some countertops require a coarser grade of sandpaper (320- to 400-grit). If the stain is deep, you can keep sanding without danger of rubbing away a veneered surface; the color goes all the way through the material. Feather the sanding so it doesn't create a noticeable depression. Finish by buffing with a soapless synthetic scouring pad. For deep gouges or damage, consult a professional countertop installer.

▶ Cultured marble countertop has burns or stains.

Most types of cast polymer (cultured marble) countertop have a protective surface that is only a thin veneer. Abrading it too much removes the coating and exposes the inner core, which is a softer material usually a different color than the surface. If very light scouring with household cleaner or 600-grit wet/dry sandpaper doesn't remove the stain, your only recourse is to replace the countertop. If light sanding removes the stain, renew the countertop by applying a coat of auto-body polish—except on surfaces where food is prepared, which should be treated with mineral oil, or left untreated.

▶ Tile countertop has stains, chips, cracks, or missing tiles.

See pages 47 and 48.

▶ Plastic laminate countertop has light scratches.

Scratches can't be eliminated, but if normal wear doesn't soften the unsightliness, try hiding the scratches by painting them with an acrylic paint. Take a sample of the laminate to the paint dealer to get a custom-mixed color to match. If you can find an appliance or auto-body touch-up paint that matches, it will dry harder. Apply the paint with an artist's brush.

▶ Plastic laminate countertop has stains.

Remove stains by rubbing mild liquid detergent or a paste of baking soda and water onto the stain with a soft brush; don't scour or use a household cleaner. If this doesn't work, lighten the stain by applying chlorine bleach or denatured alcohol with a damp cloth; rinse the area immediately.

▶ Plastic laminate countertop has burns or severe stains.

Burns and severe stains cannot be repaired. Although it's possible to patch the damaged area or replace a large section of laminate with a new piece, the easiest solution is to cut out the damaged area and replace it with an inset of a different material, such as decorative tiles or a synthetic cutting board (kits with mounting hardware are available).

Start by selecting the material and determining the exact size of cutout it requires. Then mark lines on the laminate surface for the cutout. Place masking tape over the cut lines to minimize chipping and to protect the surface, and trace the cut lines on the tape. Empty the drawer or shelf contents below the cutout area.

Drill 1-inch holes at two opposite corners for starter holes. Clamp or brace straightedge cutting guides to the countertop to guide the tools; you will be cutting through both the laminate and the substrate below it, which is typically ¾-inch material, either particleboard or plywood. To keep the cutout from breaking off and falling through the hole too soon, lay a 1x2 swivel stick across it and drive one screw

Tip   The National Kitchen and Bath Association recommends the following minimum countertop dimensions: Total frontage (length of countertop fronts) for kitchens smaller than 150 square feet—132 inches; total for kitchens larger than 150 square feet—198 inches; on each side of a sink—24 inches and 18 inches; for food-preparation area—36 inches; on latch side of refrigerator—15 inches (or a 15-inch landing space no more than 48 inches from refrigerator); on each side of a cooktop flanked by a wall—15 inches on open side and 3 inches on wall side; on each side of an open cooktop—15 inches and 9 inches; beside an oven—15 inches (or a 15-inch landing within 48 inches of oven if it does not open into a traffic lane); for a microwave oven—15 inches above, below, or beside the oven.

through the stick into the laminate top, centered inside the cutout. Rotate this board out of the way as you cut around the opening. Make the cut with a jigsaw (teeth should be pointing downward), a compass handsaw (12 teeth per inch or finer), or a router with a deep, straight bit. Cut the corners carefully; you don't want to overcut them and leave kerf marks.

Clean up the edges of the cut with a file or rasp. Cover the bottom of the hole with a piece of plywood, screwed into the bottom of the countertop from below; this will hold the inset. Seal it with primer or sealer and add shim material as necessary to flush the inset surface with the countertop surface. Attach the inset material with adhesive and seal all gaps with grout or caulk.

Cutting out damaged section

Jigsaw

Spacers

Straight-edge

1"-dia holes

Swivel stick

Preparing the cutout for inset

Tiles or other inset material

Plywood screwed to bottom of countertop

Additional backing (as necessary)

▶ Butcher-block countertop is dirty and worn.

For routine cleaning scrape with a plastic scraper, then rub with salt; rinse well and wipe dry. Rub surfaces used for food with vegetable oil; rub other surfaces with mineral oil. Let sit for 5 to 15 minutes, then wipe up excess oil.

To renew a butcher-block top, sand thoroughly with a reciprocating (or orbital) sander. Start with medium grades of sandpaper (100-grit) and finish with fine grades (200-, then 400-grit). Vacuum the block and remove all dust with a tack cloth. Protect with vegetable or mineral oil; heat the oil in a double boiler first, so it will penetrate the wood more easily.

▶ Vanity countertop is loose.

You will have to remove the countertop and reset it with caulk. To remove it, close the shutoff valves below the sink, disconnect the risers from them, and remove the P-trap. Lift the vanity top, with faucet and drain fitting attached, and carefully set it aside.

With the top removed, make sure the vanity is securely attached to the wall. If not, secure the back to the studs with screws. Then replace the countertop on the vanity to see if it wobbles. If so, mark the high spots around the top of the vanity where the countertop makes contact. Remove the countertop and plane down the high spots along the edge of the vanity; test-fit the countertop and replane as necessary until the top no longer wobbles. Apply a bead of silicone caulk around the top edge of the vanity, set the countertop in place, and press down on it. Let it set for an hour or two before reconnecting the plumbing or using it.

▶ Plastic laminate is loose and lifting.

Scrape out all debris and old adhesive from under the loose section (lift carefully). To make sure that the area is thoroughly dry, prop up the loose laminate for a day or two. Spread contact cement under the laminate, lower the laminate flap onto the cement long enough to coat it, and pull the flap up immediately. Prop up the laminate (toothpicks or matchsticks work well) long enough for the cement on both surfaces to get tacky, then press the laminate in place and smooth it down with a rolling pin.

Holding cemented surfaces apart

Toothpicks or matchsticks

Contact cement applied to both surfaces

Tip *If other techniques don't remove a stain from a plastic laminate countertop, look for a cleaner specified for plastic laminates, usually with a tylol-exyol base. Such cleaners are available from paint dealers, full-service hardware stores, or suppliers that sell plastic laminates.*

▶ Stairs squeak.

Fix squeaks by tightening loose stair parts that are rubbing together. First pinpoint the squeaks by observing the stairs closely while a helper steps on them. If a tread moves and rubs against the riser below it, drive 8d or 12d finishing nails down through the tread (and through any carpet) into the riser. If possible, force some construction adhesive into the gap before nailing it shut. For greater strength use trimhead screws (wallboard screws with small heads). To conceal the heads, slice a small flap of the tread with a knife or sharp chisel, lift the flap, drive the screw beneath it, then glue the flap down over the screw head. Drive the nails in pairs set at oppos-

ing angles. To prevent splitting, drill pilot holes before nailing. Have your helper stand on the tread while you nail.

If squeaks are caused by the back of a tread rubbing against the riser above it, insert glue-coated shims between the tread and riser. Trim them flush with a knife or fine-toothed saw and cover the gap with thin molding.

If a tread or riser is loose at either end, reattach it to the stair stringer with nails or screws, as described above. If you have access to the treads from underneath the stairs, snug wood blocks against the loose joints and attach them with glue and screws, or insert glued wedges.

▶ Handrail is coming loose from wall.

Most handrails are supported by brackets screwed into wall studs. If one comes loose, fix it immediately. A handrail must be able to support 200 pounds in any direction, along its entire length. If the screws won't retighten, replace them with longer screws that will. If the original bracket was secured with hollow-wall fasteners between studs, detach the bracket from the handrail and attach it to the closest stud with lag screws or wood screws that penetrate at least 1½ inches into the wood. Add another bracket along the span created by moving the first bracket.

▶ End of handrail is open.

A handrail that terminates without butting into a wall or newel post is dangerous; it could snag someone's sleeve and cause a fall. Fix this problem by attaching a "return" to the end of the handrail so it bends into the adjacent wall. Short sections of curved handrail that match the most common handrail styles are available for this purpose. To attach one to the handrail, make sure the ends of both pieces are cut square. Detach the handrail from the last wall bracket so you can pull it away from the wall to provide clearance for screwing in the curved section. Drill pilot holes for a double-ended screw and drive the screw halfway into the hole in the old rail. Spread carpenter's wood glue on one of the surfaces to be joined and screw the handrail extension onto the screw until it is tight. Stain the curved piece and touch up the joint to match the handrail. Re-attach the handrail to the wall bracket. If the bracket is not within 3 inches of the new end piece,

Nailing down tread — Angled nails — Riser — Pilot holes

Concealing screw head — Flap

Inserting glued shims — Shim inserted from back — Shims — Block

Securing blocks from below — Pilot holes — Wedges

Tip   *Stairways that change direction may have winders (wedge-shaped stairs) to get around the corner, instead of a level platform. This type of stairway can be dangerous because treads are so narrow at the inside corner. Codes, when they do allow such stairs, require that the narrow end be no less than 6 inches wide and that the winder be at least as wide as the regular treads at a point 12 inches from the narrow end. Make winders safer by painting the nosings white so they are easy to see, providing additional lighting, or building a banister or other barrier out from the wall at the inside corner to divert traffic away from the dangerous narrow ends of the winders.*

secure the end piece to the wall with toenailed 16d finishing nails (if there's a stud or blocking behind the wallboard), or a toggle bolt.

If you can't locate a section of curved handrail, buy a short length of straight handrail to match the existing one. Cut miter angles on the short piece and the end of the handrail. Then cut the short piece to length and attach it to the end of the railing with wood glue and finishing nails. Attach the end to the wall, as described previously. Sand the joint smooth and finish the new wood.

Attaching curved end

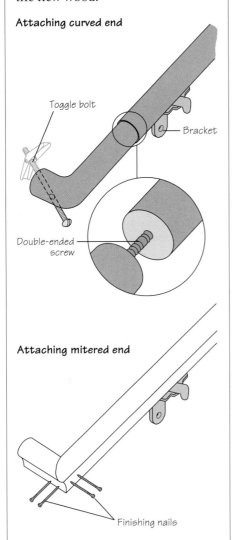

Toggle bolt

Bracket

Double-ended screw

Attaching mitered end

Finishing nails

▶ Stairs lack handrail.

Codes vary, but most require a handrail for any set of stairs with four or more risers (some local codes require one for *any* step). It must be on the open side (or sides) of the stairs, or on one of the walls if neither side of the stairs is open. It should be located at a constant height above tread nosings, usually between 30 and 34 inches. It should be able to support 200 pounds in any direction, have at least 1½ inches of clearance from the wall, and have proper termination at both ends. A balustrade on the open side of stairs must have no openings wider than 6 inches (4 inches for some codes).

To install a handrail along a wall, you will need a straight length of handrail long enough to span from top tread to bottom, two curved sections for the ends, and enough brackets to support the handrail at least every 4 feet. Measure and mark a point 30 to 34 inches up from the bottom-tread nosing. Do the same above the top-tread nosing. Stretch a string between the two points (or snap a faint chalk line if you'll be painting the wall). Attach brackets to studs every 3 or 4 feet along this line and as close as possible to the top and bottom marks. Cut the handrail to length and attach a curved section to each end. Stain and finish the rail. When it dries, attach it to the brackets.

For open stairs you can buy prefabricated handrail pieces and assemble a balustrade, have one custom-made that you can install yourself, or have a stair specialist build one for you.

Meeting handrail requirements

Minimum 6'8" headroom

Minimum 32"

1½"

30"–34"

Maximum 6" (sometimes 4")

Tip *Typical stair requirements: (1) the maximum height of a riser (distance from tread to tread) is 7½ inches; (2) riser heights cannot vary more than ³/₁₆ inch; (3) two times the riser height plus the tread width, added together, should equal 25 inches; (4) the distance between handrails or between a handrail and wall must be at least 32 inches; (5) there must be at least 6 feet, 8 inches of headroom above each riser (7 feet is optimal).*

▶ *Baluster is loose.*

If a baluster is loose at the top, force a glue-covered shim into the gap, let it dry, and trim it flush; or drive a trimhead screw (wallboard screw with small head) up through the baluster (drill a pilot hole first) into the handrail. Conceal the head by first slicing a small flap of wood, lifting it and driving the screw beneath it, then gluing it back in place.

A baluster that is loose at the bottom can be secured to the tread with a trimhead screw driven into the side at an angle (drill first), or by removing a piece of molding from the end of the tread and securing the dovetail tenon of the baluster to the tread with glue and a screw (drill first). Replace the molding.

Securing baluster at top

Block
Shim
Flap
Pilot hole
Trimhead screw

Securing with angled screw at bottom

Trimhead screw
Pilot hole
Flap

Securing tenon at bottom

End molding
Dovetail tenon
Wood screw Pilot hole

▶ *Baluster is broken or missing.*

Remove the broken baluster. If it's held in place by dowels in the top and bottom, saw the baluster in half. Lock a pipe wrench onto the bottom half, twist it sharply to loosen the glue, and lift it out. Do the same for the top. Scrape and sand old glue out of the holes in the tread and handrail. Cut a replacement baluster to length. Apply glue to the tread hole and the top dowel (not the bottom dowel). Insert the top dowel into the handrail hole, then carefully slide the bottom dowel across the tread and into the hole.

If the baluster is attached to the tread with a tenon, remove the end trim from the tread. If the tenon is loose, tap it out. Otherwise, saw the baluster flush with the tread and remove it. Then saw or chisel the tenon out of the tread cutout and sand or chisel away the old glue. Cut a new baluster to length. Check for fit, then glue and screw it into place (drill pilot holes first). Replace the tread end molding.

Removing a dowel baluster

Saw
Pipe wrench

Removing a tenon baluster . . .

. . . by tapping
End molding
. . . or sawing
Tenon

▶ *Tread is cracked or broken.*

Replacing a tread can be an ambitious job, depending on how the stairs are built. Some staircases are built like fine furniture or cabinetwork, with wedges, dadoes, and interlocking joinery. Others are built like a simple set of shelves. Proceed slowly and study how things are jointed together before you pry them apart.

To remove the damaged tread, first carefully pry off any moldings and balusters attached to the tread. Pry up the tread far enough to release nail heads, then force the tread back down, pull the nails, and remove it. If it won't budge, carefully saw or split it in half and remove it in pieces. Aligning nosings, carefully trace the outline of the old tread onto new tread stock. Cut the stock to size and install it with glue and 16d finishing nails or trimhead screws. Replace the balusters and molding pieces.

Removing tread

Baluster removed
Trim removed

Tracing new tread

Baluster cutout
New tread stock
Nosings aligned

Tip *If carpet is coming loose at the back of a tread, fix it immediately; this is a dangerous condition. Stretch the carpet back from the nosing and reattach it to the tack strip across the back of the tread by forcing a broad putty knife into the crease. If the carpet doesn't stay, tack it to the back of the tread with a row of carpet tacks.*

▶ *Newel post is loose.*

Check in the basement or crawl space to see if the newel post extends through the floor and is anchored to a floor joist. If so, tighten the bolt or screws holding it in place. If not, wiggle the post and observe carefully. If the bottom slides back and forth on the floor, secure it to the floor by squeezing carpenter's wood glue under the post and angling two 2-inch trim-head screws (wallboard screws with small heads) through the side of the post and downward into the floor. Repeat on the other exposed sides. If the post is attached solidly to the floor and wiggles against the stair tread, secure it to the tread with a ⁵⁄₁₆ by 4-inch lag screw with ¾-inch washer. First countersink a hole into the newel post with a ¾-inch bit, aiming it back toward the stair stringer. Extend the hole through the newel post with a ⁵⁄₁₆-inch bit, then complete the bore into the finish stringer and support stringer with a ⁷⁄₃₂-inch bit. Slide the washer onto the lag screw, dab some adhesive onto the threads, and screw it into the hole snugly with a socket wrench. Glue a short piece of dowel into the countersunk hole, trim and sand it flush, and finish it to match the post.

▶ *Riser is cracked or broken.*

Like replacing a tread, installing a new riser can be a big job. Study the stairs to be sure you can replicate the construction. If you want to go ahead, remove the tread (see page 57). If it won't pry loose from the riser, drill a pair of ⅜-inch starter holes into one side of the riser near the top, and use a compass saw or keyhole saw to cut the riser into two pieces horizontally. The tread should lift out, with the top piece of riser attached. Remove the rest of the riser. Note whether wedges were used to hold it in place; if so, salvage the old ones or buy new ones. Cut a new riser out of similar material, using the old riser pieces for dimensions. Install it with glue, finishing nails or screws, and wedges (if used). Replace the tread and related parts.

Tightening joist connection

Securing post to floor

Securing post to stringer

Cutting riser to release tread

Installing new riser

Tip *Carpeted stairs should be vacuumed at least once a week, more frequently if possible. Whether you use a stair-cleaning attachment or a minivacuum, it should have a beater brush built into it for agitating dirt out of the carpet as you clean.*

▶ *Stairway is too dark.*

All stairways must have a light that can be operated by a switch at both the top and the bottom. If none exists, have one installed. Avoid pendant lights that hang below the level of the upstairs ceiling. If the stairway has a light and only one switch, a second switch should be installed and the first switch replaced. There are two ways to connect the switches. One is with normal house wiring, installed behind walls or inside surface conduit. The other is to install a pair of remote-controlled switches, linked by low-voltage wiring or by radio signals. Consult an electrician or electrical-supply house.

Stairways can also be illuminated during the day with natural light. Consider a skylight above the stairwell, a window placed at the top of the stairs, or inserting wall openings between the stairwell and an adjacent room that has plenty of natural light. All require structural changes; seek help.

▶ *Stairway is weak and sagging.*

Building new stairs requires advanced carpentry skills, but there is a simple way to reinforce a weak stairway if all the parts are sound. Install a central 2x6 brace underneath the stairs. First remove any plaster or wallboard attached to the underside of the stairway. Cut a 2x6 to fit, on edge, under the center of the stairway along its entire length. It should be firmly supported at the top and bottom ends. Snugging it against the floor will take care of the bottom; attaching it to a joist hanger will secure the top. Use a bevel gauge to duplicate and mark the correct angles for cutting. To

install the brace, slide the bottom end into place first, then lift the top to a corner (not the center) of the top header and pound it over to the center with a sledgehammer. Slide a joist hanger under the top end, force the brace up as far as it will go, and nail the hanger to the header and brace. Toenail the bottom end of the brace to the floor.

To provide support for each tread, set a ¾-inch plywood cleat against the 2x6 brace and snug it up against the bottom of the tread. Screw it to the 2x6 with three 2-inch wallboard screws and secure it to the tread with finishing nails toenailed from the bottom or face-nailed from above.

Installing a 2x6 brace

Joist hanger

2x6

¾" plywood cleats

Toenailed finishing nail

Angled cut

▶ *Stairway lacks sufficient headroom.*

If a bulkhead is only an inch or two below the minimum height, you may be able to gain the headroom by beveling the bottom corner. Otherwise, the stair will need to be rebuilt—a major job.

▶ *Stairway is too steep, tilted, or narrow.*

Codes vary, but typical requirements for stair dimensions are: maximum riser height 7½ inches, no variation greater than ³⁄₁₆ inch; minimum tread depth 9 inches, plus 1-inch nosing; minimum headroom 6 feet, 8 inches above all nosings; minimum width 32 inches between handrails, 36 inches between walls; and minimum depth of landings 36 inches. Check your local building code for specific requirements.

Altering stairs to conform to these requirements usually means rebuilding the entire stairway, because changing one small dimension affects others, and many small changes have an incremental effect of changing the dimensions of the entire stairway. Consult a contractor or carpenter who specializes in stair building.

Meeting stair requirements

Maximum 7½"

Unit rise

Unit width

Nosing

Minimum 9"

Minimum 1"

Tip *If your stairway is boring, try these ideas to liven it up: (1) Paint the risers a bright color or stencil a simple design onto some of them. (2) Replace a run-of-the-mill balustrade with a new one created from stock stair parts. (3) Install strip-lighting (used for theater and airplane floors) along the stair stringer. (4) Install a skylight over the stairwell or a window at the top of the stairs. (5) Freshen up the walls with new wallpaper or faux painting techniques such as rag painting, raking, marbling, or sponging.*

▶ Fire won't draw; smoke enters room.

Open the damper (handle should be forward). Make sure the flue is not blocked with debris (leaves, bird nest, jolly fat fellow), soot, a clogged spark screen, or a chimney-top damper of which you are not aware. If smoke enters the room only for the first few minutes, stuff crumpled paper up into the chimney and light it before starting a fire. Also use more paper and kindling to start the fire; a quick, roaring blaze may be all that's needed. Exhaust fans (such as a range hood or vented clothes dryer) should not be on when you start the fire, nor a warm-air heating system if the return-air grille is nearby.

Apart from these possibilities, a smoky fireplace is most likely caused by poor chimney or fireplace design. A chimney must be at least 11 feet tall (floor to top) and rise 3 feet above the roof ridge or, if the ridge is too high, 3 feet above the highest point on the roof within 10 feet of the chimney. Exterior chimneys, especially on the north side of the house, draw less efficiently than chimneys enclosed within the house; and chimneys that terminate above eaves are less efficient than those that terminate above gables. No other appliances should share the same flue as the fireplace. The firebox should be at least 20 inches deep at the base. The optimum height depends on several variables, but if it's too high, smoke will escape into the room.

Extending a chimney involves adding sections of matching flue liner, bricks, and a cap; it should be done by a professional. You may be able to improve fireplace performance without having the firebox rebuilt by raising its floor with a new layer of firebricks or installing a metal smoke deflector or shallow hood across the top of the fireplace opening. Never use a wood "smoke board." If the fireplace is used regularly, the chimney should be serviced by a professional chimney sweep every year.

Meeting chimney requirements

Chimney cap

10'

3'

11'

20"

Altering a firebox that's too high

Metal smoke deflector

Firebricks

▶ Fire is too hot or not hot enough.

Fireplaces don't warm rooms very well. Most of the heat goes up the chimney or is absorbed into the bricks. At the same time, it draws huge quantities of warmed air out of the house. With most fireplaces the heat you feel is radiant heat from the fire itself, although some fireplaces are equipped with convective devices that circulate air around the firebox and distribute it back into the room. A fire may not feel hot because the radiant heat is blocked or deflected away. Arrange furniture for maximum exposure to direct heat, no closer to the fireplace opening than 3 feet. Build the fire closer to the front of the firebox (unless it smokes). Experiment with lowering or raising the grate.

To prevent warm room air from escaping up the chimney, have glass doors and a combustion air duct installed so the fireplace uses air from the outdoors rather than from the house.

To improve the fire itself, burn a mix of softwoods and well-seasoned hardwoods; avoid green wood. Stack logs vertically against the back of the firebox (as Europeans do). Keep kindling on hand to give the fire a boost from time to time.

If the fire burns too hot, change to softwoods. Avoid constant burning of those with high resin and pitch content; red cedar and Douglas fir burn fairly clean. Close the damper slightly to regulate draft. Install glass doors; the glass will block infrared radiation (warmest heat rays) and transmit only the "cooler" heat conducted through it. Or have a gas lighter and decorative logs installed and stop burning wood altogether.

Tip *Install a smoke detector in the same room as a fireplace or wood-burning stove. Ideally this alarm should be wired to other smoke detectors throughout the house. Never start a fire with gasoline, kerosene, or lighter fluid. Keep a fire extinguisher nearby. Never burn trash in a fireplace or woodstove, especially plastics, colored inks, or treated wood. Never leave children unattended near a fire. Don't close the damper until the fire is extinguished. Read instructions before using artificial logs. Install a carbon monoxide detector in a room with a woodstove. Empty ashes into a closed metal container. Make sure a fire screen spans the entire fireplace opening, and keep combustibles at least 3 feet from the opening.*

▶ Cold air enters room through fireplace.

Shut the damper whenever the fireplace is not in use. Install a glass enclosure (required in most new installations). Cover the fireplace opening with a decorative shield.

▶ Damper is stuck.

Wear gloves and eye protection. Pull (to open) or push (to close) hard on the handle. If it won't budge, slide a 20- to 30-inch length of pipe over the handle for greater leverage. If you can't move it, strike the pipe sharply with a sledgehammer (you may need a helper). Aim the blow straight—a glancing or angled blow could bend the handle to the side— and avoid excessive hammering. Once you've opened the damper, work the handle back and forth a few times to loosen it. Clean the rotating pins with a wire brush; apply high-temperature lubricant.

Opening a stuck damper

Chimney
Damper
Open
Firebox
Pipe

▶ Damper is missing.

See page 122.

▶ Rain comes down chimney.

Rain causes significant damage inside a chimney. It combines with the creosote present in most chimneys to produce acids that break down the flue lining and mortar. Install a metal chimney hood, or have a masonry hood custom-built. Both types should include a spark arrester (metal screening around the open areas). Measure the flue opening before buying a metal hood. Most are installed by pushing them down into the flue and require a tight fit.

Protecting chimney with metal hood

Metal raincap
Spark arrester
Terra-cotta flue
Mortar cap

Protecting chimney with masonry hood

Concrete cap
Spark arrester

▶ Chimney hasn't been cleaned for a year.

All chimneys should be cleaned periodically. The frequency of cleaning depends on whether the chimney vents an open fireplace, enclosed fireplace, or wood-burning stove; how often you burn fires; and on the type of fuel burned.

The culprit is creosote, which is formed when smoke and hot gases cool and make contact with even cooler surfaces. It builds up rapidly inside a chimney if the smoke is relatively cool to begin with (which is common with slow-burning stoves), and the fire never burns hot enough to heat up the chimney and force the smoke out quickly. Built-up creosote is a fire hazard.

When creosote builds up to ⅛ inch on flue walls, the chimney should be cleaned. If you burn hot, blazing fires in an open fireplace, such accumulation may take a year or more. If you have a woodstove and burn slow fires, soot and creosote may build up to dangerous levels as quickly as every two weeks, depending on the type of fuel used. Have your chimney inspected and cleaned by a professional.

▶ Sparks fly onto rug or floor.

All fireplaces should have a protective screen or glass doors that cover the entire fireplace opening. Many homes have a freestanding, portable screen open at the top. This may not be sufficient protection; replace it with a permanent screen attached to the fireplace. Follow manufacturer's installation instructions. Most require boring two to four holes into the brick with a masonry bit and inserting expansion bolts or lead shields. If you drill on the inside of the firebox, wear gloves, goggles, and a hat for protection from falling soot and debris.

If the draw mechanism for a screen is fouled or stuck, clean the track and any wheels with a stiff brush. Apply a high-temperature lubricant recommended by a fireplace dealer.

Tip *To burn efficiently, firewood should be seasoned. Most woods take from nine months to two years to season. Ways of recognizing green wood and seasoned wood are: (1) Seasoned wood is much lighter in weight. (2) When struck together, two sticks of green wood will sound dull; two sticks of seasoned wood will resonate with a light ring. (3) The ends of seasoned wood are darker colored than green wood and they have slight cracks. (4) The bark of seasoned wood peels back easily, revealing no greenish wood underneath.*

▶ *Hearth is too small.*

A fireplace hearth should extend 20 inches into the room in front of the fireplace opening and 12 inches to each side (16 and 8 inches for openings less than 6 square feet in area).

Extending a hearth is more complicated than removing some floorboards and gluing a few tiles or bricks to the subfloor. Most codes require at least ½ inch of noncombustible backing under the tiles or other masonry material, which means removing some of the subfloor and providing structural support to install new subflooring at a lower level. Consult a professional familiar with local requirements.

Meeting hearth requirements

Extending a hearth

▶ *Fireplace is old and hasn't been used in years.*

Have it inspected by a licensed fireplace specialist, such as a chimney sweep, fireplace contractor, or brick mason, before using it. If you've never used it, the inspection may turn up such surprises as a missing or blocked chimney, a chimney that terminates in the attic, or a gas-burning fireplace that was never intended for fires.

▶ *Firebox bricks are cracked or crumbling.*

Firebricks and fireclay mortar are intended to withstand extreme temperatures, but eventually deteriorate and must be replaced. If only a few mortar joints are failing, scrape out the loose mortar with a cold chisel or similar tool. Mix some mortar with fireclay and water, according to label directions for fireboxes. Pack mortar into the open joints with a trowel, then smooth the joints with a jointer or an old spoon (see page 127).

If the bricks are deteriorating (tapping them with a metal tool produces a dull thud instead of a sharp retort), the firebox needs to be rebuilt. This is best left to a professional brick mason, unless you have considerable experience laying bricks yourself. Use firebricks and fireclay mortar, and observe the layout pattern as you remove the old firebricks.

▶ *Fireplace is too small.*

Fireplaces in many older homes, especially Victorians, are small because they were intended to burn coal. Provided everything is in safe working order, you can build in such a fireplace a reasonably sized wood fire that generates the same amount of heat and ambience as a larger fireplace. You could also burn coal.

If you want the firebox enlarged, it will most likely involve rebuilding the entire fireplace and chimney as well. Consult a fireplace specialist.

Never enlarge a small firebox or fireplace opening without enlarging the chimney flue. (The area of the fireplace opening should not exceed 10 to 12 times the area of the flue opening.)

If you want to make the fireplace appear larger by extending or rebuilding the facade, plan it carefully. A large facade may overwhelm the smaller firebox. In general, stepped designs or variations in materials are more successful than a large, unrelieved expanse of the same material. Be sure not to place anything flammable too close to the firebox (see opposite page).

▶ *Glass doors are dirty and smoky.*

Buy some stove-glass cleaner, which contains chemicals for cutting through soot and creosote that ordinary glass cleaners don't have, and use according to label instructions. If you can't find it at a hardware store, try a fireplace or woodstove dealer.

▶ *Fire screen is damaged.*

If it's a freestanding screen, replace it with glass doors or a new fireplace screen that attaches to the fireplace. If you already have that type of screen and it doesn't work properly, dismantle as much of it as you can and look for replacement parts at a hardware store or fireplace dealer.

Tip *Fireplaces with gas lighters should have a removed or permanently propped-open damper to ensure a safe vent for combustion fumes or leaking gas. Brush ashes away from the holes of the gas burner after each use.*

▶ Gas lighter doesn't light.

Most lighters consist of a gas valve located outside the fireplace and operated by a removable key, and a perforated gas/air mixing chamber (burner) located in a decorative log inside the fireplace. If the log won't light when you turn on the valve, the holes in the perforated chamber are probably blocked by accumulated ashes. Instead of trying to unclog them, buy a replacement chamber at a home center or other supplier. It looks like a pipe with holes in it. Be sure to get one specified for your fuel source, either natural gas or LP. Make sure the valve is shut off when you remove the original chamber and install the replacement.

Some lighters, usually installed in a prefabricated fireplace, have a standing pilot light or electronic ignition that enables them to light automatically. If the unit won't light, consult the manufacturer's operating instructions or call a fireplace technician.

▶ Mantel is too close to fireplace.

All combustible materials, such as a wood mantel, must be at least 12 inches from the fireplace opening. Check local codes for required clearance above a wood-burning stove installed in a fireplace; it may be more than 12 inches.

If the mantel is attached to the face of the wall, you can probably detach it and move it up. Look for bolts, screws, or brackets under the mantel and remove them (a helper or brace should support the mantel). Move the mantel to the required height, mark where holes should be drilled or brackets attached for installing the support hardware, and reinstall it. Patch

holes and cracks from the original installation.

If the mantel rests on a brick shelf or it is otherwise impractical to detach and move it, install a sheet-metal deflector between the mantel and the fireplace opening. Have a sheet-metal shop cut a rectangle from 20-gauge sheet metal, 4 to 6 inches wide and long enough to span the fireplace opening. It should be bent lengthwise at a 135-degree angle, 1½ inches from one edge. This creates a flange that can be bolted to the face of the fireplace. The rest of the shield flares upward for 3 or 4 inches, enough to shield the mantel from direct heat. Have the exposed edge and corners folded; otherwise they're too sharp. To paint the shield, etch the metal with vinegar, rinse, and wipe dry. Spray-paint it flat black or a color to match the fireplace facade.

Attaching metal shield

Wood mantel
20-ga sheet metal
Expansion bolts
3"–4"
Less than 12"
1½"
135°

▶ Mantel is loose.

Some mantels rest on the brick fireplace facade, some are supported by wood posts (pilasters) attached to the sides of the fireplace opening, and some hang on the fireplace wall supported by decorative brackets (corbels) or hidden hardware. Methods of attachment vary, so inspect closely to determine what fasteners have come loose and need tightening or replacing. The connections most likely to fail are wall fasteners, such as lag screws, angled through the mantel top or bottom and driven into wood framing inside the wall. If the hole drilled through the mantel is still sound, try drilling through it into the wall at a slightly different angle to create a new pilot hole for the lag screw. If the hole is not sound, drill a new one nearby and angle it toward the stud, or drill holes between studs and attach the mantel to the wallboard with expansion bolts. After tightening existing screws, create additional support by adding more lag screws (there may be other framing members hidden inside the wall), an unobtrusive cleat under the mantel, or decorative brackets at the ends of the mantel.

Boring for lag screw

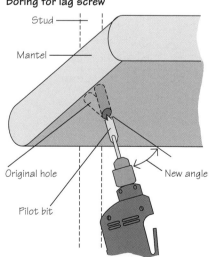

Stud
Mantel
Original hole
Pilot bit
New angle

Tip *To protect carpets and flooring in front of a fireplace from occasional sparks or embers, place a fireproof hearth rug in front of the hearth. They come in a wide variety of decorative patterns and colors.*

▶ *Wood-burning stove is old and needs upgrading.*

Have it inspected by a professional such as a licensed chimney sweep, stove installer, or local building inspector. Safety and air-quality regulations are constantly being upgraded, and wood-burning stoves are not foolproof devices that you simply install and forget about. Having it inspected will make you aware of innovations in safety and efficiency, especially for installa- tions made prior to July 1992. Some of the things to inspect for include: a noncombustible base; minimum clearances to combustible walls and furniture; proper size and type of flue; allowable horizontal runs and changes in direction of the flue pipe; condition of the doors, legs, hinges, grate, and draft louvers; combustion efficiency; and the installation of an insulated chim- ney liner for fireplace inserts.

Meeting wood-burning stove requirements

Horizontal run sloped toward stove

Noncombustible shield

48" clearance to combustibles

Less than 48"

Working doors and louvers

Noncombustible base

▶ *Brick facade is painted an undesirable color.*

Removing paint from bricks is diffi- cult because it penetrates deeply and gets partially baked on by the heat. The easiest way to solve this problem is to repaint the bricks a more desirable color. Scrape off loose or flaking paint, wash the surface with TSP, and paint with a high-quality latex masonry paint.

If the paint is already deteriorat- ing, you may have success with a paste-type paint stripper; follow label directions. You will need to make several applications, and still may not remove all the paint. Try staining the residue with a wood stain to match the exposed brick. Or give up and paint the mortar a mor- tar color and the bricks a brick color with flat latex paint. Paint the mor- tar first with a brush, then the bricks with a sponge or short-nap roller.

If the paint has not deteriorated and you do want it removed, have a professional sandblast the bricks.

▶ *Wood-burning stove with catalytic combustor emits dark smoke.*

The catalytic combustor, located at the base of the flue pipe, is intend- ed to "clean" the smoke by remov- ing pollutants before it goes up the flue. To work properly, the combus- tor must be cleaned regularly and replaced after 10,000 to 12,000 hours of use (three to eight years). Always follow manufacturer's in- structions. Most suggest cleaning the combustor with a soft-bristled brush at least twice a year and re- moving it for a major cleaning every two to three years. Follow the removal and cleaning instructions carefully; combustors are very frag- ile and should not be scraped, hit, washed with compressed air or a high-pressure hose, or returned to use until they are completely dry.

Tip *Transform an ordinary brick facade by covering it with tile, facing bricks, marble, cultured stone, plaster, or other noncombustible material. Then add a mantel. You can make one from a slab of marble, solid-surface countertop material, or wood boards and molding (at least 12 inches from the fireplace opening); order a kit; or look in architectural salvage yards.*

► Foundation has cracks.

Hairline cracks are normal for concrete foundations. Larger cracks, up to ⅛ inch wide, may indicate settling but should not be of concern unless they widen and shift over time. To test, glue a glass microscope slide over the crack with epoxy glue and check in a few weeks to see if concrete movement breaks it. If so, consult a foundation specialist. Patch small cracks on the outside of the foundation with a concrete patching compound. Apply a latex bonding agent to the area first, and feather the compound as you apply it over the crack. Cracks wider than ¼ inch and any crack that is wider at one end than the other require attention. Consult a professional.

► Foundation has white powder.

Efflorescence is a white powdery substance left on concrete and brick walls by moisture migrating through them. In and of itself it is insignificant; it does little damage to the masonry and can be removed with a stiff brush (avoid wire brush for brick). A new wall may have this problem temporarily while the concrete or mortar cures. If efflorescence is recurrent, it might indicate the presence of leaks or excessive moisture that could cause structural problems. Block the source of moisture by plugging cracks in specific areas, or by installing a drainage system on the outside of the foundation wall and sealing it.

► Foundation is sagging, leaning, or uneven.

The cause is poor foundation design and/or unstable soils. Consult a qualified foundation specialist, such as a structural engineer, a soils engineer, or a general building contractor experienced in foundation repair.

► Sill is not bolted to foundation.

Install anchor bolts no more than 6 feet apart (4 feet in earthquake or hurricane areas) and within 12 inches of each end of every sill board. To install the bolts, drill through the wood sill with a ½- or ⅝-inch spade bit, depending on the size of bolt. Then drill a 5-inch-deep hole into the concrete with a rotary hammer, using the same size bit. Use a piece of flexible tubing or an old basting syringe to blow concrete dust out of the hole (wear eye protection). Insert an expansion bolt into the hole and tighten the nut until the washer digs into the sill.

Drilling hole

Rotary hammer

Clearing the hole

¼" ID plastic tubing

Tightening the bolt

5"

Expansion bolt

Tip *When working in a crawl space, make sure lights and power tools are plugged into a GFCI-protected receptacle. Wear gloves and heavy clothing, such as a jumpsuit, to protect against insulation fibers, insects, dust, and chill.*

▶ Sill is rotted.

Replacing an entire rotted sill should be left to a professional, but you might be able to replace 2 or 3 feet of affected wood yourself. First make sure the cause is eliminated (termites, earth contact, moisture). Remove enough siding and sheathing on the outside of the house to expose the damaged sill. With a helper, two jacks, two short posts, and a 6-foot 4x4 beam, shore up the floor joists that bear on the damaged portion of sill. Set the jacks on 2x12 scraps, about 18 to 24 inches from the foundation wall. Rent jack posts if you're working in a basement. Raise the joists just enough to take pressure off the sill. With a reciprocating saw or handsaw, cut through the sill at both ends of the rot and remove the damaged portion. Cut a piece of pressure-treated 2x6 to the same length, coat the ends with preservative, apply three beads of caulk along the bottom, and tap it into place with a sledgehammer. Seal gaps with caulk. If the new sill is thinner than the old, place cedar shims under the joist ends to make up the difference. Remove the shoring and replace the siding and sheathing.

Replacing rotted section of sill

▶ Wood is within 8 inches of the ground.

Building codes require that all wood, except pressure-treated lumber specified for ground contact and certain grades of redwood or other durable species, be at least 8 inches above the ground. If siding, framing lumber, posts, or other wood members are closer than 8 inches to the ground, fix the problem by excavating soil away from the wood, replacing exposed wood with pressure-treated lumber (LP-22 for ground contact), or building up the foundation wall or piers with new concrete. Because these tasks may require shoring up parts of the house, building forms, or pouring concrete, consult a foundation specialist before proceeding.

If you are excavating soil from around the outside of the foundation, the ground should slope away from the house 1 inch per foot for 10 feet. If this is not possible, create a concrete gutter against the foundation that can carry water away.

Meeting clearance requirements

▶ Post is not centered on concrete pier.

The post will exert uneven pressure on the concrete footing and eventually cause it to lean. It is not difficult to move the post over to the center of the pier so long as it remains plumb and stays centered under the girder. First provide temporary shoring by jacking up short posts on each side of the main post; set the jacks on scraps of 2x12 or similar pads. Raise the beam just enough to take pressure off the original post. Then remove the toenails, brackets, or other connecting hardware from the post and tap it into place with a 5-pound sledgehammer (not a claw hammer). If the post is rotted or split, replace it with a new one cut just a hair longer than the space. With a level, plumb the post in two directions. Secure the post with new brackets or 12d HDG common nails toenailed into the support pier and girder. Remove the shoring.

If moving the post would move it off center under the girder, don't move it. Leave it alone or, if the pier is tilting, have a new footing and pier installed.

Moving post

Tip *All decay problems associated with wood structural members under the floor, such as termites, rot, and fungus damage, can be traced to a single cause: moisture. The moisture, however, can come from sources far above the crawl space or basement area. Leaky roof gutters, open cracks in the siding, rotted windowsills, unsealed porches, poorly caulked shower stalls, and leaking pipes can contribute to serious structural damage. Solving foundation and crawl-space problems includes addressing these conditions.*

▶ Post is not attached securely to pier or beam.

Attach posts to beams (girders) with metal framing connectors, available in a variety of sizes. Choose a post-to-beam bracket that fits the size of post (for example, a rough 4x4 is slightly wider than a surfaced 4x4) and can be attached after the post and beam are in place. Nail with 16d joist-hanger nails. For earthquake reinforcement, add a ¾-inch plywood triangular brace to each side of the post. Nail it to the post and beam with 8d or 10d common nails.

Securing post to beam and pier

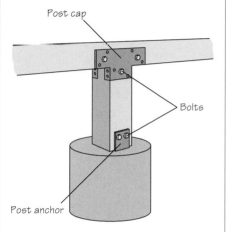

Post cap

Bolts

Post anchor

Adding plywood braces

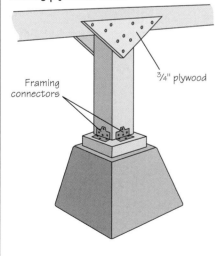

Framing connectors

¾" plywood

▶ Cripple wall does not have earthquake bracing.

In areas that require earthquake reinforcement, the short walls between a foundation and first floor should be well braced. If solid sheathing was not installed on the exterior side of the wall, nail ½-inch plywood panels to the crawl-space side. First be sure the sills are bolted to the foundation (see page 65). Then install 2x4 blocking between the studs along the sill to provide a nailing surface flush with the studs and plates. Nail each block to the sill with at least six 12d HDG common nails. Then cut sheets of plywood to fit horizontally along the wall; they should rest on the sill, not the foundation, and extend to the floor joists. Center vertical joints over studs. Nail the plywood to the studs, plates, and bottom blocking with 8d common nails, spaced every 4 inches along the edges, every 8 inches in the field. To provide air circulation, cut a 3-inch-diameter hole in the plywood at the top and bottom of each stud bay.

Installing plywood bracing

Joists

3" ventilating holes

Plates

½" plywood

Foundation wall

Sill

Blocking

Anchor bolt

▶ Powder-post beetles may be present.

While you are inspecting for termites, look for small piles of fresh powdery sawdust (frass) or random patterns of tiny holes in wood. They indicate powder-post beetles, which are structurally harmful and very difficult to control. Some types prefer hardwood and will attack flooring, furniture, and cabinets; others enjoy any type of wood. If you find such activity, call an exterminator.

▶ Termites may be present.

Inspect the foundation area for signs of termites and other insects once a year when the soil temperature is 50° to 55° F. The most obvious signs of infestation are earth tubes between the soil and wood. They are usually found along the foundation wall or interior piers but can be freestanding. They should be knocked down, but consult an exterminator first.

If you don't find tubes, it may mean that termites have found easier access to the wood structure. These paths are often hard to detect. Look for joints and cracks in the foundation, especially on the outside where stucco or brick veneer extends to the ground. Look for concealed posts or columns, such as porch or stair supports. With an ice pick or sharp awl, probe any wood near these points of access. The surface may appear sound, but the inside may be riddled with hollow channels and pockets. Other signs of termites are weakened wood, discarded insect wings on the ground, fresh coarse sawdust, and wood that has a hollow sound when tapped. If

Tip *Clear away all wood and other cellulose debris (paper, cardboard) from the crawl-space area. It attracts termites and other pests. Do not stack firewood or lumber close to the house. Remove nearby tree stumps. Trim tree limbs that touch the house.*

you find any suspicious signs, call an exterminator.

Even if you find no evidence of insect pests, you should be aware of conditions that promote them. Examine any wood for evidence of moisture or rot. Remove all wood and related material from the ground. Eliminate sources of crawl-space moisture. Patch or plug foundation cracks, gaps around pipes, and other potential passageways between the earth and wood.

Inspecting for termites

Stucco or brick veneer

Firewood

Buried wood debris

Earth tube

Foundation crack

Wood on ground

▶ *Wood structural members have streaks, stains, or rot.*

Several types of rot thrive in moist, unventilated areas. Once established, its growth is accelerated by humidity. If you discover rot, find the source of moisture and eliminate it first. Spongy or crumbly wood indicates severe rot and should be replaced immediately. Whitish streaks or cottonlike fibers indicate dry rot, a type of fungus that spreads rapidly and attacks wood. Dark gray or blue streaks indicate a faster-growing but less harmful type of fungus; its presence, however, indicates conditions that will attract the slower-growing but more dangerous types. Brownish streaks or stains indicate previously wet areas.

To treat rotted wood, eliminate the cause of moisture, allow the wood to dry, scrape or wipe away the rot, and apply preservative to the area, according to label directions. If the rot has caused more than surface damage, cut out all the infected wood at least 12 to 18 inches beyond the rotted section and replace it with pressure-treated wood. (For information on repairing joists, see page 32.)

▶ *Wires are sagging below floor joists.*

House wiring presents a danger in crawl spaces if it is not attached safely to floor joists or other framing members. Reattach sagging wires with staples approved for electrical cables, nailed no more than 42 inches apart. Use caution around wires, no matter how harmless they appear. Make sure the circuit is grounded and that wires terminate in electrical junction boxes or fixture boxes. Wear gloves, use tools with wood or rubber handles, and avoid moist ground. Call an electrician if you are not comfortable with doing this yourself. Some local codes prohibit running house wiring across the bottoms of floor joists or require that it be protected by metal conduit. Other wires (telephone wires, TV cables) should also be securely attached.

▶ *Floor above crawl space needs insulation.*

See page 33.

▶ *Insulation is falling.*

Push the insulation up between the joists and support it with wire insulation supports, sometimes called "tiger tails" or "tiger teeth." Place one under the insulation every 16 to 24 inches, wedging it between the joists.

▶ *Insulation is installed upside down.*

In most climates floor insulation should be installed with the vapor barrier facing up toward the living space. If your insulation was installed with the paper on the bottom, first check to make sure that the exposed paper is indeed the vapor barrier—some insulation has paper on both sides. It should be labeled clearly. Also, in climates with warm winters it's preferable to have the floor insulation reversed. If neither of these situations apply and your insulation is upside down, you can remedy the problem by cutting slits into the exposed vapor barrier to allow trapped moisture to escape.

Tip *There are three types of termites in the United States: subterranean, drywood, and dampwood. Most damage is caused by subterranean termites, which are found in all states except Alaska; they live in colonies in the ground. Drywood termites are found in states along the southern coasts and border, in a large arc sweeping from Virginia and the Carolinas to Florida and across the southern border area into California. Dampwood termites are found west of the Rocky Mountains, throughout the Southwest, and in southeastern Florida.*

► *Crawl-space area has puddles or moisture.*

This condition contributes to mildew problems in the house, cold floors, structural damage under the house, and even mold in the attic. For temporary relief, install a 6 mil polyethylene moisture barrier over the dirt floor of the entire crawl space. Overlap seams 6 inches and seal with duct tape. Run the sheeting up the foundation walls at least 4 inches and seal with tape. (See page 33 for more information about crawl-space vapor barriers.) A sump pump will remove excess water; many communities require one for a crawl space or basement. The sump pit should have a liner, and the outlet pipe should discharge water at least 15 feet from the house.

Eliminating the source of moisture depends on the cause (condensation from high humidity, leaky pipes, excessive groundwater, a high water table). Prevent condensation by improving ventilation. Add screened vents around the foundation (no more than 25 feet apart) so there is at least 1 square foot of vent area (allow for reduced airflow because of screens) for every 150 square feet of crawl space. Corners should have a vent on each wall, and vents should be placed across from each other to ensure airflow. Inspect under bathroom and kitchen areas, repair leaky pipes, seal the floor around bathtubs and toilets, and avoid overflowing fixtures. To keep external groundwater away from the foundation, grade the soil so that it slopes away from the house 1 inch per foot for 10 feet or more. Repair leaky gutters and downspouts, and divert water at least 8 feet away from the house with leaders or underground drainage pipes that open to daylight (but not onto a neighbor's property). Seal foundation walls. Avoid sprinklers and excessive watering around the foundation area; plant large shrubs at least 3 feet away. Provide diversion drainage, such as a splash block or dry well, for the condensate from an air conditioner placed next to the house. A final, drastic measure is to install footing drains around the perimeter of the house (consult a professional).

Installing a vapor barrier

6" overlap
Duct tape
Rock weights
Plastic sheeting

Adding vents

Reciprocating saw
New screened vent

Diverting surface water away from house

Caulking gun

4'–6'
Drain
Window well
8' minimum
4" drainage pipe
10'
10"
Downspout

Tip   *Although excessive moisture in a crawl space usually comes from other sources, it is natural for some subsurface moisture to rise to the ground surface by means of capillary action, even if the water table is as deep as 10 feet below grade.*

▶ Basement walls have moisture.

Determine whether the cause is condensation or seepage; treatment varies. To find out, tape squares of aluminum foil or plastic sheeting to any suspicious areas of the wall, below grade level, when it is dry. When the wall is damp again, check the test patches. If they are damp on the surface, the problem is condensation. If they are damp underneath, it is seepage. (It could be both.)

To solve a condensation problem, increase ventilation and eliminate sources of vapor, such as from a clothes dryer or bathroom, by venting them directly to the outside. Insulate cold-water pipes. Keep basement windows closed on hot, humid days. On nonhumid days, raise the temperature slightly. If there is no seepage problem, finish the walls with insulation and wallboard as a long-term solution. As a last resort, install a dehumidifier.

Solving seepage problems requires eliminating the source. On the outside of the house, check all gutters, downspouts, windowsills, hose bibbs, and siding joints for leaks; repair any you find. Make sure window wells are sloped away from the house and have proper drainage. Provide leaders for the downspouts to divert water away from the house at least 8 feet (use solid, not perforated, pipe). Grade the soil around the foundation so that it slopes away from the house 1 inch per foot for 10 feet or more. Move plants and shrubs 4 to 6 feet from the foundation and replace them with grass or a 6-inch layer of packed clay, which is impermeable to surface water. Remove large tree roots next to the foundation. If you

suspect a leaky water pipe, turn off the valve at the meter before a vacation and check afterward to see if the seepage stopped. If so, excavate the pipe and fix the leak. If these measures don't solve the problem, it could be lack of adequate waterproofing and footing drainage around the foundation, a drain blocked by silt and debris, a high water table, or an overloaded community storm sewer. Consult a professional. See also page 69.

On the inside of the wall, repair obvious cracks, holes, and deteriorated mortar joints with an expansive mortar or hydraulic cement, according to label directions. Avoid using waterproofing paints unless seepage is eliminated completely, especially on block walls.

Testing for source of moisture

Plastic

Seepage

Patching cracks and holes

Plug

Trowel

Hydraulic cement

▶ Basement floor has moisture.

Water may be seeping imperceptibly through the walls and accumulating on the floor, so test and if necessary repair the walls (see left). If water regularly leaks in through the joint between the walls and floor, or up through floor cracks, the problem is most likely blocked foundation drains or a high water table. Try sealing the cracks with hydraulic cement, according to label directions, and installing a sump pump; avoid finishing the basement. A permanent solution, if possible, would require excavating around the foundation, waterproofing the walls, and installing a new drainage system, and perhaps installing a new basement floor over drain rock and moisture barriers. Consult a professional.

▶ Sump pump cycles on and off repeatedly.

A sump pump should cycle on and off no more than every 15 minutes, even after heavy rains. If it does, the water it discharges may be flowing right back to the basement, possibly undermining the soil beneath the foundation. Extend the outlet pipe as far as you can, at least 15 feet from the house or, if allowed, into a public storm sewer. If the pump continues to cycle rapidly, the problem is excessive moisture. See above for solutions.

▶ Basement floor has cracks.

There are many specialty products available for sealing cracks in concrete, such as expansive mortars, hydraulic cements, and epoxy-based sealers. Loosen and vacuum

Tip *Quick ways to make basement rooms more attractive: (1) Box in ducts or paint them bright colors. (2) Paint the ceiling with a light hue in graduating intensities, with the darkest shades around the edges and lightest tints in the center. (3) Paint the ceiling flat black and nail on wood lattice, stained or painted a light color. (4) Use one continuous floor covering in a light, neutral color to unify and simplify the space. (5) Cover a long wall with mirrors. (6) Stop paneling short of the ceiling to make the ceiling seem higher. (7) Conceal support* away all debris in the crack. Some products require widening the crack and undercutting the edges with a hammer and cold chisel to provide better adhesion. Apply epoxy sealers to narrow cracks with the applicator supplied with the sealer. Apply hydraulic cement with a trowel, according to label directions.

If the floor has extensive cracking, sloping, or damage but is structurally sound, you can have a self-leveling compound (liquid underlayment) applied. It levels itself and hardens to a smooth, water-resistant surface without troweling.

Patching cracks

Applying self-leveling compound

▶ Basement windows have moisture.

Moisture on the inside surface indicates condensation problems in the basement (see opposite page). If moisture collects between the panes of a double-glazed window, the moistureproof seal around the window glass has failed. Replace the glass unit. (See page 98.)

▶ Joint between floor and wall has gap.

In some cases this joint is intended as a weep joint to channel moisture to the base of the walls, where it collects in a trough and flows to a sump for automatic discharge. If a trough or other collection device is not present, the gap should be sealed. Use expansive mortar or hydraulic cement, applied according to label instructions.

▶ Stairs are too steep and narrow.

Most basement stairs are considered secondary stairs, which can be steeper and narrower than the primary stairs between the main floors of a home. If you convert your basement to living space, however, you may have to upgrade the stairs with safer dimensions. You may want to do this in any case. See page 59 for recommended stair dimensions. If there is not enough room for a straight-run stairway with wider treads and lower risers, consider adding a landing near the bottom and turning the stairs out into the room. Lengthening stairs also requires lengthening the stairwell ceiling opening; make sure

there is available space on the first floor. It may be more convenient to leave the present stairs and build a new stairway elsewhere.

Improving stairs

Old steep stairs

posts in built-in cabinets or room dividers, or incorporate them into peninsula countertops. (8) Place lights on the floor and direct them upward against a wall to heighten it. (9) Replace ceiling lights with wall sconces to accentuate the walls rather than the ceiling. (10) Install a brightly colored metal or plastic handrail in the stairway. (11) Replace the door at the top of the stairs with a French door.

▶ *Basement has no emergency exit.*

All bedrooms must have an emergency egress. Some codes require an emergency exit for finished basements used for any purpose. The minimum requirement is either a door to the outside or a window with a clear opening at least 20 inches wide, 24 inches high, and 5.7 square feet in area; the sill can be no higher than 44 inches from the floor. Most basement windows must be enlarged by lowering the sill. To do this requires cutting through the concrete or masonry foundation wall, a job for professionals. The window well must also be enlarged, which offers opportunities for terracing or other landscaping, but may require a guardrail. It is also possible to add an exterior door by breaching the foundation wall and installing a prefabricated metal stairway with hatch cover.

Enlarging a window and well

Header
Terraces
Guardrail
Drain
Maximum 44"
Area = 5.7 sq ft

▶ *Basement ceiling is too low.*

Most codes require a minimum ceiling height of 7½ feet for habitable rooms (bedroom, family room, rec room, kitchen), and 7 feet for hallways and bathrooms. There should be 80 inches of clearance beneath ducts, headers, and other ceiling obstructions. (Measurements are from finished surface to finished surface.) If the ceiling is too low, the only solution for creating finished rooms is to lower the floor. This requires breaking through the existing concrete floor, excavating to the required depth (stopping 2 feet from the foundation), building short concrete retaining walls, and pouring a new concrete floor. This is major work, but the payoff is added living space and the opportunity to correct drainage, plumbing, and moisture problems.

Meeting clearance requirements

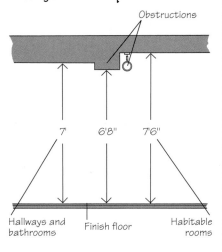

Obstructions
7' 6'8" 7'6"
Hallways and bathrooms   Finish floor   Habitable rooms

▶ *Basement is too dark.*

Strategies for brightening any room apply to basement rooms: Paint walls and ceilings light colors, install more light fixtures in the ceiling or on walls, and install large mirrors on walls opposite windows.

Maximize the natural light from small windows by clearing away shrubs, widening the window well (beware of creating a tripping hazard; add a guardrail or other barrier), and using light muslin or other gauzy material for curtains. To get the most light, add or enlarge windows—the most difficult solution. Take advantage of a basement in a hillside home by having large windows installed in the downhill wall. In conventional basements, cluster several small windows together in one area. Replace small windows with larger windows (and larger window wells); see left. You can also cut an opening in the ceiling to admit light from the room above.

▶ *Window wells present security risk.*

Install grates or plastic bubbles over the wells, or replace the window glass with panels of polycarbonate, a strong shatterproof plastic. Have the panels cut to size by a plastics supplier. Consider double-wall panels for additional strength and insulation, if you don't mind the fact that they obscure the view (they still admit light). If you wish, you can leave the window glass in place and install the polycarbonate panels on the outside like storm windows, although there is risk of condensation forming between the panes. First drill screw holes around the perimeter of the panel. Then apply a bead of silicone caulk around the window sash, and bed the panel in the caulk. Screw it in place with HDG wallboard screws. Run a second bead of caulk around the edge of the plastic. Gouge the screw heads to prevent unscrewing. Frame the edge with strips of molding to give a more finished look.

Tip *If the basement has a furnace or gas water heater, the wood joists above the appliance should be protected with a layer of ⅝-inch, Type X wallboard or similar fire-resistant material.*

For quick (but unattractive) security, attach ½-inch hardware cloth (heavy screening) over the window; nail it to the sash with 1-inch HDG fencing staples.

▶ *Basement is too cold.*

First take measures to keep cold out of the basement. Seal all gaps, cracks, and joints with caulk or weather stripping. Place fiberglass blanket insulation above the mudsill, against the rim joist. On the outside of the foundation wall, install foam insulation that is suitable for ground contact, from the floor line down to the frost line; or install insulation on the basement side of the wall if all moisture problems have been eliminated. Replace single-pane windows with double- or triple-glazed units. Install plastic shields (bubbles) over window wells.

If your home has a warm-air heating system, install one or two registers in the basement by tapping into ducts exposed in the ceiling. If the ducts are rigid, cut an opening in the sheet metal for a register boot: Trace the boot outline on the duct. With aviation snips, cut an opening 1 inch smaller than the outline, snipping slits around the opening to create tabs, and bending every other tab outward. Slide the end of the boot inside the bent tabs and reach inside it to bend the other tabs against its side. Secure three or four of the tabs to the boot with sheet-metal screws, seal the joint with metallic duct tape, and wrap duct insulation around the boot. Attach a register grille to the boot and adjust the heat level.

If the ducts are flexible, look for a joint between two sections, remove the tape and screws holding it together, and insert a Y-shaped fitting between the two sections.

Attach a register boot to the free branch of the Y fitting. Finally, install return-air vents for the basement in ducts that return cold air to the furnace plenum, as close to the floor as possible.

If there's no central heating system, install baseboard heaters or have a wood-burning stove or fireplace installed. Run the flue out the top of the basement wall and up the side of the house, then box it in.

Insulating a basement

Flashing Siding Sill Fiberglass insulation

Joist

Protective stucco

Frost line Foam insulation

Adding a heat register

Opening

Duct

Tabs

Register boot

▶ *Basement needs finishing.*

Do not install wallboard, insulation, flooring, or other finish materials unless all moisture problems have been eliminated completely and the basement remains dry for at least two seasons. The floor and walls should be installed over moisture membranes, such as 6 mil polyethylene sheeting or rigid foam insulation. Consult a qualified professional experienced in finishing basements in your area.

▶ *Window well traps animals.*

If birds, squirrels, or other small animals get stuck in a window well from time to time, provide an escape ramp made from a 2x4 covered with carpet, chicken wire, or other material that offers secure footing.

Assisting trapped animals

Tip *According to most real-estate appraisers, the return on investment for finishing an attic or basement is approximately 50 percent. It is considerably higher if the remodeling job includes a new bathroom.*

▶ Attic has moisture.

First look for roof leaks. Active leaks during a rainstorm and points of daylight visible from the attic are obvious signs; you should also inspect the roof for damaged or missing shingles and deteriorated flashing, and make appropriate repairs (see page 112). Leaks in the winter may be caused by ice dams forming along the roof eaves and diverting melted snow under the shingles. Solve this problem by installing more ceiling insulation; this prevents heat inside the house from migrating through the ceiling and warming the attic enough to melt the snow on the roof.

Another source of moisture is condensation formed when warm vapor from inside the house rises through the ceiling and insulation, then contacts cold surfaces in the attic. Solve this problem by sealing cracks and gaps where pipes and other conduits penetrate the ceiling, by installing a vapor barrier between the ceiling material and insulation, or by providing more ventilation in the attic (see right).

▶ Roof boards are rotted.

Roof boards and framing members can rot from condensation formed in the attic during the winter. Prevent condensation by stopping the source of moisture, which is vapor migrating through the ceiling (see page 17), and increasing attic ventilation (see right and opposite page). Then replace the rotted boards.

▶ Attic lacks ventilation.

An attic should have 1 square foot of unobstructed attic vent for every 150 square feet of attic area. Vents should be positioned to promote cross-ventilation—for instance, two gable vents placed opposite each other. If prevailing winds are reliable, place the downwind vent higher than the upwind vent. Eave vents placed opposite each other allow some air circulation, but are much more effective when combined with several gable vents or a continuous ridge vent. Install attic vent chutes to improve circulation from eave vents. Vents should not be covered in the winter. Instead, use self-closing louvered vents, which open and close as breezes move air through the attic.

Installing gable vents

Gable vent

Installing eave and ridge vents

Ridge vent

Plastic vent chute

2" air space

Eave vents

Continuous soffit vent

Tip   Attics are exposed to severe temperature extremes. During hot weather, temperatures can reach as high as 150° F in a poorly ventilated attic. During cold weather, a poorly ventilated attic can turn water vapor to frost and ice, which eventually melts or forms condensation on attic surfaces.

▶ Attic overheats in hot weather.

Install a roof fan, attic gable fan, or several roof turbines. Roof fans and turbines require cutting a hole in the roof. Mark the position, between two joists and near the ridge, by driving a nail up through the roof boards and roofing. From above, use the nail to lay out cut lines on the shingles. With a utility knife, cut through the shingles and under-layment and remove them. Cut through the roof sheathing with a reciprocating saw or compass saw, after drilling a starter hole with a ¾-inch spade bit. Set the fan or turbine housing into place by sliding the flashing under the shingles on the uphill side of the roof hole (you may have to remove nails). Replace any damaged or missing shingles. Secure the flashing with roofing nails; cover the heads with roofing cement.

Fans require electrical wiring. Most have automatic switches, so the minimum wiring requirement is a feeder line from any source directly to the fan. Many local codes, how-ever, require that you provide an override switch in a convenient location, either next to the attic access or downstairs.

▶ Attic floor needs more insulation.

At least 10 to 20 inches (R-30 to R-60) of ceiling insulation is now required for most climates, so you may need to add some. Con-sult your local code for the exact requirement. Before insulating, seal all gaps, cracks, and bypasses be-tween the living space and attic with caulk (use sheet metal for gaps around chimneys and flues). If the present insulation was installed with a vapor barrier, new fiberglass batts should be the kind without paper or foil facing, or else slit the facing in several places before lay-ing the batts over the existing insu-lation. If there is no vapor barrier present, consider pulling up the old insulation and installing the new over a vapor barrier, especially in climates with cold winters. Use 4-mil polyethylene, pressing it into place so it hugs the ceiling and sides of the joists. Then install batts or loose insulation over it. Install new batts at right angles to the old.

Do not block vents with insula-tion. Protect vents along the eaves with plastic-coated or foam baffles to maintain at least 2 inches of air space against the roof. Maintain 3 inches of air space around recessed light fixtures (unless they are clearly labeled for contact with insulation). Apply insulation to the scuttle hatch or attic door and weather stripping around the opening.

Cutting roof hole

Shingles removed

Rafters

Securing housing

Roofing cement

Adding insulation

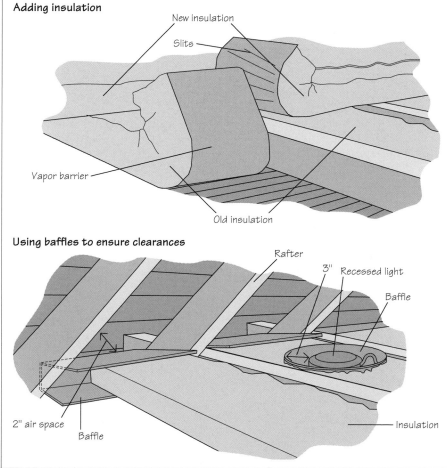

New insulation

Slits

Vapor barrier

Old insulation

Using baffles to ensure clearances

Rafter

3" Recessed light

Baffle

2" air space

Baffle

Insulation

Tip   *If an attic contains living space, the places that should be insulated are the walls around the living space, the ceiling of the living space, and the floor of the rest of the attic. If there is no living space in the attic, insulation should always go on the attic floor and not between the rafters.*

▶ Attic has snow in it.

Sometimes snow blows into a ridge vent, producing a line of powdery snow underneath. This is not a serious problem, but you can block the snow and still allow air to pass through the vent by inserting strips of 1-inch-thick fiberglass filter material (available in rolls, or cut from furnace filters) in the ridge vent openings. Replace it every few years when it gets clogged with dust and debris.

▶ Insulation has dirty smudges.

Smudges may appear where the insulation has filtered dust out of air leaking up from the rooms below. Such air leaks, called bypasses, contribute to heat loss and attic vapor problems and should be sealed; the smudges are a convenient way to find them. The most likely bypasses are around pipes, flues, electrical wires, light fixtures, chimneys, and wall intersections. Seal cracks with caulk, large gaps with foam insulation. Cover gaps around a chimney or flue with sheet metal and seal with high-temperature furnace cement.

Sealing bypasses

Pipe

Insulation rolled back

▶ Attic is dark and stuffy.

Attics should be well ventilated to prevent condensation problems during cold weather and overheating during hot weather. Provide gable or eave and ridge vents. Install a gable fan or roof fan. See also page 74.

▶ Attic has limited access or egress.

Most codes require a 22-inch by 30-inch scuttle if the attic has 30 inches or more of headroom. If you want to add another one, the best place is over a hallway or closet—joist spans in such a place are short and the location is accessible but out of the way. With a framing square, mark lines for a rectangular cutout. There should be no wires, ducts, or other obstructions over the opening. Cut lines should be on the inside faces of joists, not centered beneath the joists. Remove insulation from above the cutout and carefully saw along the cut lines with a handsaw. Set the cutout piece aside. Cut and remove the section of joist that passes over the opening and install 2x4 or 2x6 headers to support the cutoff ends of the joists, attaching with screws or a nailing gun; hammering might jar the ceiling. Attach molding to the ceiling around the edge of the opening so that it provides a lip for the cutout hatch to rest on. Apply insulation to the top of the hatch with adhesive; attach weather stripping around the opening.

If an attic is used for sleeping, it must have an emergency egress from the bedroom. A window that has 5.7 square feet of unobstructed opening qualifies, so long as it is at least 20 inches wide, 24 inches high, and no more than 44 inches above the floor. If it doesn't open onto a section of relatively flat roof, provide an escape ladder that can be stored under the bed and hung from the sill in an emergency.

Cutting scuttle opening

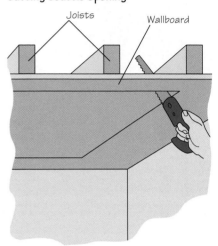

Joists

Wallboard

Installing headers and trim

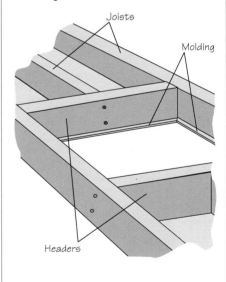

Joists

Molding

Headers

▶ Chimney has open gap around it.

There should be at least 1 inch of clearance between a chimney and any combustible material, such as wood framing or sheathing. This clearance creates a gap around the chimney where it penetrates the ceiling and roof. Roof flashing takes care of the roof gap. The ceiling gap is usually filled with noncombustible material, such as plaster or fiberglass. The best way to seal the gap is with strips of sheet metal. Apply a bead of caulk to the tops of the framing members, then nail the metal strips to them so they butt tightly against the chimney. With high-temperature caulk, seal both the joint around the chimney and the joints between metal strips.

Sealing gap around chimney

Sheet metal

High-temperature caulk

▶ Chimney bricks have white or black powder.

White powder is probably efflorescence and indicates that the bricks have been in frequent contact with moisture. Inspect roof flashing around the chimney and take measures to eliminate attic moisture (see page 74).

Black powder is soot, caused by smoke escaping through joints or cracks in the chimney. This is a fire hazard. Have the chimney inspected and repaired before you use it again.

▶ Attic floor sags or bounces.

The floor is probably supported on ceiling joists not designed for an attic floor load. This is a structural problem; consult a professional.

▶ You want to convert attic to living space.

This is a major project. Before you involve an architect and contractor, you may want to do a quick feasibility check of your own. If the roof is supported by trusses, which create a web of braces and supports throughout the attic, go no further. Every member of this engineered roof system is vital and cannot be cut or moved.

Is there enough floor area and headroom? Codes specify the minimum size of a room intended for certain uses (80 square feet for a bedroom, for example); however, at least one-half of that area must also have the minimum headroom, which is 7½ feet for most habitable rooms. Furthermore, there is a minimum ceiling height, usually 5 feet. Any floor space outside that limit cannot be counted in calculating the room size. Finally, all of these dimensions are between finished surfaces; you must take into account alterations to the floor, ceiling, and walls. Dormers are one way to overcome height limitations, but as a rule of thumb there should be at least 9 feet of headroom in the unfinished attic to make a conversion feasible.

Other considerations are the size of floor joists, strength of the foundation and first-floor walls, availability of space for a stairway, location of plumbing and mechanical connections, and potential for windows and skylights.

Calculating floor area

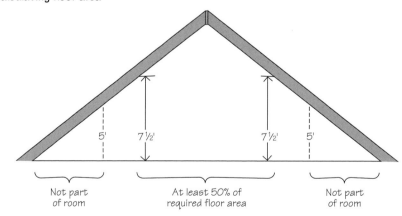

5' 7½' 7½' 5'

Not part of room — At least 50% of required floor area — Not part of room

▶ *House has ants.*

The most effective ant control is bait. Place ant baits where the ants are thickest and don't use any other controls for about a week. The ants will carry the bait back to their nest, which will poison it and stop the invasion from that nest. Another control is to apply an insecticide for ants (containing diazinon, chlorpyrifos, or propoxur) along baseboards, under the sink, around windowsills, and in other areas of access. Insecticides with pyrethrins have a repellent action; spray them across ant trails to control access. Follow label precautions.

To control ants permanently, follow trails to the central colony and destroy it. Apply a residual spray or granules (such as diazinon) around the perimeter of the house periodically to discourage future ant attacks. Be sure all cracks and openings on the outside of the house are caulked or otherwise sealed; this won't control ants by itself, but is essential for overall pest control. For limited control try spreading talcum or baby powder or cucumber peelings around areas that attract the ants.

▶ *House has fleas.*

Flea problems are linked to pets. As adults, fleas live on the host pet, but during the rest of their life cycle (egg, larvae, pupa), they inhabit various areas inside or outside the home, such as pet sleeping areas, baseboards, edges of rugs, and shady, moist areas under shrubs and along pet walkways. The simplest control is to apply an insect growth regulator to these areas, according to label directions. For more complete control, you must simultaneously treat the pet and all indoor and outdoor areas likely to harbor fleas.

Eradicate fleas on your pet with regular applications of a shampoo, spray, or dust product that contains a flea control agent such as carbaryl, tetramethrin plus sumithrin, pyrethrins, or malathion. Follow label directions and cautions exactly; be sure that the product is specified for use on animals. At the same time treat indoor areas by washing (or disposing of) the pet's bedding material; spraying or dusting the sleeping area with an insecticide specified for fleas; vacuuming all floors, carpeting, and furniture in rooms where the pet goes (dispose of the vacuum bag immediately); and treating the rooms with an insecticide spray or a total-release aerosol. Control fleas outdoors by applying insecticide to crawl spaces, pet sleeping areas, and other areas that animals frequent. Mint, garlic, cedar, and eucalyptus aromas may repel fleas. If infestations persist, consult a veterinarian or pest control specialist.

▶ *House has cockroaches.*

These pests infest kitchens, bathrooms, and other areas where food and water are available. They hide in walls, under sinks, behind refrigerators, within piles of grocery bags, around pipes, behind paneling or loose wallpaper, and in similar dark places; they rarely are seen during the day. To control cockroaches, eliminate all food and water sources (see right). Seal cracks around pipes, baseboards, sinks, cabinets, and other hidden areas with caulk or foam insulation. Remove all food and utensils from the kitchen. Then sprinkle finely powdered boric acid, which is very safe and effective, in cracks and other potential hiding places, following label directions. Reline the shelves with fresh paper, and replace the food and utensils.

▶ *House has flies.*

Flies feed on and lay their eggs in decaying organic materials, so the first line of defense is to maintain sanitary conditions in and around the home and garden, especially garbage cans. Keep cans clean by lining them with garbage bags or newspapers; attach a resinous pest strip to the bottom of the garbage can lid. Rinse bottles and cans thoroughly before placing them in recycling bins.

Next make sure that all doors and openable windows have tight-fitting screens that are in good repair. Inside the house control isolated flies with a flyswatter (and good aim). You can kill larger numbers of flies quickly with a spray containing d-trans allethrin, tetramethrin, pyrethrins, or resmethrin; follow label directions. For temporary control spray flies with hair spray—it doesn't kill them, but it immobilizes them so they can be disposed of easily.

Discourage flies from entering the house by spraying outdoor areas where flies land or congregate, such as around screen doors, lights, and south-facing walls, with a residual insecticide that contains chlorpyrifos, diazinon, or malathion. Pesticide strips work best in enclosed rooms where the vapors can build up; they are not very effective on porches or other well-ventilated spaces. Avoid using them near food or where infants or the elderly are confined. Control fruit flies (called vinegar flies) by removing any spoiled fruit or vegetables. If you leave fruit out to ripen at room temperature, control fruit flies with a simple trap: either a long-necked wine bottle with ½ inch of wine in the bottom, or a bowl of water with a small amount of apple juice and liquid detergent in it.

Tip *Good housekeeping is the best defense against pests (although occasional pests do not mean you're a bad housekeeper). Clean kitchen countertops, floors, shelves, and cabinets frequently, especially in corners and hidden areas. Store food (including pet food) in screw-top jars; wipe around lids after closing jars. Keep lids on garbage cans. Vacuum carpets frequently. Clean clothing before storing it. Close door and window screens tightly. Keep the house ventilated and moisture under control.*

▶ House has spiders.

Spiders are generally harmless and even beneficial. Only a few, particularly the black widow and brown recluse, are dangerous (but rarely fatal). However, because of the nuisance of webs and the disconcerting appearance of spiders, most people want them out of the house. Remove all spiderwebs and keep other insects (their prey) under control. Seal cracks and other entry points into the home; keep screens repaired. Remove debris from around the perimeter of the house and store firewood at least 10 feet away. Indoors, spray infested areas with an insecticide containing propoxur or chlorpyrifos, following label instructions carefully.

▶ House has silverfish.

Silverfish feed on starchy materials such as paper, book bindings, wallpaper paste, cotton or linen clothing (not wool or fur), and stored grains or cereals. They thrive in damp, humid conditions; some species prefer cool places like basements, others warm places near hot-water pipes or heaters. They are nocturnal. You are likely to notice them if you lift an object, such as a book or cardboard box, under which they've been hiding. To control, seal cracks around pipes, baseboards, and cabinets. Throw out unnecessary books, magazines, or papers. Move books around in bookcases periodically. Use a spray containing diazinon or chlorpyrifos to treat baseboard gaps, door and window frames, closets, behind drawers and shelves, behind and around the edges of bookshelves, and holes where pipes go through walls. Dusts such as boric acid or silica aerogel are also effective. Wait two or three weeks; if infestations recur, repeat the treatment. Bait packets also work, but are effective only when spaced no more than 1 to 3 feet apart. Follow all label instructions.

▶ House has clothes moths or carpet beetles.

Clothes moths and carpet beetles are not much nuisance themselves, but you'll know their presence by holes in sweaters, moth-eaten upholstery, and damaged carpets. The larvae (but not adults) damage household fabrics more often than any other insect pest. The adult moths, unlike other types of moths, prefer dark corners and are not attracted to light. The adult beetles resemble small ladybugs. Despite their names, neither pest infests only one type of material; they like it all.

Use the same control techniques for both pests. Start with a thorough search for the wormlike larvae in clothes, carpets, blankets, wool rugs, upholstered furniture, felt piano parts, animal-bristle brushes, feathers, animal skins, and accumulations of lint or pet hair in hidden areas. Eradicate the larvae by dry-cleaning or laundering the fabric, throwing out the damaged article (spray with insecticide first and seal in a plastic bag), or applying a spray with pyrethrins directly to the fabric, according to label instructions. To avoid staining, make sure it is specified for use with fabrics. To stem further activity, spray a residual insecticide containing propoxur, diazinon, or chlorpyrifos onto closet floors and corners, over empty shelves, along baseboards, behind heaters, and in cracks and other hidden places. Vacuum carpets frequently, moving furniture occasionally to vacuum underneath; dispose of the vacuum bag promptly if you suspect eggs or larvae. When storing clothes, blankets, and other susceptible items, clean them thoroughly first; then spray the garments with a moth-proofer containing tetramethrin and sumithrin and wrap them in plastic. Dry-clean or launder them before using again. Store woolen items in a tight container with mothballs, crystals, or flakes. Placing mothballs in a closet, or lining it with cedar, is not enough; the garments must be enclosed in a tight container. Wrap the mothballs in paper so they don't touch the fabric. Outdoors, remove or clean sources of hair, feathers, and animal debris.

▶ House has pantry moths or beetles.

Certain moths and beetles infest stored food, such as flour, spices, cereal, beans, nuts, dried fruits, candy, and even pet food. Although you may see the smallish moths (¼- to ½-inch wingspan) flying in your home in the evening, particularly in dimly lit areas, the reclusive habits of these pantry pests make it difficult to detect a problem unless you search. Telltale signs are tiny holes or webbing in food or packaging. Pay close attention to opened packages and boxes that have been on the shelf for a long time. If you find only one infested package, simply seal it in a plastic bag and throw it in the garbage. If infestation is widespread, you can save lightly contaminated items (throw out anything heavily infested). Kill the insects by freezing the food for three days or spreading it on cookie sheets and warming it in an oven set at 120° to 130° F for two hours. Keep an eye on it to avoid scorching the food. Boil dried fruit for about one minute, then spread it to dry before storing it again.

For serious infestation, remove all food, packages, and utensils from cabinets and shelves. Thoroughly

Tip   *How to handle and store poisons: (1) Read the label before using the product. (2) Store in a locked cabinet, never under the kitchen sink or near food. (3) Don't let insecticide sprays drift onto food or utensils. (4) Wash your hands and face immediately after using the product. (5) Keep the container handy in case you must identify the product for a doctor or poison control center if it gets in someone's mouth or eyes.*

clean the storage areas by vacuuming and scrubbing with soap and hot water. Dispose of crumbs in a sealed plastic bag. Spray corners and other hidden areas with a short-lived insecticide containing tetramethrin and sumithrin, or pyrethrins. It should be specified for food cabinets. Consider applying a residual insecticide containing chlorpyrifos or diazinon, but only to cracks and crevices. Allow it to dry thoroughly before replacing food and utensils. After an infestation clean shelves frequently and store all food in sealed containers.

▶ House has wood-boring insects.

Termites, powder-post beetles, carpenter ants, and carpenter bees are insects that bore into wood for food or nesting places. They should be eradicated when first detected. They are not restricted to the foundation and crawl-space areas—drywood termites infest attics, carpenter ants work throughout the structure, powder-post beetles invade hardwood furniture and flooring, and carpenter bees infest exterior siding and trim. Telltale signs of infestation are holes in the wood, small piles of fine sawdust (frass), weak wood, and discarded wings from swarming activity. The best control is inspections every 2 to 10 years, depending on where you live. Survey the foundation, outside and inside. Look for termite tubes, frass, small holes in wood, and soft, crumbly wood. For prevention: remove all wood debris from under and around the house; keep firewood piles as far from the house as possible; remove dead trees, branches, and stumps; eliminate sources of moisture from the crawl space, attic, and similar places; use pressure-treated lumber for ground

contact; and maintain 8 inches of clearance between all other wood parts of the house and the ground. See also page 67.

▶ House has dust mites.

All houses contain dust mites, which feed on human skin debris commonly found on mattresses and in house dust on floors. They produce asthma symptoms in sensitive people. It is impossible to eliminate them, but there are ways to control them. Try to maintain humidity below 70 percent (humans require 35 to 50 percent relative humidity). Do so by using exhaust fans in the bathroom and kitchen, controlling moisture in the basement or crawl space, venting gas heaters properly, and, if necessary, using a dehumidifier. Frequent vacuuming may control mites, but is also likely to stir them up. It is more effective to replace carpets with wood floors, area rugs, or other floor coverings. Consult an allergy specialist for other controls.

▶ House has mice.

Mice are difficult to control because they're nocturnal, can fit through cracks as small as ¼ inch, and can survive on meager food supplies. Practice general sanitation, remove debris from outside the house, and seal cracks and other openings on a regular basis. Droppings and greasy smudges along trails, such as baseboards, indicate the presence of mice. Eliminate them with traps or poison bait. Spring traps work best if you start by placing them baited but unset along trails and close to food sources for a few days. Experiment with such baits as peanut butter, dried fruit, gumdrops, or bacon to see what is preferred. When you set the traps, tie the bait to the trigger

or press it firmly in place. Use several traps (you may need as many as three per mouse) and space them no less than 6 feet apart. Make sure children or pets can't get to them. When placing traps along a wall, set single traps at right angles to it, with the bait toward the wall, or pairs of traps end-to-end, with bait facing opposite directions. Check traps daily; wear plastic gloves. Place carcasses in plastic bags and deposit them in the garbage or bury them. Poison baits are also effective, so long as they are specified for mice. The fastest-acting type, and safest to use around pets and desirable wild animals, is one with cholecalciferol. Place baits in the same kinds of places as traps, according to label instructions. If you have children or pets, place the bait in a wooden box with a lockable lid. Cut 2½-inch-square access holes in opposite ends of the box, then set the box against a wall so the holes are in line with the mouse trail. Check daily and replenish bait as needed. Cats that are skilled in hunting (most pet cats aren't) also help.

▶ House has rats.

Because rats are larger than mice, they are easier to exclude from the house by sealing openings. They are harder to trap, however, because they are more wary of new food or other items in their territory and, in the case of roof rats, can nest high in inaccessible places. Follow similar control procedures as for mice. Traps must be larger and can be spaced farther apart. Be especially careful where you place them if children or pets are in your home; you may need to set them in locked boxes, as with poison bait for mice (see above). For roof rats, place traps and bait up high, such as on tree limbs or fence tops, and tie them in place so they won't fall.

Tip *In cold climates subterranean termites live below the frost line and stay there during the winter. They can survive for months without a fresh food supply, which in their case is cellulose from wood materials.*

For safety, convenience, comfort, and appearance, all the doors and windows in your home should work properly and be in good repair. This chapter will help you solve more than 110 door and window problems, from a squeaking door to a broken drapery cord.

▶ *Door squeaks.*

Oil the hinges with light penetrating oil or silicone spray. To get the lubricant inside the hinge, raise the pin slightly by placing a nail under the hinge pin and knocking it upward with a hammer. Then apply the oil around the pin at the top of the hinge. Wait a few minutes for it to penetrate, then hammer the pin back in place. If squeaking persists, open the door fully, prop the bottom so it won't sag, and remove the hinge pin by knocking it all the way out with a hammer and a 16d nail. Smooth the pin and inside of the hinge barrel with steel wool, lubricate them, and reassemble. Repeat for the other hinge.

▶ *Door binds.*

If the door binds on the hinge side, check the hinge screws first and tighten any loose ones (see Tip below). If a head protrudes because it's too large, use a longer screw with a smaller head. If part of a head protrudes because the screw is driven at an angle, remove the screw, fill the opening with glued matchsticks or toothpicks, and, after the glue dries, drill a pilot hole straight into the jamb and install the screw. If the door still binds, check for hinge leaves that are recessed (mortised) too deep and shim them out. To shim a leaf, loosen the screws, insert thin cardboard under the outside half of the leaf, and tighten the screws. Increase the shim thickness by folding the cardboard or adding layers. Use trial and error—slight increments amplify door movement elsewhere. If removing the bind causes sticking elsewhere, see following.

Straightening an angled screw

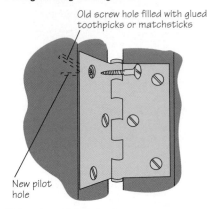

Old screw hole filled with glued toothpicks or matchsticks

New pilot hole

Shimming a hinge leaf

Jamb

Cardboard shim

▶ *Door sticks on latch side.*

First check for loose hinges and tighten the screws (see Tip below). If there's a gap along the hinge edge when the door is shut, keep it shut, remove the pin of the hinge closest to the gap and, with pliers, bend the hinge knuckles of the jamb leaf slightly toward the jamb; replace the pin. Another way to move the knuckles toward the jamb is to place a shim under the jamb hinge leaf along the edge closest to the doorstop (do this with the door open).

If the gap is too narrow (thinner than a dime) to move the door any more and the door still sticks, it's time to lubricate, sand, plane, or saw the edges—in that order. First locate exactly where the door sticks or binds. If it barely sticks, rub a candle over the bulge or apply silicone lubricant. If it still sticks, wrap coarse-grit sandpaper around a woodblock and ease the high spots with it, allowing for a layer of touch-up paint or finish. If the bottom sticks, tape a sheet of coarse sandpaper to the floor and work the door back and forth over it. As the sandpaper wears, place thin cardboard under the new paper so it will remove more of the door bottom.

To remove more wood, plane or saw the edge. Mark how much wood must be removed with the door in place; then remove the door (see Tip, opposite page) and stabilize it on edge (to plane) or lay it on sawhorses (to saw). Try to rent or borrow a power planer. It is easier to control than other tools, works quickly, and leaves a smooth edge for repainting. Whether using a hand plane or power planer, work with the grain and start at the corners, working toward the center. If you use a saw or you must plane an entire edge, trim the hinge edge instead of the latch edge; you won't have to take off the latch hardware and you don't run the risk of cutting off the 5-degree bevel that a latch edge must have. Trimming an edge with a saw may also leave scarring marks, which are hidden more easily on the hinge edge. After trimming, deepen the hinge mortises with a sharp chisel, touch up the edge with sandpaper, and repaint.

Tip   *If a screw turns but won't tighten, remove the screw. Then pack a few matchsticks, some toothpicks, or some short pieces of solder into the hole and replace the screw with a slightly longer one. For a more permanent repair, remove the hinge leaf, enlarge the hole to ⅜ inch by drilling, and glue in a ⅜-inch hardwood dowel. Let the glue dry, trim the dowel flush, drill a pilot hole in it for the screw, and replace the hinge leaf.*

Note: If the sticking problem is seasonal, be aware that adjusting the hinges or trimming the door may cause other problems during the off season.

Bending knuckles

Pin removed

Jamb casing

Door

Knuckles bent toward jamb

Shimming hinge leaf

Door

Shim

Using a power planer

Direction of grain

Wedge

Planing ends

Plywood door buck

▶ Door sticks against center of head jamb.

Hold a level or straightedge against the head jamb to see if it is sagging. If so, it's probably because shims were placed between the jamb and header (overhead framing member), transferring weight from the header to the jamb. To solve the problem, you need to remove the shims. On the side of the door that is least noticeable, score the painted joints of the head casing with a utility knife, then carefully pry off the casing. Remove any shims from the cavity above the head jamb by splitting them with a chisel and pulling the pieces out. The head jamb should spring back toward the header. If nails prevent it from moving, locate the nail heads on the bottom side of the jamb and tap them upward with a nail set and hammer. Replace the casing, patch nail holes and cracks, and repaint.

Removing shims

Head casing

Header

Shims

Wallboard

Nail heads

Doorstops

Jamb

Side casing

▶ Door won't close tightly.

If the door closes all the way but doesn't latch, the latch bolt isn't aligned with the strike plate. First close the door and check to see if the latch reaches the strike plate. If not, put enough shims behind the strike plate so that the latch bolt engages it. If they are not aligned, close the door and use a pencil to mark where the top and bottom of the latch bolt engage the strike plate. Compare these marks with the top and bottom of the strike plate hole. If the marks fall within the hole limits, the strike plate is too far back. If it's just a slight misalignment, enlarge the hole with a file. If a larger adjustment is necessary, remove the screws and plate, pack the screw holes with glued matchsticks, set the plate in the new location, drill pilot holes, and screw. You may also have to enlarge the hole in the doorjamb with a chisel to accommodate the latch.

If the marks show that the strike plate is too high or too low, measure the discrepancy. If it's less than 1/8 inch, enlarge the strike plate hole with a file. Otherwise, move the plate up or down the required distance by removing the plate, trimming away wood with a knife or sharp chisel, and reattaching the plate in the new location. Patch the resulting gap with spackling compound or wood putty, and touch it up with paint or stain. Bear in mind that this problem may be seasonal and the repair may cause misalignment during the off season.

If the latch bolt is aligned with the hole but doesn't engage it, the spring that drives the bolt is broken or jammed. Disassemble the lockset and clean all working parts with a

Tip To remove a door, open it about halfway and slide a shim under the latch edge to stabilize it. Remove the lower hinge pin first, then the upper, by grabbing the top of the pin with pliers and pulling upward, or tuck a chisel under the top of the pin, or insert a 16d nail below it, and knock it upward with a hammer. With the pins removed, slide the door away from the hinges and carry it out. If the door is solid-core, have someone help you stabilize and lift it.

light solvent. Lubricate them with a silicone or other nonstick lock lubricant and replace the spring if broken. See page 97.

Marking latch bolt position

Strike plate

Latch bolt   Pencil marks

Filing strike plate

Enlarging strike plate mortise

Enlarged hole
New screw hole
Plug

▶ *Door sags.*

Check the screws in the top hinge and tighten any that are loose. If they are tight, shut the door and, while observing from the side where the hinge knuckles are exposed, check to see if there is a wide gap between the door and jamb near the top hinge. If so, remove the door (see page 82) by pulling the hinge pins and, using pliers, bend the knuckles of the top hinge back toward the jamb. Rehang the door. If it still sags, realign the hinges (see below), or trim the bottom.

▶ *Door wanders and won't stay still.*

The door wanders because the hinges are not aligned plumb. To steady the door, try stiffening the hinges by removing the pins, one at a time, striking them with a hammer to bend them slightly, and replacing them. If the door still wanders, you'll have to realign the hinges by working on the door-jamb leaves. Pull the hinge pins and remove the door. Suspend a small plumb bob from the first knuckle on the top hinge to the lowest knuckle on the bottom hinge and note the direction(s) in which the hinges are out of alignment; or hold a 6-foot level vertically against the hinges, checking it in two directions (a shorter level with a straightedge also works). Move one of the leaves away from the jamb (by inserting shims behind it) and/or move one farther out from the doorstop (by enlarging the mortise with a chisel and plugging old screw holes so screws won't drift back into them—see Tip, page 82). Before rehanging the door, straighten the bent hinge pins or buy replacements.

Note: Because moving hinges far enough to make them plumb may cause other problems, such as a sticking door or misaligned latch, it may not be worthwhile to make them perfectly plumb; adjusting them slightly may be enough.

Checking plumb alignment

Adjusting hinge

Cardboard shim

New holes

Tip *Most interior doors are either "flush" (the face is plain and smooth) or "panel" (individual panels are set into a cross-shaped frame). Flush doors are hollow, with two "skins" (veneers) of thin lauan plywood. Panel doors vary in style and number of panels. Traditionally they were made from solid wood, which meant they were costly. Panel doors with hardboard facings made to resemble traditional panel styles are now available at much cheaper prices—about the same as flush doors.*

▶ Door bottom needs trimming.

At one time or other almost every home has a door that needs to be trimmed at the bottom: it drags on new carpet; it won't clear a new threshold; the door frame has shifted over time; or central heating requires airflow under the doors. If the door has not been removed, open it and measure ½ inch above the finish flooring at both bottom edges of the door (½ inch clears most carpets; ¾ inch is recommended if the home has central warm-air heating). Remeasure with the door closed. Remove the door (see page 82). If the door has been removed, measure from the head jamb down to the finish flooring along both sides of the door frame and transfer these measurements to the door, less ½ inch or ¾ inch for clearance. Allow for any gap that existed at the top of the door. (This method assumes that both the frame and the top of the door are square and that the floor level at the doorway is the same as where the door swings open; if not, adjust measurements accordingly.)

Run a length of masking tape along the bottom edge of the door face, to prevent the saw from splintering the door face, and scribe a cut line over it, between the marks. Lay the door on sawhorses with the best side facing up if you trim with a handsaw, down if you trim with a circular saw or jigsaw. To minimize splintering with a handsaw, duplicate the cut line on the side of the door that faces down and score that line with a utility knife. For a circular saw or jigsaw, score the cut line and clamp a straightedge to the door to guide the saw. After sawing, sand the cut edges smooth and apply sealer or paint to the bare wood.

Measuring from floor

Marks

Marking door for trimming

Side that faces down

Best door face

Masking tape

Trimming with circular saw

Guide

Tape

C-clamp

▶ Door has gaps around edge.

When they are shut, interior doors normally have about ³⁄₁₆ inch of clearance around the edges (thickness of a nickel). The door should "float" within the opening, rather than fit snugly all around; however, it should fit snugly against the doorstops.

If the gap is too wide, it may be unsightly. Remove the door (see page 82) and take the hinges off it. Plug the hinge mortises with wood strips. Attach a strip of wood (wide enough to reduce the gap to ³⁄₁₆ inch) along the hinge edge of the door with glue and nails. Then cut new hinge mortises into the strip, sand the strip smooth (especially along the joint), and finish it to match the rest of the door.

▶ Door is warped or coming apart.

It's often easier to buy a replacement door than to repair one; you may be able to find a used door or a door second at a reasonable price. If not, remove the door (see page 82). To repair a bowed door, set it on sawhorses, convex side up, and distribute weights (books, bricks) near the center of the door. Leave it there for two or three weeks. For warped doors that are twisted as well as bowed, attach wires and a turnbuckle to eye hooks screwed into opposite corners. Place a 2x4 under the wire and increase tension daily for three or four days. After it's straight, remove the hooks and fill the holes with putty. If the door is still warped when you hang it, install a third hinge midway between the top and bottom hinges.

To repair a panel door that's coming apart, remove the door and set it on sawhorses. Try squeezing the door parts together with bar clamps—paint and debris may have

Tip *Most doors have butt hinges, which have two leaves of identical size that open flat. For interior doors, the most common size is 3½ inches. The leaves are recessed flush into mortises cut into the doorjamb and door edge. Most mortises are now cut with a router, which leaves corners rounded because the bit rotates in a circular motion. For this reason, butt hinges are available with rounded corners, in addition to the traditional kind with square corners for mortises cut with a chisel.*

clogged the cracks. Remove the clamps, separate the pieces as far as you can without breaking the joints, and inject aliphatic adhesive (carpenter's wood glue) into the joints with a glue syringe. Clamp the stiles together with a bar clamp placed at each rail on alternating sides of the door. Use 2x4 fillers to avoid marring the door. Alternately tighten clamps a little bit until the joints are all tight. Wipe away excess glue, let dry overnight, remove the clamps, and paint or seal the door.

Straightening a warped door

Turnbuckle

Gluing joints of a paneled door

Glue syringe   Pry bar

Open joints

Clamping the door

2x4 Filler

▶ *Door is hard for children or an elderly person to open.*

Replace the doorknobs with lever handles, which come in many attractive styles. With some styles, you may need to replace the entire lockset. There are also lever handles that clamp onto an ordinary door-knob. To make opening a door convenient for a person in a wheel-chair, you can have automatic door openers installed on certain interior doors. They can be activated by a remote-controlled device, much like an automatic garage-door opener.

▶ *Door opening is too narrow for wheelchair.*

If the opening is wide enough with-out the door itself blocking part of it, replace the existing hinges with offset hinges. They let the door swing out of the way when it opens fully, so it clears the opening. If the opening is still too narrow, the only solution is to widen the doorway and install a new door. Consult a carpenter.

Using offset hinges to swing door out of the way

Doorstop   Offset hinge

Clear opening

▶ *Door needs replacing.*

Buy a new door the same size as the opening or slightly larger. The stan-dard height for new doors is 6 feet, 8 inches; widths range in 2-inch in-crements from 2 feet to 3 feet. If the old door fits perfectly, use it as a template for trimming the new one to size. If one edge of the new door is beveled, make it the latch edge and trim the other edge. If not, make the trimmed edge the latch edge and bevel it 5 degrees. If the old door does not fit well or is miss-ing, measure the doorway dimen-sions and use them to mark cut lines on the new door. Check the door opening for square by measur-ing the diagonals, or by holding a framing square against each cor-ner; adjust dimensions accordingly. Allow for 3/16-inch clearance at the top and each side, 1/2 to 3/4 inch for the bottom. Score the cut line with a utility knife, or cover it with masking tape to minimize splinter-ing; clamp a straightedge to the door as a saw guide. Use a power saw to trim the door. If you are trimming the latch edge, set the saw blade to a 5-degree bevel.

After trimming the door, mea-sure and mark for the hinge mortises. Take measurements from the old door or measure the distance from the head jamb to the hinge mortises in the door frame, then subtract 3/16 inch to allow for the top clearance. Cut the mortises with a 1½-inch chisel; start by scoring and deepen-ing the cut lines, then chisel away enough waste so that the hinge leaf will recess flush into the mortise. Next drill holes for the doorknob or other latching hardware. Instructions supplied with the doorknob should provide dimensions for the diameter and centering of the holes. Install the hinges and doorknob, and hang the door to test it for fit; make adjust-ments as necessary.

Tip *To reduce sound transmission between rooms, replace hollow-core flush doors with solid-core flush doors or solid panel doors.*

Take down the door, remove the hardware, and paint or finish as desired. When the finish dries, install the hardware and hang the door.

Measuring door opening without square corners

Trimming door edge

Cutting hinge mortise

▶ Edge of door seems to be wrong color.

If the whole door is painted one color, the edges should be the same color. If the two sides of the door are painted different colors, paint the edges to match the rooms they face when the door is open—hinge edge one color; latch edge, top, and bottom the other.

▶ Bifold doors bind or won't close.

First shut the doors as far as possible and see if there are gaps between the doors and side jambs. If there are, move the bottoms of the doors toward the jambs by lifting up on them and sliding them over. To move the tops, locate the pin holder at each end of the overhead track, and loosen the setscrews that lock them in place; slide the holders toward the jambs and retighten the screws. If the doors still bind, they are too wide for the door opening. Trim one of the center panels along its nonhinged edge.

Adjusting bifold door at top

Adjusting bifold door at bottom

▶ Bifold doors don't align at the center.

This problem is prevented by a pair of guides attached to the backs of the center panels, near the floor. One or both may be missing or loose. To find replacements at the hardware store, look for bifold hinges.

If the gap where the two doors meet is uneven, adjust it by moving the pivot pin at the bottom outside corner of either door toward the jamb or away from it.

▶ Bifold door scrapes head jamb.

Move the bottom outside corner of the door toward the side jamb by lifting up on it and sliding the pivot pin a few notches toward the jamb. You will have to adjust it by trial and error. If adjusting the door causes the bottom edge to bind against the side jamb, adjust the top instead. Locate the pin holder at the end of the door track, and loosen the setscrew that locks it in place. Slide it slightly toward the center of the track and tighten the setscrew.

Straightening bifold door

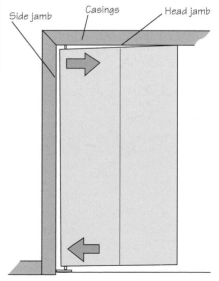

Tip   *Door talk: A "two-eight by six-eight" (2-8 x 6-8) door is 2 feet, 8 inches wide (not 28 inches wide) and 6 feet, 8 inches high. Door widths from 2 feet to 3 feet are 2-0, 2-2, 2-4, 2-6, 2-8, 2-10, and 3-0.*

▶ Bifold doors scrape carpet.

If there is enough clearance above the doors, raise them by rotating the threaded pivot pin that is located at the bottom outside corner of each door. If the turning knob does not rotate easily, lift up on the door while you turn it, or use pliers to rotate it. If the top of the door hits the track before the bottom clears the carpet, you will have to trim the bottoms of the doors. See page 85.

▶ Bipass doors rub together.

First make sure that the rollers for each door are attached securely and centered in the overhead track. Then check the door guide, which is a small cleat attached to the floor that keeps the doors separated from each other at the bottom. If it's missing or the center divider is broken, buy a replacement and screw it to the floor in the center of the door opening. If the doors still rub together, one door must be warped. Remove both doors and reverse them.

▶ Bipass doors drag on floor or don't hang straight.

If a door hangs too low or is tilted, you can adjust it by raising or lowering it where it hangs from the roller. Look behind the door where the hanger is attached. If it has a cam-type adjusting mechanism, loosen it with a wrench or screwdriver and adjust the cam. If not, the hanger should have slotted screw holes for the screws holding it to the door. With a helper, loosen the screws, move the door edge up or down so the screws change position in relation to the hanger, and tighten them. If you don't have a helper, improvise a foot lever or use wedges to raise the door as you adjust the hanger screws.

Adjusting door height

Door track

Door guide

Foot lever

Adjustable hangers

▶ Bipass doors rattle.

Lightweight hollow-core doors move easily with breezes or vibrations, causing them to rattle. The noise is usually caused by the door bottoms bumping against the door guide, but check other places as well. To muffle the noise, attach short pieces of self-sticking weather stripping to the guide where the doors rub against it.

▶ Bipass doors have gap in center or on sides.

If the doors aren't wide enough to cover the entire opening (they should overlap at least ¼ inch), widen one of the doors by attaching a strip of wood to the edge that rests against the side jamb. Use lattice for a narrow gap (up to ¼ inch) or 1x2 for wider gaps. Doors are 1⅜ inch thick, and most wood strips are 1½ inch wide; therefore, you will have to rip the strip to size. Attach it with glue and finishing nails, and smooth the joint by filling gaps with wood putty or spackling compound and sanding it. Then paint or finish the strip to match the doors. Another solution to the gap problem is to attach thick doorstops or other molding strips to the side jambs, in front of the doors, so they conceal the gaps. Attach bumpers to the door edges to keep the doors from closing too far.

▶ Pocket door rattles.

Check the bottom of the door pocket to see if the door guide or anchor is missing; it's a small shoe or pair of bumpers that stabilizes the door and keeps it from scraping against the sides of the pocket. If there is none, you may be able to find a new one where pocket-door hardware is sold. Otherwise, improvise one from a door guide for bipass doors (see left), or buy two glide buttons intended for the bottom of chair legs. To install the guide or glide buttons, you will need to remove the door. First pry the doorstop from the side jamb; then pull the door all the way into the opening, lift it, and tilt it (as shown) to release the rollers from the overhead track. With the door removed, center the guide in the door pocket

Tip *Properly installed bifold doors have ½ inch of clearance at the bottom, ⅛ inch between each door and the jamb at its side, and 1/16 inch between the doors when they are shut. The door fronts should be set back from the face of the casings approximately ¾ inch.*

and screw it to the floor; or nail the glide buttons to the sides of the pocket at the floor. Replace the door and doorstop.

If there is a guide and the door rattles against it, attach self-sticking weather stripping to its inside edges to muffle the sound and limit door movement. If it rattles against the doorstop, stick the weather stripping on the inside edge of the stop.

Removing a pocket door

Installing door guides

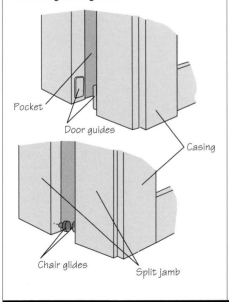

▶ Pocket-door latch won't align with strike plate.

If the door latch is too low to align with the strike plate, push up on the overhead track to see if it is loose and sagging, causing the door to droop. If so, push the door into the pocket and tighten the screws that attach the track to the framing. If the track is secure, see if you can adjust the hanger screws to move the door up or down. If not, you will have to enlarge the strike plate hole with a file so the door latch fits into it, or move the strike plate up or down (see page 83).

▶ Pocket door doesn't glide easily.

Remove the door (see opposite page). Inspect the rollers attached to the top of the door for worn, sticking, or broken wheels. If a wheel is defective, replace the whole roller mechanism. If the rollers spin freely, inspect the track for debris, looseness, cracks, or dents. Clean out all debris. If the track is loose, tighten the screws that hold it to the framing. This is a good job for someone with long, thin arms, as access to some screws is only through the 2-inch-wide door pocket. If the track is dented or cracked, replace it.

▶ Pocket door doesn't recess all the way into pocket.

Remove the door (see left) and inspect the back of the pocket for debris that might block the door. Then inspect the track for dents or other obstacles that might limit door movement. If the pocket and track are clear, measure the width

of the door and the depth of the pocket; the door might be too wide. If not, remove the bumper from the back edge of the door and replace it with something thinner, such as a plywood scrap, to allow the door to travel farther into the pocket. Rehang the door and reattach the doorstop.

▶ Pocket door doesn't block sound.

Pocket doors are not effective at blocking sound because of the loose fit, the hollow pocket cavity, and the need for clearance at the bottom to allow the door to slide back and forth. To reduce sound transmission, apply weather stripping to the doorstop and, if necessary, against the jamb where the door latches. Then apply it to the sides of the jamb where the door slides into the pocket when it's opened. Use the vinyl-cushion type of weather stripping for both places, and paint it to match the trim. To reduce sound transmission at the bottom, lower the door as much as possible by adjusting the hangers. At least one of the rooms adjacent to the door should have carpet; if only one room does, the carpet should terminate under the door, not in front of it. Replacing a hollow-core door with a solid door will also reduce sound transmission, but it may be necessary to reinforce the track for the heavier door (most track and door hardware is designed to hold doors up to 125 pounds).

Tip *Installing a pocket door requires a framed opening larger than other door openings because there can be no studs, wires, pipes, or other obstructions inside the recessed pocket area of the wall. Twice as much wall covering must be removed, and a header twice as long as an ordinary door header must be installed. Consult a carpenter or building contractor.*

▶ *Pocket door comes off track.*

An obstruction may be causing a roller wheel to jump the track, or the bottom of the door may be too low to clear the floor completely. First check the track by opening the door all the way and feeling along the track for debris or dents. Remove any debris. Repair dents by removing the door and the track, then pounding out the dent with a hammer, using a sledgehammer or other heavy block of metal in back of the track as you pound on it. If the track is clear, raise the door to clear the floor by adjusting the hanging mechanism. If the door still jumps the track, a roller wheel is probably worn or broken. Remove the door and inspect the rollers. If a wheel is defective, replace the whole roller mechanism.

▶ *Exterior door admits drafts.*

Install weather stripping around the top and sides, and a door shoe with vinyl gasket seal on the bottom (see right). If the door fits loosely between the jambs, install vinyl V-strip or metal spring-type weather stripping; it won't show when the door is shut. Install the top piece first, fitting it flush to the side jambs. Install the side pieces next, cutting the tops at an angle to fit snugly against the top strip; the nailed edge faces outward. Don't cover the strike plate; install a short piece of stripping against the doorstop instead. If the door fits snugly, apply gasket weather stripping to the doorstop around the outside of the door. The tubular vinyl type is easiest to install; the nail-on type lasts longer.

▶ *Exterior door leaks at bottom.*

To prevent water from coming under the door, install an aluminum threshold on the floor and a door shoe with a metal drip shield and vinyl gasket on the bottom of the door. First take down the door (see Tip, page 82), then remove the old threshold. If it is metal, remove the screws and lift it out; if it is wood, saw through the threshold at both ends, pry out the middle section, and remove the remaining end pieces. Mark the new threshold for cutting by setting it against the door opening and transferring measurements onto it. Cut it with a hacksaw. Set the threshold in place and mark the screw locations on the subfloor for drilling pilot holes. Remove the threshold, drill the holes, dab some caulk into each one, and set the threshold back in place. Drive the screws part way in, dab some caulk under the heads, then drive them tight.

   With the threshold in place, rehang the door and close it to check for clearance between the threshold and bottom of the door. If the bottom clears, measure the height of any gap. Subtract that distance from the thickness of the new door shoe when you trim the bottom of the door for the shoe. If the bottom doesn't clear, mark on each edge of the door a point that is level with the top of the threshold. Measure above these marks a distance equal to the thickness of the shoe and make new marks; connect the new marks with a line. Remove the door and trim the bottom along that line (see page 84).

Cut the shoe to length with a hacksaw (cut the vinyl gasket with a knife), attach it to the bottom of the door with the screws provided, and rehang the door.

Cutting old wood threshold

Measuring for new threshold

Subfloor

New threshold

Cut lines

Installing door shoe

Notch for stop

Threshold

Door shoe

Vinyl gasket

Tip   *To increase the effectiveness of gasket weather stripping with a nail-on flange installed around a door, apply a thin bead of acrylic latex caulk under the flange before screwing it in place.*

Tip   *If you are installing adhesive-backed rubber or foam weather stripping around a door, be sure the temperature is above 50° F. If the temperature is lower, the adhesive may not stick.*

▶ *Exterior door leaks at top.*

An exterior door not protected by a porch or overhang is exposed to direct rain and any water running down the wall above it. Install a drip cap and drip flashing to divert water away from the top of the door. First remove a strip of siding and underlayment paper from above the door casing. Measure the siding cutout carefully. It should be as wide as the drip cap material is high, and long enough to extend ¾ inch beyond the door on each side. Then cut a piece of drip cap (or a strip of 1x2 redwood with a beveled top) and a piece of galvanized drip-cap flashing, both long enough to fit within the cutout. Set the flashing in place first, slipping the back flange up under the siding and underlayment paper. Then tuck the drip cap up under the flashing and attach it to the wall sheathing with 8d HDG nails driven up at an angle from below. Set the nail heads, fill them with caulk, and paint the drip cap to match the house trim. If leaking persists, have a small sheet-metal shield fabricated and installed above the door, or have a permanent overhang constructed.

Cutting siding

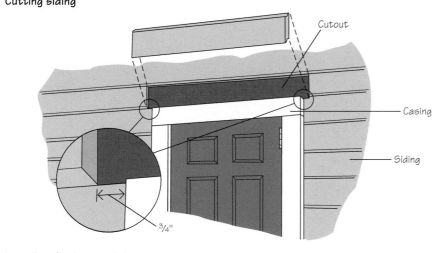

Installing flashing and drip cap

▶ *Exterior door sticks.*

First check the hinges for loose screws and the edges for excessive gaps, as with an interior door (see page 82). If it still sticks, do not trim the door unless you are sure that the problem is permanent and not seasonal. If the weather is humid or rainy, wait until a drier season. If the door still sticks, trim it. If not, make sure the gap is wide enough for a new coat of paint; remove the door and reseal all four edges and both sides with two coats of sealer or one coat of primer and one of paint. If the gap is too narrow for the buildup of paint, trim the door before resealing it.

▶ *Exterior-door jamb is cracked.*

Even for cracks as long as 2 feet, it is easier to splice in a new section of jamb than to replace the entire damaged jamb. First remove the exterior casing next to the damaged area. Then, with a pencil and square, mark cut lines across the jamb above and below the crack. If damage is confined to the outer half of the jamb, make a vertical cut line between these marks along the doorstop. With a circular saw or reciprocating saw, cut through the jamb at both horizontal lines; if you made a vertical line at the doorstop, stop the cuts there and use a jigsaw to complete the cuts. Remove the damaged section of jamb. Next nail or glue shims or a filler block behind the cut ends of the jamb, leaving enough shim material above and below the cuts to fur out the new patch. Cut a patch from identical jamb stock or other replacement lumber, apply glue to the back of it, set it into the cutout area, and nail it with 16d

Tip *A wood door exposed to the weather can soak up water like a sponge, especially at the bottom, unless all surfaces are sealed. The most vulnerable surfaces are the top and bottom edges, which are also hidden from view. If a door has not been painted in some time, it is worthwhile to remove the door entirely and paint all six surfaces (two sides and four edges) with a clear sealer or a coat each of primer and paint.*

finishing nails; set the nail heads well below the surface. Plane or sand the patch so it is flush with the rest of the jamb, then finish to match.

Cutting out damaged section

Installing patch

▶ Exterior-door panels are cracked.

An old door may not be worth repairing; consider buying an insulated steel-clad door to replace it. For slight cracks or surface damage, sand the area, apply wood filler with a putty knife, let it dry, sand it smooth, and touch up the repair to match the rest of the door. If the joints are coming apart and you feel the door is worth repairing, repair it in the same way as an interior door (see page 85).

▶ Exterior door needs painting or varnishing.

Start early in the day so the paint will be dry by evening. Remove the door (see Tip, page 82), set it on sawhorses, and remove all hardware. Thoroughly scrape and sand away all loose paint and varnish; wear a dust mask and eye protection. If you wish to refinish a painted door with a stain or natural finish, use a water-soluble paint stripper, following label directions carefully. When the old finish has been scraped or stripped, vacuum the door and remove any remaining dust with a tack cloth or solution of TSP and water, mixed and applied according to label directions. Then prime, seal, or stain both sides and all four edges of the door. Let the first coat dry, sand it lightly with 200-grit sandpaper or fine steel wool, and apply the finish coat. When it dries, replace the hardware and rehang the door. If the finish isn't dry, leave the door ajar overnight. Screw a panel of ½-inch plywood to the inside of the door opening for security.

▶ Threshold is damaged or rotted.

Remove the old threshold by sawing through it at both doorstops, prying out the center section, and chiseling away the short end pieces. Next mark the new threshold for cutting. Use the pieces of the old threshold as a template for marking the new, or hold the new threshold against the door opening and transfer cut marks onto it with a pencil and square held against the sides of the door opening. Cut out the new threshold and finish it with a sealer or paint. When the finish dries, apply caulk to the bottom of the threshold, set it in place, and nail or screw it to the floor. To install a metal threshold, see page 90.

▶ Threshold gasket is missing or worn.

Some metal thresholds include a vinyl gasket that may get worn or damaged. Buy a replacement gasket where thresholds are sold. Slip the old one off, vacuum out the channels in the threshold, cut the new gasket to length with a utility knife so it fits flush against both door jambs, and press it into place so the flanges are locked into the two channels in the threshold.

▶ Threshold screws won't tighten.

Try longer screws. If they won't tighten, the screw holes for the threshold are probably lined up over a gap between the subfloor and wall sheathing, leaving little wood for the screws to bite into. Remove the screws and, with the threshold in place, insert a thin pencil (or a nail with chalk on the

Tip *Many exterior doors have a sill under the threshold, which slopes downward away from the house. Be sure that the joint between the sill and threshold is sealed tightly with a bead of caulk and that both pieces of wood are well sealed with paint or a clear wood finish.*

point) into each hole to mark locations on the subfloor. Remove the threshold. If the problem is a gap, widen it to ¾ inch and insert a 1-by board into the gap. It should be deep enough to rest on the rim joist or other framing below the subfloor. Nail it to the framing with 8d or larger nails (predrill first). Caulk any gaps around the strip. Set the threshold in place, mark where the holes line up over the new strip, and remove the threshold. Drill pilot holes into the marks, moving them toward the center of the wood strip if they align over a crack or open joint; dab caulk into the holes, and set the threshold in place. Drive the screws in most of the way, dab some caulk under the heads, and then tighten them.

Inserting filler strip

Metal threshold

Finish floor

Siding

Subfloor

Filler strip

Rim joist

▶ *Double French doors don't align.*

The latch in one door may not be aligned with the strike plate in the other door, keeping them from shutting securely. To solve this problem, start by shutting the doors and observing how wide the gaps are around the tops and sides. Knowing where the gaps are will help you make adjustments later. If the alignment is only slightly off and the door gaps are not objectionable, simply enlarge the hole in the strike plate with a file. For larger adjustments, move the latch edge of each door up or down by slipping cardboard shims beneath the hinge leaves or bending the hinge knuckles. (See page 82 for specific techniques.)

▶ *Double doors have exposed gap between them.*

If there is a gap between double French or patio doors that are exposed to the exterior, a strip of molding on the exterior will keep out rain and keep the doors aligned. Attach it to the fixed door if the doors open inward; to the moving door if they open outward. Flat molding, such as a doorstop, is the easiest type to install. Cut a piece the same length as the door, prime or seal all sides and edges, apply a bead of caulk along one side, and nail it to the exterior side of the door so half of it extends beyond the edge of the door.

An astragal, which is T-shaped in profile, is stronger than flat molding, but you will need to trim back the door edge to install it. After cutting the astragal to the same length as the door and priming or sealing it, remove the lockset hardware from the door (or the strike plate if the doors open inward). Then measure the width of

the astragal flange and trim that amount from the edge of the door. Set the saw blade at the same bevel as the flange. Apply a bead of caulk to the back of the astragal near the front edge, and nail the flange into the edge of the door with 6d finishing nails. Bore out the astragal where it covers the hole in the door edge for the lockset, paint the astragal, and replace the door hardware when the paint is dry.

Installing molding

Gap

Molding

Door swing

Installing an astragal

Door swing

Beveled side

Astragal

Tip *According to the National Association of Home Builders, the life expectancy of an exterior door protected by a porch or overhang is 80 to 100 years. The same door, without such protection, would last from 25 to 30 years.*

SOLVING DOOR & WINDOW PROBLEMS

▶ Double glass doors don't lock securely.

With a pair of French doors, one door serves as a fixed panel and the other door opens and closes against it. Install heavy-duty throw bolts at the top and bottom of the fixed door; they should be long enough to slide at least 1 inch beyond the strike plates or cleats attached to the head jamb and floor. Install a lockset in the moving door that includes a 1-inch dead bolt. A single lock assembly, called a cremone lock, includes lock bolts at all three points—top, bottom, and latch. Avoid locks that require a key to open from the interior side as well as exterior; many codes do not allow them because they present an escape hazard during emergencies.

▶ Sliding glass door doesn't glide smoothly.

Start with routine maintenance by giving the bottom door track a thorough cleaning; dig out stubborn debris with a screwdriver, vacuum out the track, and buff the channel with fine steel wool. Apply a light coating of silicone spray or aerosol furniture polish to the top track. If the door still balks, inspect the top and bottom tracks for bent or dented areas. Bend such spots back into shape with a hammer; place a woodblock in the track to back up the blows. If the tracks pass inspection, the problem is faulty door wheels. Loosen the adjusting screws for the wheels and, with a helper, remove the door by lifting it up and pulling the bottom outward (you may need to hold the wheels up until they clear the track). Place the door on padded sawhorses, supporting the frame so

the glass doesn't take the weight. The wheels should feel solid and spin freely. Remove worn or loose wheels by loosening or removing the setscrews that hold them in place; replace them with roller units from the same manufacturer.

Hammering out a dent

Replacing a wheel

Adjusting screw

▶ Sliding glass door lacks safety glass.

Codes developed in recent years require that doors have safety glazing such as laminated safety glass, tempered glass, or plastic panels (except panes less than 3 inches wide). Check to see if your glass door is labeled as safety glass in one of the corners. If not and the doors are standard height (6 feet, 6 inches for 6-foot 8-inch openings), you should be able to buy replacement doors with safety glass that will fit in the same frame. To conserve energy, consider buying double-glazed units.

▶ Sliding glass door lacks security lock.

The style of latch in most older patio doors is not very strong. For extra security install a keyed lock or thumb latch designed for installation near the top of the door. Mount it on the face of the metal frame farthest from the latch side; drill holes for the two sheet-metal screws that hold it, and screw it to the frame. Then shut the door and mark where the lock bolt strikes the top metal jamb. Drill a hole at the mark, slightly larger than the diameter of the lock bolt. Mark and drill a second hole with the door open 2 to 4 inches; this allows you to lock the door with it opened slightly for fresh air. Another way to lock the door is with a "charley bar," an adjustable rod that lies in the floor track and blocks movement of the door.

▶ Screen/storm door opens too far or not far enough.

To limit door travel and prevent a storm door or screen door from blowing against the house wall, install a chain retainer. Attach one end to the head jamb, then open the door as far as you want it to reach, and stretch out the chain to determine where to attach it to the door frame. Close the door and attach the chain. If the door has a chain that doesn't allow it to open as far as you'd like, loosen the chain from the head jamb and reattach it at a point closer to the hinge end of the jamb.

Tip *French doors and other glass doors should have safety glass. Doors in most older homes don't. It is possible to replace each of the panes with tempered glass or laminated safety glass (double-glazed for energy conservation and sound control), especially if the outside putty is already loose and deteriorating. It may be easier, however, to buy a replacement door.*

▶ Screen/storm door closes too fast or too slow.

Regulate the speed of the door by adjusting the automatic door closer. If it's the pneumatic type, which has a horizontal tube or piston, close the door and turn the adjusting screw at the end of the tube. If it doesn't have a screw, remove the pin that holds the tube to the door. Holding the tube in one hand, use pliers to rotate the plunger that was held by the pin—clockwise to increase tension and door speed, counterclockwise to slow the speed. If the door has a hydraulic closer (vertical barrel), use a screwdriver to rotate the adjusting screw at the bottom of the barrel to change speed.

Adjusting a pneumatic closer

Adjusting screw

Adjusting a hydraulic closer

Adjusting screw

▶ Screen/storm door won't fit in opening.

A door opening may be too narrow for the new screen door or storm door closest to it in size. If the door is wood, trim it along the hinge edge, allowing for a ³⁄₁₆-inch gap on both sides. Most aluminum doors have a sleeve on the hinge side that makes it possible to adjust the door to any width within a 1- to 2-inch range.

Measure the width of the door opening at the top and bottom, and subtract ¼ to ⅜ inch from each dimension. Adjust the hinge sleeve so the width of the door is the same as these dimensions at the top and bottom, drill pilot holes, and secure it with the screws provided.

Adjusting hinge sleeve

▶ Screen/storm door frame is tarnished.

Restore tarnished aluminum with aluminum or copper cleaner, following label directions. Do not scrub with abrasive powders or a scouring pad.

▶ Screen/storm door sags.

If the door is wood, buy a cable-and-turnbuckle kit for reinforcing sagging screen doors. With the turnbuckle fully open, attach one end to the top corner of the door on the hinge side, the other end to the bottom corner on the latch side. Tighten the turnbuckle until the door sag is gone. An aluminum door can be fixed in the same way, but you may also be able to fix it by replacing a bent or broken corner key. This is a metal reinforcing bracket located inside the door frame at each corner. (Not all aluminum doors have them.) A buckled corner reveals which key needs to be replaced. Remove the door and disassemble the buckled corner. Look for a replacement key at door shops or hardware stores that sell the type of door you have.

▶ Doorknob is loose.

If the lockset is an old-fashioned mortise style with a porcelain, glass, or heavy brass doorknob, loosen the setscrew on the side of the knob that secures it to the square spindle. Back off the setscrew far enough for the knob to turn freely without operating the latch. Screw the knob clockwise until it is snug but not tight against the door, then tighten the setscrew. Be sure the screw is tightened against a flat side of the spindle, not a pointed corner (you may have to back the knob away from the door one-eighth turn).

If the lockset is the cylindrical type, one of the knobs will have a

Tip *If you are decorating a room, don't forget the doorknobs. Most locksets have several styles of doorknobs that are interchangeable. Remove the old doorknob and take it to a locksmith or hardware store to find a replacement with the same fastening method.*

slot on the side of the shank, just behind the knob. Push a screwdriver into the slot to release the knob. Then remove the decorative rose that covers the lockset by depressing a spring clip at the edge. This will expose a mounting plate with two screws. Tighten the two screws, snap the rose back in place, and push the knob onto the spindle so the keeper snaps back into the slot on the shank.

Locating setscrew for mortise lock

Removing knob from lock cylinder

Tightening screws of cylindrical lock

▶ Key doesn't slide into lock smoothly.

First check to be sure it's the right key and that the key isn't bent. If the weather is cold, the lock could be jammed with ice formed from accumulated moisture. Start by chipping away as much ice from the keyhole as possible. Then heat the key with a match and insert it in the lock; you may have to repeat this operation until it goes in all the way. Turn the key carefully; don't force it. If the problem is not ice, lubricate the keyhole and key with a nonsticking lubricant such as silicone spray or powdered graphite. If that doesn't work, look inside the keyhole for a foreign object. Remove it with a piece of thin, stiff wire.

▶ Latch bolt gets stuck in lock.

Check to see if the latch bolt is binding against the latch plate in the edge of the door (see page 83 for adjusting the alignment). If so, inject some graphite powder or silicone spray into the latch mechanism to lubricate the edges of the plate. If the latch bolt still binds, insert a thin screwdriver between the latch bolt and plate and carefully enlarge the gap by prying them apart. If necessary, dismantle the lockset to remove the latch assembly so you can lubricate it and adjust alignment of the bolt.

▶ Key is broken in lock.

If enough of the key is protruding, pull it out with needle nose pliers. If the pliers can't grip it, try raking out the broken piece with the blade of a coping saw, or pulling it out with stiff wire formed into a hook. If none of this works, try to dismantle the lockset and push the piece

out from the backside with a piece of thin, stiff wire. *Note:* Some locksets can't be disassembled while the door is shut.

▶ Key turns and nothing happens.

The mechanism connecting the lock cylinder to the tailpiece or spindle may be broken, or the tailpiece has snapped off. Disassemble the lockset and check to see if the tailpiece is intact. If it is not, buy a new cylinder with tailpiece. If it's intact, turn the key in the cylinder to see if it moves the tailpiece. If not, take the assembly to a locksmith and have it repaired or replaced. If the key does turn the tailpiece, the tailpiece is not engaging the deadbolt assembly or the dead bolt is defective. Try reassembling with the tailpiece properly engaged in the dead-bolt hole. If it still does not work, replace the dead-bolt assembly or the entire lockset.

Checking lock assembly

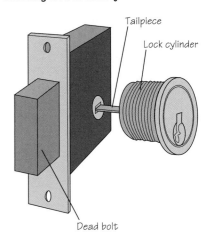

Tip *Lock your house whenever you leave. An unlocked home is an invitation to burglary. In fact, many insurance policies will not honor a claim for theft if there was no evidence of forced entry.*

▶ Key won't turn in lock.

Don't force it. If it's a newly made replacement key, check it against the original for minor discrepancies; get a new key made. If it's not new, the problem may be that the lock cylinder is turned slightly from a vertical position. Open the door from the inside and locate the setscrew on the door edge that holds the cylinder in place (with some models you may have to disassemble the lockset), loosen it, and return the cylinder to its original position; tighten the screw. If the key still won't turn, the tumblers are probably damaged; have the cylinder replaced.

▶ Latch bolt of mortise lockset retracts but won't extend.

A mortise lock has a one-piece rectangular body that is recessed into a large cavity cut into the edge of the door. Occasionally the spring inside breaks, eliminating the thrust that forces the latch bolt back after you retract it by turning the handle. To remove the lockset, remove one of the doorknobs by loosening the setscrew that holds it to the spindle and screwing off the knob. Remove the other knob and spindle from the other side of the lockset. If the lockset has a dead-bolt knob, remove it by loosening the setscrew and sliding it off the spindle; then loosen the setscrew for the lock cylinder (located on the latch plate), and pull the lock cylinder and spindle out from the other side of the door. Next remove the two mounting screws from the latch plate and remove the lock assembly. One side has three screws; lay down the lockset so the screws face up, loosen them, and remove the cover plate. Locate the broken spring and take it to a locksmith to get a replacement. Set the new spring in place, holding

it under tension with needle nose pliers so it fits behind the latch linkage. Carefully reassemble the lockset and reinstall it in the door.

Removing mortise lockset

Lock cylinder   Setscrew   Latch plate   Dead bolt   Latch bolt

Placing new spring

▶ Security bolt doesn't align with hole.

First tighten any loose mounting screws. They are located on the lock housing if the lock is surface-mounted, and on the latch plate if the lock is inside the door. If the lock is secure, you may need to adjust the strike plate as described on page 83. However, consider the possibility that this is a temporary problem due to a change in the weather or slight shifting of the house. If the door gradually starts to bind, leave it locked and do not use the door for a week or two—it may fix itself.

▶ Dead bolt is keyed on both sides.

This type of dead bolt, which requires a key to open it from the inside, is intended to discourage intruders from breaking nearby glass and reaching in to turn the lock handle. However, such locks also prevent occupants from making a quick escape in case of emergency and are often prohibited by local codes. Replace the double-key dead bolt with a conventional dead bolt. To improve security, replace glass in the nearby window with breakproof glazing.

▶ Lock is not heavy enough.

A dead-bolt lock should have at least a 1-inch throw, be constructed of solid (not stamped) metal, and have a heavy-gauge strike plate with screws long enough to reach the stud behind the jamb. If the existing lock lacks these attributes, buy a lock designated as "heavy-duty" to replace it. First remove the old lock to use as a template in selecting the new lock so you can use the same holes bored in the door. If you have to enlarge a hole, use a hole saw.

▶ Bathroom door is locked and someone's inside.

If a child is locked in the bathroom or someone falls and is unable to reach the door for help, you need to be able to unlock the door from the outside. If the doorknob is the type with a small hole in the center, push a nail or similar device into the hole to unlock the door. If the doorknob cannot be unlocked, remove the door by extracting the hinge pins, if they are exposed. If they aren't, pry loose the doorstop on the latch side just enough to slip a plastic credit card against the latch to force it open.

Tip *Fumbling for extra keys is awkward and unnecessary. You can have both locks in one door—or all locks in the house—keyed to a single key if they have compatible cylinders. For one door, remove the dead bolt or lock, whichever is easier, and take it to a locksmith along with both keys. Have the locksmith replace the lock cylinder and key it to the same key that operates the other lock. If the cylinder can't be changed, buy a dead bolt with a compatible cylinder and have it keyed to the key of the other lock.*

▶ *Window glass is broken.*

Wooden frames: Work from the outside, except for windows that have removable wood strips on the interior side of the glass. First, wearing gloves and eye protection, remove all loose pieces of glass; then remove the glazing compound by chipping it away with a putty knife. If it doesn't chip easily, heat it with a hair dryer or heat lamp to soften it. With a putty knife or needle nose pliers, pry out the metal points that hold the glass in place. As you work, the remaining pieces of glass will loosen; be wary and remove them as you work your way around the window. Pull out the rest of the glass, using pliers for stubborn pieces. Scrape away all old putty and paint, and brush out the rabbet (groove) thoroughly. Measure the width and height of the opening for a new pane of glass, subtracting ⅛ inch from each dimension for clearance. Before you go to the glass dealer, paint any bare wood in the rabbet with fast-drying primer. Bring a scrap of glass to the store to be sure the replacement glass is the same type (see Tip on opposite page for windows that require safety or tempered glass).

To install the new pane, first make a thin rope (¼ inch) of glazing compound and press it into the rabbet; this cushions the glass and provides a tight seal. Next press the new pane firmly into place and secure it with glazing points, spacing them 4 to 6 inches apart; push them into the wood with a stiff putty knife. Apply new glazing compound around the window; work it into a rope and press it into place with your fingers, then smooth it with a putty knife held at a 45-degree angle. Check other panes to see how far to extend it onto the glass. Let it cure for at least a week, then paint it.

Aluminum frames: Remove the sash. If the glass is held in place by beveled strips around the outside edges, pry them off, remove the broken glass, apply sealing mastic around the interior perimeter of the new pane, press it into place, and reinstall the strips. If the frame consists of U-shaped channels with no removable strips, disassemble it by loosening the screws from both corners of one side and removing the side. Pull out the broken glass and vinyl gasket surrounding it. Slip the gasket around the new glass, slide it into the frame, and replace the side piece.

Removing putty

Sash

Applying glazing compound

Rabbeted edge

Inserting glass

Glazing points

Smoothing compound

▶ *Double-glazed window has moisture or haze between panes.*

Air with water vapor has seeped into the sealed cavity between the two panes and has condensed on the cold glass. It is difficult, if not impossible, to have the window repaired. It is also difficult to replace only the glass unit; you'll probably have to replace the entire sash, unless the window is a fixed window fabricated on-site. Check to see if your window has a guarantee.

▶ *Window glass is wavy or distorted.*

Because it is technically a liquid, all glass eventually slumps and deforms. This condition adds to the charm of older homes; but if you find it annoying, you can replace the offending panes (see left). While you're at it, you might consider double-glazed replacement windows with low-E glass to increase energy efficiency, sound insulation, and sun control. The replacements should match the design and proportion of existing windows to retain the style of the home.

▶ *Plastic glazing is faded or scratched.*

Most plastic windowpanes collect scratches over time, and some types discolor or develop a haze. Replace older panes with new acrylic panes if you want plastic that stays clear longer. Use polycarbonate for windows vulnerable to burglars or active play (such as basement windows); it is more expensive than acrylic and tends to become hazy over time, but it is very durable and shatter resistant. Have either type of pane cut to size by a plastics

Tip *To temporarily seal a cracked window until you can replace the glass, apply clear shellac to the crack.*

Tip *If you have broken a double-glazed (insulating) window, replace the entire sash or have a professional glazier repair it.*

supplier and install it like a glass pane with glazing points and putty (see opposite page). To install it like a storm window, drill screw holes around the perimeter of the panel, apply a bead of silicone caulk around the window frame, bed the plastic panel into the caulk, and secure it with 1-inch HDG wallboard screws. The screw holes should be slightly larger than the screws so the plastic can expand and contract. Give it a finished look by covering the edges with molding.

▶ Window admits too much sun.

Direct sunlight coming through a window can cause glare, fading, and overheating problems. The most effective control is to shade the window from the outside. If an awning, overhead, or shade tree isn't feasible, provide exterior sun control with a sun screen or shading fabric. You can order a screen that will fit over the window and block 70 percent or more of the sunlight, or you can replace the insect screening with shading fabric.

Another way to block the sun is to apply sun-control film to the inside of the window. (Older films were applied to the outside; modern films applied to the inside perform much better.) Reflective films, which are silver or slightly tinted, block heat, glare, and ultraviolet rays, but reduce visibility from the inside. Low-E films also block heat, glare, and rays, but do not discolor the window and have the added benefit of reducing heat loss through the window during winter. Both types are self-sticking. To apply, first clean the window thoroughly, then measure it. With a utility knife and straightedge, cut the film 1 inch larger in both directions. Spray the window with soapy water (½ ounce clear dishwashing liquid to 1 quart water). With a

helper remove the protective backing from the film, being careful not to wrinkle the film or let it stick to itself, and spray the adhesive side of it with the soap solution. Stick the film on the window, spray the exposed side with soap solution, and use a squeegee to smooth it in place. Trim the edges ¹⁄₁₆ inch in from the sash, and smooth the film again with the squeegee, working outward from the center.

Installing a shade screen

Smoothing window film

Squeegee   ¹⁄₁₆" space

▶ Window film is difficult to remove.

If you want to remove old film and it doesn't peel off easily, start by loosening ¾ inch of film along the top with a razor blade. Then mix a solution of 1 part ammonia to 1 part water and spray it behind the

loosened flap to soften the stubborn adhesive. Wearing rubber gloves, start at one corner and pull the loosened flap downward diagonally, spraying behind it as you go. When the film is removed, spray the same solution onto any remaining adhesive and rub it in with your gloved hand for 3 to 6 minutes; then scrape it off with a razor blade. Wash the window with soap and water.

▶ Single-glazed windows allow heat to escape.

Single-glazed windows in older homes account for a significant amount of heat loss during cold weather (and heat gain in warm weather). One way to reduce heat loss is to replace the old windows with energy-saving, double-glazed, insulating windows. However, there are simpler, less expensive ways that are almost as effective. First apply weather stripping to eliminate infiltration of cold air. If the windows are double-hung or sliding (not casement), install storm windows on the outside. Choose a combination style that has operable windows and insect screens so you can leave the units in place all year. To install, measure the inside dimensions (jamb to jamb) of the window, and trim the mounting flange of the storm window to fit. Drill screw holes around the outside edge of the mounting flange, apply a bead of silicone caulk to the front edges of the top and side window stops, and set the storm window in place, pressing it against the caulk. Slide the storm window as high as it will go and secure it with screws. Force the adjustable windowsill down over the original sill, making sure the weep holes are clear.

Another type of secondary window, called an interior insulating window, is installed on the interior and is less obtrusive than a storm

Tip *Safety requirements for windows: (1) For emergency egress, bedroom windows must have 5.7 square feet of unobstructed openable area, be at least 20 inches wide and 24 inches high, and be no more than 42 inches above the floor. (2) Windows within 18 inches of the floor must be safety glass. (3) Windows at the bottom of stairs must be at least 36 inches above the floor. (4) Windows within 16 inches of a door must have tempered or safety glass. (5) Windows above a shower or tub must have tempered or safety glass.*

window. It can be used on any type of window. Installation kits include an acrylic panel that you cut to size and magnetic or self-fastening edging that you attach to the borders of the panel for sealing it against the window. Follow manufacturer's instructions carefully to ensure a tight seal.

Other ways to reduce heat loss are to apply low-E film to the interior side of the window glass (see page 99) and to install heavy floor-to-ceiling draperies. You can also eliminate some heat loss due to metal window frames by covering the insides of the frames with wood trim.

Installing a storm window

Stops
Storm window/screen
Mounting flange
Adjustable sill

Installing an interior insulating window

Acrylic panel
Steel strips applied to wood stops
Magnetized sleeve around edge

▶ Window glass has condensation on surface.

When warm, moist interior air contacts cold window glass, condensation forms. Install an interior insulating window to keep house air away from the cold glass (see page 99). If the house has high humidity, it is likely to be caused by things that you can control. Reduce the sources of water vapor, such as an unvented clothes dryer, bathroom shower, or stovetop. Increase air circulation to further reduce condensation.

▶ Window sash is rotted or joints are coming loose.

A broken or deteriorated sash should be replaced, but you can repair some damage. If the joints are slightly loose, remove the sash and gently squeeze the joints together by hand at the top and bottom of the window to see if they move. If not, clean them out as much as possible and try again. Then clamp the top and bottom together with bar clamps and apply gentle pressure. At each joint that is coming loose, drill two ⅜-inch-diameter holes through the stiles into the rails, vacuum out the holes, and glue dowels into them. Trim the dowels flush with the edge of the window and touch up with sealer, primer, and paint. Restore damaged glazing compound around the windowpanes and repaint it.

Fill rotted cavities with wood filler or epoxy compound. These materials are different from spackling or other patching compounds; they include potent chemicals and are applied in two steps that require mixing two materials (resin and hardener) each time. The wood must be dry. Remove loose and rotted material. Drill several ³⁄₁₆-

inch-diameter holes through the rotted wood into sound wood. Vacuum, then paint sealer or primer onto the damaged section. After it dries, wearing rubber gloves, apply the first mixture according to label directions. Apply the second mixture, a paste filler, according to label directions and smooth it with a putty knife. After it dries, sand it smooth and touch up the area with primer and two coats of finish paint.

Doweling a sash joint

Rail
Stile
Dowels
Clamp

Applying wood filler (step 1)

Consolidant
Shallow holes
Part B
Part A

Applying wood filler (step 2)

Rubber glove
Putty knife
Plastic film
Temporary form
Paste filler
Part B
Part A

Tip *Window terminology: glazing is a pane of glass or plastic; sash is the frame, usually movable, that holds the glazing; divided lights are multiple panes within one sash; muntins are the strips of wood that divide the sash into panes; true divided lights are sashes with multiple individual panes, as opposed to a single pane with a grid placed over it to resemble individual panes.*

▶ Window sash is stuck and won't open.

The window is probably painted shut. Break the paint bond by scoring all the joints, inside and out, with a putty knife, paint zipper, or pizza cutter. If the sash still sticks, carefully pry it open by inserting a pry bar under both bottom corners and lifting (pry at top and bottom corners for casement windows). Work double-hung sashes up and down to loosen them. Scrape paint and debris out of the channels and coat them with candle wax, silicone spray, or white lithium grease (used for auto maintenance).

▶ Windowsill is rotted or split.

If the sill is badly damaged, replace it. Remove the bottom window sash and interior trim (casings, stops, apron, and stool). Work carefully; score the paint joints with a utility knife and pry gently. Use a hacksaw to cut exposed nails to release the trim pieces. Measure the dimensions of the old sill while it is in place. Then saw through it near both ends, remove the center piece, and pry away the end pieces. Save any wedges. Lay out the measurements on the new sill and cut it. If you use a circular saw, be careful not to cut past layout marks at the corners. Bevel the ends slightly so they will fit against the window jambs without binding. Test the sill for fit by sliding it into place or tapping it with a hammer and woodblock; don't force it. Remove it and sand the ends if necessary, then prime or seal the wood on all sides. After it dries, install it, and replace the wedges. Drive 12d HDG finishing nails through the bottom of the sill into the exterior casings; toenail 16d finishing nails into the interior edge and facenail them as needed. Caulk all joints on the exterior and apply the final finish.

If a sill is slightly damaged or cracked, repair it with wood filler or epoxy compound (see opposite page).

Removing old sill

Interior casing
Jamb
Stop
Rough sill
Old sill
Stool
Apron

Cutting new sill

Cuts beveled toward bottom

Tapping new sill into place
Primed sill

Nailing sill

▶ Double-hung window sash sticks.

Brush and vacuum the side channels thoroughly, especially corners; remove built-up grit or paint with a sharp chisel and sand the wood smooth. Rub candle wax into the channels, or lubricate with silicone spray. If the channels are too narrow and pinch the sash, place a woodblock against the stops wherever they bind and tap it sharply with a hammer. In some cases you may have to pry off the stops and renail them farther from the sash.

▶ Window latches don't lock securely.

Windows provide easy access for intruders because they are often open or the latches don't lock securely. Double-hung windows are especially vulnerable because the ordinary butterfly latch that holds the two sashes together can be flicked open from outside with a table knife. Replace the latch with a safety lock or improvise a pin latch by drilling a hole through the sash into the side jamb, near the top; insert a 12d nail into it when the window is closed. To secure the window when it's open for ventilation, move the sash to the open position and drill into the jamb through the same sash hole. You can also install a ventilating window lock. It has a sliding bolt that stops the sash at a certain point or slides out of the way so you can open the window fully.

    Secure a sliding window with one of several devices that clamp into the top or bottom track and stop the sash from sliding any farther. Casement windows latch fairly securely when they're shut because exterior trim covers the joint

Tip   *Technically, a windowsill is the sloped ledge outside the window. Inside, the sill is not visible, as it is covered with a ledge called the window stool. Most people refer to the stool as the sill, however.*

between sashes, but you can fortify them with sliding bolts at the top and bottom of both sashes. Basement windows provide convenient access. Cover the window glass with polycarbonate plastic or decorative safety bars. At least one window should have movable bars that can be unlocked from the inside and swung out of the way in an emergency.

Securing a double-hung window

Ventilating lock

Security lock

Strike

Butterfly latch

12d nail

Securing a casement window

Slide bolts

Securing a sliding window

Sliding sash

Fixed sash

Track lock

▶ *Double-hung window sash is too loose and rattles.*

To prevent side-to-side movement, install weather stripping in the sash channels, either vinyl V-strip or the metal spring-type (see opposite page). If the window has weather stripping on the outside, install spring tension devices in the side channels. Screw them to the channels or the edge of the sash, depending on the type. They press against the sides of the sash and hold it steady.

If the sash rattles back and forth, move the stops closer to it. To nudge a stop less than 1/16 inch, set a woodblock against the stop and strike it with a hammer along its entire length until the paint breaks loose and the stop moves. Drive three or four finishing nails into it to hold it in the new position. To move a stop farther (1/16 inch or more), pry it loose, scrape the jamb smooth with a chisel, and renail the stop closer to the sash. Place a thin cardboard shim between the stop and sash as a temporary spacer.

▶ *Double-hung window is hard to lift or won't stay up.*

If the sash glides easily (see page 101), the lifting mechanism is faulty. For most windows installed before 1940, the mechanism consists of a counterweight, pulley, and sash cord on both sides of the window. One or both cords may be broken, or the pulleys jammed. Buy new sash cord to replace broken cords. To install it, remove the lower sash by prying off one of the side stops and easing out the sash. If an unbroken cord is still attached, free the knotted end from the sash groove, keep

tension on it while the counterweight pulls it upward, and insert a nail through the knot to hold it against the pulley.

To tie new cord to a weight, or to rescue a dropped weight, remove the access plate located in the jamb. If it's covered by the parting bead that separates the upper and lower sashes, pry out the bead with a chisel, or pull it out with pliers (using wood strips to pad the jaws). Now you can remove the upper sash, if necessary. Inspect the pulley and replace it if the wheel won't turn. Thread new sash cord over the pulley and down the weight cavity; tie the end to the weight. Rest the sash on the sill and pull the free end of the cord far enough down the sash groove to lift the weight within 2 inches of the pulley. Cut the cord where it touches the sash 2 inches below the groove and knot it. Replace the access plate, repeat the operation for the other broken or missing cord, and reassemble the window. If you use chain instead of cord, attach it to the sash groove with screws.

There are several types of lifting mechanisms in post-1940 windows, including tension-spring and spiral lift units. To repair a tension-spring unit, remove the lower sash and unhook the pull tapes from it. Remove the faulty spring unit from the side jamb, replace it with a new unit, reattach the pull tapes to the sash, and reassemble the window. A spiral lift mechanism has a spiral rod inside a long tube located in the sash channel. To adjust tension, swing the lower sash outward, detach the spiral rod from the sash (keep a tight grip on it), and tighten or loosen it a few turns; then reattach it. To replace a unit, detach the spiral rod from the sash and the

Tip *Types of windows: A <u>fixed window</u> doesn't open; a <u>double-hung window</u> has two sashes that move up and down; a <u>single-hung window</u> has only one sash (the lower) that moves up and down; a <u>casement window</u> opens like a door, with hinges on the sides of the sash; a <u>double casement window</u> has two sashes that open like double doors; an <u>awning window</u> swings outward at the bottom; a <u>hopper window</u> swings inward at the top.*

tube from the jamb; then attach the new tube to the jamb, wind up the spiral rod, and attach it to the sash.

Removing lower sash

Attaching cord

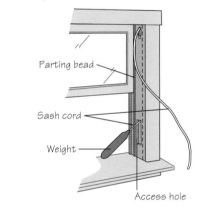

Replacing a tension-spring unit   **Adjusting tension of spiral lift unit**

▶ *Double-hung window is missing access plate or parting bead.*

You may find an access plate at a used-window dealer or architectural salvage yard. Take the remaining cover plate out of the window and bring it along as a sample. If you can't locate a replacement, take one from a less conspicuous window (closet or back room) of the same kind. Using it as a pattern, fabricate a replacement out of a scrap of wood, then install them both.

If a parting bead is missing or broken, buy a new bead at a lumberyard. Bring along a scrap piece of the remaining bead to make sure the new one is the same size. If not, look for a salvage yard or used-window dealer who has the same size bead.

▶ *Double-hung window admits draft and needs weather stripping.*

For double-hung windows, use metal spring-type weather stripping, in either a V shape or an offset angle; it is durable and unobtrusive. Attach it with nails provided with the material; the nailed edge should face out. First raise the lower sash and install strips in the side channels beneath it. They should extend 1 inch above the sash when it is shut. Lower the upper sash. Nail strips into the side channels above it, extending them 1 inch lower than the sash when it is shut. Nail strips to the top of the upper sash and bottom of the lower sash. Check for gaps around the edges and pull the free side of the strip out with your fingers to fill the gaps.

If the windows fit too tightly along the edges to install weather stripping in the channels, apply

tubular vinyl weather stripping to both sashes around the outside edges. Seal the joint between the two sashes by applying a strip under the bottom of the upper sash.

Applying metal spring-type weather stripping

Applying tubular vinyl gasket

Tip   *An open double-hung window without a screen is a temptation for young children to crawl through. To childproof such a window: add a screen; secure the lower sash and open only the top sash; or limit how far the lower sash can open (4 inches is safe) by attaching a safety lock to the top, or drilling a hole through the sash into the side jamb near the top and inserting a nail through both holes.*

▶ *Double-hung window latch won't lock.*

Make sure that the sashes are aligned horizontally. If the upper sash is stuck, score the painted joints and lower it slightly, then try to slide it all the way into the top channel. If it won't go all the way up, paint buildup and grit are probably blocking it; chisel them away and smooth out the channel with sandpaper. Make sure the lower sash is not binding against the interior stool. If the sashes are aligned and the latch still won't lock, loosen the piece attached to the upper sash and move it to the right or left. Plug the old screw holes with glue-coated matchsticks and drill new pilot holes. If the latch is defective, replace it with a safety lock.

▶ *Casement window sash flies open in wind.*

Install a casement operating mechanism that will hold the window open in any position. One type is operated by a crank, the other by loosening and tightening a thumb knob attached to a sliding rod. Both types have a primary bracket that attaches to the interior stool with screws, and a secondary bracket that attaches to the bottom rail of the sash.

▶ *Casement window sash sticks or binds.*

Look for paint buildup between the sash and frame; remove it by scraping with a sharp chisel or paint scraper. Sand the area smooth, touch up bare wood with primer or sealer, and apply candle wax or a nonsticking lubricant. If the problem isn't paint, open and shut the window a few times and mark any places where it binds. Remove the sash and the weather stripping, then plane $\frac{1}{16}$ to $\frac{1}{8}$ inch of wood from the marked areas. Touch up the bare wood with sealer or primer and finish paint.

▶ *Casement window sash is loose.*

If it has conventional hinges, inspect them for loose screws and tighten them (see page 82). Replace faulty hinges. If the sash pivots on levers at the top and bottom, check them for loose joints and replace a defective unit (see opposite page). If a replacement is not available, repair loose joints with new rivets. Remove a loose rivet by chiseling off the head, or drilling through it and driving out the body with a punch. Insert a new aluminum hollow rivet and squeeze it with a rivet tool.

Removing rivet

Cold chisel
Hammer
Rivet

Installing a new rivet

Rivet tool
Hollow rivet

▶ *Casement window crank interferes with blinds.*

Replace the handle with a more compact type such as a disk handle (a small disk with a knob) or butterfly handle. Both are harder to crank because of reduced leverage.

▶ *Casement window mechanism doesn't work properly.*

If it's just hard to crank, replace the handle with a longer one that offers more leverage. First make sure the sash isn't sticking or binding. Then, to remove a handle, loosen the setscrew at its base; pull off the handle. Slide on the new one and tighten the setscrew. If a crank turns and nothing happens, loosen the setscrew, rotate the crank slightly, and tighten the screw in the new position. If that doesn't work, remove the handle and inspect the teeth on the shaft. If they are stripped, replace the operating mechanism. If not, replace the handle.

The mechanism itself may be corroded or worn and need replacing. Models vary, but removing most operating mechanisms involves unscrewing the cranking unit from the window frame or stool and slipping the arm out of a track at the bottom of the sash. Some models have a wood stop that covers the gears; carefully pry it off to gain access to the mounting screws. After removing the operating mechanism, secure the loose window sash by shutting and latching it. Inspect the gears and arm of the operating unit. If they are stripped or damaged, take the unit to a window dealer or home center and buy a replacement. If they appear sound, clean the unit with kerosene, wipe it dry, and coat moving parts with silicone spray or other nonsticking lubricant.

Tip *Most casement windows open outward, making it possible to decorate them with almost any type of window treatment. If they open inward, the decorative treatments are restricted to those that don't interfere with window movement. Curtains or blinds attached to the window sashes, traditional draperies installed alongside the windows, and Roman shades mounted high enough to clear the window are options that work well.*

Straighten the arm if it is bent. Clean out the track, lubricate it, and reassemble the window.

Unscrewing handle

Setscrew

Removing older-type operator

Sash

Removing newer-type operator

Operator arm   Support arm

Sash

Cranking mechanism   Stool

▶ *Casement window admits draft and needs weather stripping.*

Metal spring-type weather stripping is the least conspicuous and most durable type for casement windows. Install the side strips first, cutting them flush with the sill and head jamb. Nail along the exterior edge so the free edge faces inward. Cut the ends of the top and bottom strips at a slight angle, so they don't force the side strips shut, and install them, concealing the bottom strip by applying it to the bottom of the window sash. If the window is too tight for weather-stripping the channels, apply tubular or cushion vinyl stripping (which is less attractive) to the window stops.

For steel casement windows, which have narrow frames, you can buy weather stripping that slips over the metal flanges. Miter the joints by cutting the ends at 45-degree angles, and attach the strips with an adhesive recommended by the manufacturer.

Applying weather stripping

Stop

Metal spring-type weather stripping

Sash

Stop

Tubular gasket

Viewed from indoors

▶ *Gliding-window sash sticks and won't slide easily.*

Remove the sash by lifting it up and swinging the bottom out from the tracks; you may need to adjust a setscrew at the top of the sash before lifting it. Clean out the tracks. Scrape away accumulated grit and debris with a toothbrush or nylon scouring pad, and vacuum thoroughly. Hammer out any dents; back up the blows with a woodblock to keep from denting the track more. Inspect the bottom of the sash for debris, loose screws, nicks, or worn wheels; clean it and remove obstructions. Free stuck wheels with a few drops of penetrating oil, or remove them and buy replacements from a window dealer. Apply silicone lubricant to the tracks and reassemble the window.

▶ *Gliding-window latch won't catch.*

Check to see if the latch is aligned with the strike hole. The sash may be riding up on accumulated debris or an obstruction, raising the latch too high to engage the strike hole. If so, clean out the track, as described above. If the latch is faulty, remove the screws that hold it in place and take it to a window dealer for a replacement.

▶ *Aluminum window frame is tarnished.*

Clean with aluminum cleaner, a mild abrasive cleaner, or fine steel wool and mild detergent. The oxidation that forms on aluminum does not deteriorate the metal—it actually forms a protective surface that inhibits further oxidation—so you're cleaning the metal for cosmetic purposes only. If you wish to paint aluminum window frames, you do not have to remove the oxidation. Lightly sand the frame

Tip   *Many gliding windows are vulnerable to break-ins even when locked, because the sashes can be removed simply by lifting them up and inward. To avoid this possibility, slide the movable sash open and install a sheet-metal screw in its upper track. Adjust the screw until it protrudes enough to prevent the sash from being lifted when it is shut.*

to smooth it, then prime with zinc chromate or a water-based metal primer specified for aluminum.

▶ Jalousie window is vulnerable to break-in.

Jalousie windows, where allowed, should not be placed near doors or where an intruder can reach them easily; they are easy to break into. The intruder simply reaches in, bends back the holding clips, and removes all the panes. If a window is vulnerable, replace it with a more secure type, install security bars on the inside, or have the holding clips soldered or secured so they can't be bent back to release the panes.

▶ Jalousie windowpane is broken, missing, or loose.

To remove a damaged pane, crank the window open until all of the panes are horizontal. Both ends of the pane rest in a channel with a clip wrapped over the top edge. Push the clips downward and slide the glass out of the channels. Buy a replacement pane or have one cut from tempered glass and buffed around the edges. Slide the new pane into place and bend the clips over it. If a pane is loose, remove it. Then bend the clips with pliers and pull them down as small a distance as possible while you slide the pane into place.

Sliding jalousie pane into place

▶ Jalousie window won't close tightly and admits drafts.

Although grooved gaskets that slip over the edges of individual panes are available, it is difficult to seal a jalousie window. The best solution is to remove the window and replace it with a double-hung or sliding window. Because jalousies can't be sealed tightly and the panes are susceptible to coming loose and falling out, many communities don't allow them for house windows except for enclosing porches or in climates where energy performance of windows is not a concern.

▶ Windows need upgrading or replacing.

Replacing old windows with new ones can solve many problems, including heat loss and gain, air infiltration, noise, condensation, carpet fading, and tired-looking windows. Replacing old windows is also very expensive, however, and in some cases may jeopardize the historical integrity of a home. Before you elect to replace windows completely, consider the following options for upgrading your present windows. Although most of the repair techniques are described in this chapter, some of the projects are beyond the scope of this book, and you should consult a professional.

For improving energy performance, consider weather stripping, an interior film, an exterior storm-window/screen combination, an interior insulating window, heavy draperies, or an insulating shade.

To upgrade performance, consider overhauling or replacing the lifting mechanism of a double-hung window, repairing or replacing the cranking mechanism of a casement window, and overhauling the track and sash of a gliding window.

To improve the appearance of a window, consider replacing cracked or distorted glass; repairing rotted wood with an epoxy filler; painting a metal window frame; adding snap-on muntins to a plain window; exchanging old, dull hardware for decorative replacement latches, cranks, and lifts; cleaning or replacing screens; installing exterior shutters; or adding a flower box.

If you choose to replace old windows, consider all of the replacement options when talking with a dealer or contractor. They include: new sash only (fits inside old jambs); new sash and side-jamb liners (fit inside old jambs); new sash and side jambs (fit inside old jambs); new sash and jamb set (remove old jambs); and complete window unit (sash, jambs, and casings—requires complete tear-out).

▶ Window opening is too small for new window.

Although replacements for most windows may be ordered in custom sizes to fit any opening, there are times when you may want to install a new window that is larger than the existing opening. In planning such an installation, keep in mind that making an opening longer by lowering the sill is fairly easy to do; making it wider by more than 1 or 2 inches is very complicated and involves replacing the header above the opening.

▶ Screening is torn or has hole.

Seal a tiny hole or tear with a drop or two of waterproof glue that dries clear. Apply it in layers; wipe away excess. If the screen is metal and the wires are not torn, simply restore the original weave by pushing individual wires back into place with an awl or sharp nail. You can also repair a small hole by darning it with a few strands of screening.

Tip *If the window screens in your home are showing their age, replacing all of the screening at one time will give your home an immediate face-lift. Screening fabrics of fiberglass and other materials come in many attractive patterns and colors. Replacing the screening also provides a good opportunity to repair and repaint the frames.*

Cover larger holes with a patch. If the screen is plastic or fiberglass, sew the patch in place with a few strands taken from the same kind of screening. (You can also iron on a fiberglass patch: set the iron at a high temperature, lay the screen on solid backing, place a cloth over the patch, and press it; practice on scraps first.) To patch a metal screen, cut the patch 2 inches wider than the hole, remove some strands from around the edge of the patch, and bend the protruding ends 90 degrees. Lay the patch over the hole, push the bent ends through the screen, and crimp them.

Patching small holes

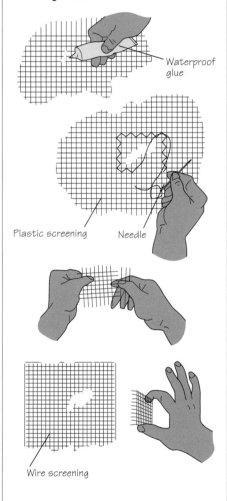

Waterproof glue

Plastic screening   Needle

Wire screening

▶ *Screening in wood frame needs replacing.*

To replace the screening in a wood frame, pry off the screen bead (wood strips) from the frame, and remove the staples that hold the screening. Remove the screening and dust out the groove. For doors or large window screens, bend the frame by setting a piece of 1-by lumber under each end and holding down the center with clamps on both sides. Lay new metal screening over the frame and staple or tack it to one end. If the screening is fiberglass or vinyl, fold it under to make a 1½-inch hem before stapling it to the frame. Stretch the screening taut and staple it to the other end. Remove the clamps and 1-by pieces and staple the sides, starting at the center and working toward the ends. Nail the screen bead to the edges with 3d HDG finish nails. If the old bead is damaged, replace it with new bead; prime and paint it first.

Removing screen bead

Screen bead

Clamping frame

Staples

Stapling sides

▶ *Screen is hard to see through.*

Remove the screen from the window. Clean it with soapy water and a brush (brass bristles for metal screening, nylon bristles for plastic or fiberglass screening). Let it dry in the sun. Although all screens distort the view somewhat, changing the screening fabric to a different color may improve visibility. A black screen is the least obtrusive; it seems to recede into the background. It also changes the look of the window dramatically, however; so if you want your screens to match, you'll have to change them all. Light-colored screens can be difficult to see through when they are new because the shiny surface attracts the eye, but as they age they become darker and less distracting.

▶ *Screening in metal frame needs replacing.*

To replace the screening in a metal frame, buy a piece of fiberglass, aluminum, or vinyl screening at least 1½ inches larger all around than the old screen. Lay the old screen on sawhorses with the interior side facing up. Remove the vinyl spline that holds the old screening in place; start at one end and pull carefully to avoid breaking it. (If it's damaged or brittle, buy a new length of spline.) With the spline and screening removed, vacuum out the groove. Lay the new screening over the frame and trim off the corners diagonally. If the new screening is metal, use the convex wheel of a screen splining tool to press the screening into the groove along one side of the frame. Then, using the concave (grooved) wheel, press the vinyl spline into the same groove. Use short, choppy motions. Repeat the process for one end, then the second side, and finally the other end, keeping the

Tip *When replacing window screens, you can get sun control by using shading fabric instead of traditional insect screening. Some types reduce visibility; others allow almost as much visibility as regular insect screening while blocking as much as 60 percent of the sun's rays. Shading fabric will also keep out insects.*

screening taut. If the screening is fiberglass or vinyl, use the grooved wheel to press both it and the spline into the groove in one pass.

Removing old screening from metal frame

Spline

Installing spline

Convex wheel

Diagonal cut

Spline

Grooved wheel

▶ Aluminum screen frame is tarnished or bent.

Clean tarnished frames with aluminum cleaner, a mild abrasive cleaner, or fine steel wool and mild detergent. It is normal for aluminum to oxidize, so the frames will stay clean only a short time. A frame that is bent or damaged can be repaired, but it is easier to find a replacement. Window dealers and most home centers carry replacement screens in standard sizes. If you can't locate one, have a window dealer fabricate a new one.

▶ Wood-frame screen is weak or loose at joints.

Renew old screens by reinforcing the joints with metal angles or straps available at any hardware store. Place them on the inside, and paint them to match the screen.

▶ Screen doesn't fill opening or fit snugly.

Even small gaps around a screen allow insects to enter. If a wood-frame screen is too small, fill the gaps with wood strips nailed to the edges. If the screen has an aluminum frame, look for a replacement screen at a window dealer or home center. One of the standard sizes may be just what you need. If not, you can have a window shop fabricate a larger screen, or you could build out the frame by attaching strips of extruded aluminum framing stock. Buy it at a window shop, cut pieces to length with a hacksaw, and screw them to the frame.

▶ Shade rolls up too quickly.

Roll up the shade, leaving it in a locked position. Carefully lift the flattened pin (spear) out of the slotted bracket. Make sure the little flipper (pawl) is locked against the ratchet teeth and the spear is not exerting tension on the bracket as you lift it out; if it is, stop, unroll and then roll up the shade again until it locks, and lift the spear out of the bracket. With pliers, rotate the spear counterclockwise a few turns while steadying the shade with your other hand. Make sure that the ratchet teeth are locked by the pawl at the end of each turn; start each turn by twisting the spear clockwise a bit to release the pawl before turning it counterclockwise to release spring tension. Return the shade to the brackets and test it. If it is too

fast, repeat the process. If it is too slow, tighten the tension by rotating the spear clockwise a few turns.

▶ Shade doesn't catch.

A shade catches when the ratchet teeth at the end of the roller are locked in place by a little flipper (pawl) that falls against them. If the shade doesn't catch, it's usually because the pawl is gummed up and can't move freely. To clean it, roll up the shade and carefully remove it by lifting the end with the flattened pin out of the slotted bracket. Brush the grit and grease away from the pawl and lubricate it with graphite powder or silicone spray. With a pair of pliers, wind the flattened pin (spear) a few times and return the shade to the brackets.

Cleaning out the pawl

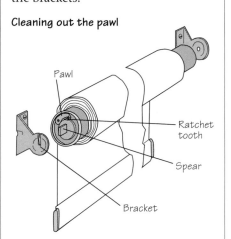

Pawl

Ratchet tooth

Spear

Bracket

▶ Shade winds up too slowly or not far enough.

You can control the speed of a shade by adjusting the tension of the internal spring. To do this, roll up the shade as far as possible and leave it in a locked position. Lift the end with the flattened pin (spear) out of the slotted bracket. With pliers, turn the spear clockwise a

Tip *To clean a plastic or plastic-coated window shade, remove it from the window and lay it flat. Scrub both sides with hot water and an all-purpose cleaner. Sponge to rinse, then dry. Roll up at once to smooth the fabric, then unroll and air-dry. Spot-clean with an art-gum eraser.*

few turns while holding the shade with your other hand. Make sure the pawl is locked against the ratchet teeth each turn before releasing the pliers, or the spear will unwind completely and you'll have to start over again. Return the shade to the brackets and test it. If it's still too slow, tighten the spear some more; if it's too fast, release the tension by backing off the spear a few turns.

Increasing tension on the spring

▶ Shade wobbles or doesn't wind up straight.

If the shade winds up crooked, check to see if the brackets are level. Roll up the shade, leaving it in a locked position, and set a level on it. Note which bracket is lower and how far; decide whether it should be moved up or the other bracket moved down. Remove the shade by lifting the end with the flattened pin (spear) out of the slotted bracket. Remove the nails or screws of the bracket to be moved, set it in the new position, and secure it with nails or screws. Replace the shade and test it. If it still wobbles (or was level in the first place), check for bent pins, worn bracket holes, or a loose spear. Straighten bent pins with pliers; replace worn brackets. Replace the shade if the spear is loose or the roller is faulty.

▶ Shade is loose or needs replacing.

If the fabric has become detached from the roller but is otherwise in good condition, restaple it to the roller. First roll the shade up, leaving it in a locked position, and remove it from the brackets. Then, without releasing the ratchet from the pawl, unroll the shade onto a long table or the floor by turning the roller. Staple the loose end of the shade to the roller with a staple gun, or attach it with tacks. Carefully roll up the shade by hand without releasing the ratchet, and return it to the brackets.

If the shade fabric is torn or otherwise needs replacing, take the whole shade, roller and all, to a shade store and have it repaired.

▶ Shade comes loose from brackets and falls.

The brackets are too far apart. Try bending them toward each other. If they are loose, remove the nails and secure them with screws or hollow-wall fasteners (see page 19). If the shade still comes loose, remove one of the brackets and move it closer to the other one.

▶ Blinds have worn cords and tapes that need replacing.

Buy new ladder tapes and cord at a hardware, variety, or drapery store. Be sure the new tapes are appropriate for the slat width. Remove the blinds from the window and lay on a work surface. Release the tapes and cords from the bottom bar. Untie the knots at the bottom of the lift cords and pull the ends of the cords up just to the headbox. Remove the slats, wash them, and set them aside to dry. Release the tapes from the tilt tube; some loop over prongs, others are held by clips. Cut the new tapes to the same

length and number of slats as the old, including any loops you need to sew for attaching the tops to the tilt tube. Attach the new tapes to the tilt tube and slide the slats into position.

To replace the old cords, which are still in the headbox, cut the loop at the bottom of the lift cord and remove the equalizing buckle. Attach each end of the replacement cord to the two cut ends of the lift cord by butting the ends together and wrapping tape around them. Then find the two free ends of the lift cord in the headbox and thread them down through the slats. As you pull on them, the old cord will pull the new cord into place. Pull until the looped end of the new cord is at the same height as the old one was. Cut the free ends of the new cord and attach them to the bottom bar the same way as the original cord was. Attach the tapes to the bottom bar as the old ones were. If the blinds have a tilt cord instead of a vertical bar, replace it with new cord—just lift it off the pulley and loop the new cord over it.

Replacing cords and tapes

Tilt tube · Ladder tapes · Headbox · Lift cord · Bottom bar · Tilt cord · New cord · Tape · Equalizing buckle

Tip *To clean miniblinds, wash them in the tub or shower with mild detergent and water. Dry metal parts with a hair dryer and coat them with mineral oil to prevent corrosion. To clean larger venetian blinds, wipe both sides of each slat with a mild detergent, an all-purpose cleaner, or a venetian blind cleaner. Scrub the tapes with a soft brush and warm soapy water, then rinse.*

▶ *Blinds rise unevenly or don't operate smoothly.*

Pull on one side of the lift cord, then the other, until the bottom bar of the blinds is level. Then adjust the equalizing buckle on the cord so it hangs evenly. If the blinds still rise unevenly, the cord is not threading through one of the pulleys properly. Remove the cover from the headbox at the top of the blinds and inspect the pulleys and cord channels for obstructions. Have repairs made by a window-covering specialist.

▶ *Curtain rod sags.*

Rods over 48 inches long should have a center support. Wire hooks for this purpose are available from hardware stores or fabric stores that have drapery supplies. To screw in the hook at the right level, stretch a string between the bottoms of both ends of the curtain rod and mark the wall at the midpoint of the string. Measure up from the mark a distance equal to the depth of the hook; screw the hook into the wall at that point.

▶ *Curtain rod bracket has come loose from wall.*

If the bracket is attached to wood trim and the screws have pulled loose, deepen the hole by drilling all the way through the trim and wallboard and slightly into the stud or header behind it. Reattach the bracket with longer screws (1½ inches for wallboard walls, longer for plaster walls). If the bracket is attached to wallboard or plaster where there is no wood framing to back up the screws, use expansion bolts or other hollow-wall fasteners (see page 19).

▶ *Traverse rod has broken or excess slides.*

Drapery hooks hang from slides in the traverse rod; there should be a separate slide for each hook (except end hooks, which are attached to the corners of the rod and the carriers). To remove a broken or extra slide, take down the draperies. Push down on the gate at the end of the rod and slip the slide out. Replace a broken slide with an exact duplicate. The slides on decorative rods are attached to a ring; replace the entire ring. Rehang the draperies.

▶ *Traverse rod cord is loose and lacks proper tension.*

Locate the pulley yoke attached to the wall at the bottom of the window. Raise the tension pulley and hold it in place with the lock button on the side of the yoke or, if it has none, insert a nail through the hole in the pulley shaft. Then locate the master carrier in the traverse rod and pull the knotted end of the cord to take up the slack. Tie a new knot in the cord and trim the excess. Release the tension pulley.

▶ *Draperies don't draw evenly.*

If two-way draperies don't part evenly in the center, the cord has probably slipped position in the underlap carrier. Release the cord from the bridge under which it is hooked, slide the carrier to the proper position (the same distance from the center of the rod as the master carrier), and rehook the cord under the bridge.

▶ *Traverse rod cord is broken or frayed.*

Replace a damaged drapery cord with new cord, available where drapery rods are sold. First unhook and take down the draperies. Then

remove the old cord by untying both ends from the master carrier and releasing it from the bridge (a friction hook) of the underlap carrier. Thread one end of the new cord through either hole in the master carrier, knot it, and thread the rest of the cord through the rod, pulleys, and tension pulley (as shown). Secure the second end of the cord to the master carrier with a temporary knot. With the underlap carrier and master carrier at equal distances from the rod ends, secure the cord to the underlap carrier by hooking it under the bridge. Before tying a final knot in the second end of the cord, raise the tension pulley in the pulley yoke as far as it will go and secure it with the lock button or a nail. Then pull all of the slack out of the cord, tie the final knot in the end, and trim off the excess. Release the tension pulley and hang the draperies.

Threading drapery cord

One-way traverse

Tip *A considerable amount of heat can be lost through windows on a cold night. Various types of window coverings are available that insulate as well as decorate. Pleated shades, which have an insulated air space between two layers of fabric, compress into a very tight formation when they are raised, much like miniblinds. Window quilts, which insulate like blankets, can be concealed in a valance when they're rolled up.*

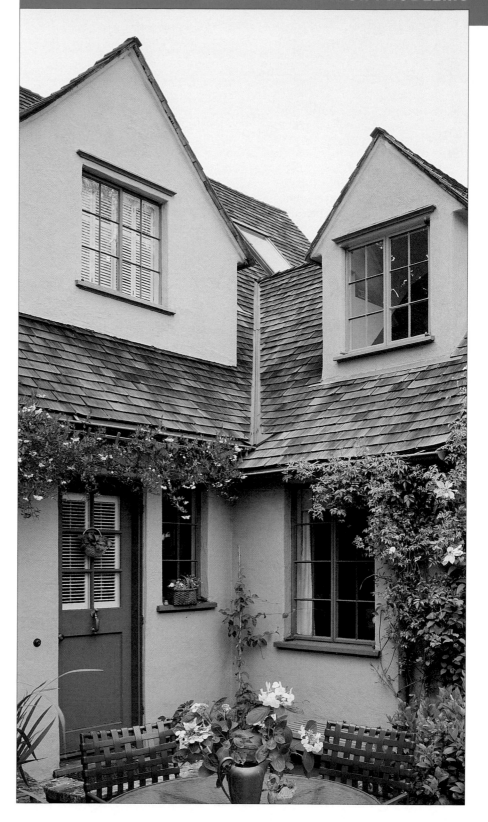

From roof shingles to patio pavings, the areas outside your home develop problems that often need immediate attention. This chapter provides information for solving more than 180 such problems.

▶ Roof leaks.

The first step in fixing a roof leak is to find it. The actual leak is seldom directly above the area where the ceiling is dripping. To pinpoint the source, inspect the attic during a storm or, at a more convenient time, have someone spray the roof with a hose while you search the attic. Look for water migrating along rafters, pipes, or other attic features and follow it upstream.

When you find the point where water penetrates the roof sheathing, mark it clearly with bright chalk for future reference. Transfer the location of this point to the surface of the roof. One way is to drive a 16d nail straight up through the leaking area, but only if you'll be fixing the leak right away. Otherwise, take two measurements—one from the roof ridge down to the leak, the other laterally from the leak to a nearby feature on either side, such as a pipe, chimney, or gable wall— and transfer the measurements to the surface of the roof.

Once on the roof, examine the area around the nail or measured coordinates for broken shingles, loose flashing, cracked caulk, or other problems. If none is apparent, look for those problems farther up the roof slope. (For especially mysterious leaks, wait for dry weather and then have someone watch the chalked area in the attic while you spray the roof with a hose, working slowly upslope and wetting small areas until water flows into the attic.) Once you have verified the source of the leak, mark it, and repair it during dry weather. You can temporarily protect it during a storm by covering the leak area with a tarp; it should extend up and over the roof ridge. Anchor it well with bricks, timbers, or similar weights, or by tying it down.

▶ Roof leaks around chimney.

Deteriorating chimney flashing, or a chimney that was not flashed properly in the first place, is a source of many roof leaks. Such a leak may not be noticed for many months if the chimney is enclosed by interior walls. If you suspect a leak, make an attic inspection during a storm or while someone sprays water on the roof, and note where water runs down the chimney bricks. Then climb up onto the roof and check that side of the chimney for defective flashing. (Inspect other areas also, as the leak may originate upslope from where it penetrates the roof.) If the chimney leaks on the side, it may have the wrong kind of flashing. It should have step flashing—a series of L-shaped pieces installed over shingles and covered by the shingles above them. (See page 123.) If the upslope side of the chimney leaks, the roof may lack a cricket (a peaked bulge that diverts water away from the chimney). If so, whatever flashing protects the upslope side of the chimney may not extend far enough up the slope under the shingles to repel the rapid buildup of water behind the chimney. Replace it with a cricket, new flashing, and new roofing material.

Another cause of leaks around a chimney is lack of counter flashing, or cap flashing, to protect the top of the primary flashing. To install new counter flashing, buy a 10-foot length from a sheet-metal shop. Cut and install in stair-step fashion short sections that overlap the primary flashing and each other. The top of each section should be anchored in the mortar joints between bricks. First chisel out ¼ to ½ inch of mortar. Then run a bead of roof caulk into the deepened joint, press the bent top of the flashing into it,

and secure it to the mortar with two 1-inch concrete nails. Hold the nails with needle nose pliers and drive them sharply with a 2- or 3-pound hammer. See also page 121.

Installing step flashing

Base flashing • Step flashing • Roofing

Flashing a cricket

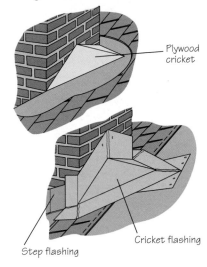

Plywood cricket

Step flashing • Cricket flashing

Installing counter flashing

3" overlap

Counter flashing

Tip *Roof safety: Wait until the roof is dry. Wear sneakers or other soft-soled shoes. Inspect any ladder for damage or weakness before using it. Set the feet on solid ground at a distance away from the house equal to one-quarter the total height. Don't place the ladder near power lines. When you climb to the top, tie the ladder to the gutter or another anchorage so it won't slide to either side. If the roof slope is greater than 5 in 12, use a safety rope. Tie one end to a tree or post on the side of the house opposite where you'll be working; toss the other end over the roof to the ladder.*

▶ *Composition shingle leaks.*

For a temporary repair, slide a flat piece of aluminum or galvanized flashing under the damaged shingle. It should extend 4 inches beyond the crack or hole on each side. Secure it with roofing cement or a nail, or by bending the metal slightly so it is held in place by friction. If a nail has popped up and poked a hole through the shingle, pull the nail, fill the nail hole with caulk, and drive a new nail nearby.

Inserting metal flashing

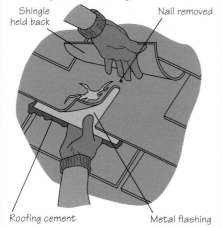

Shingle held back

Nail removed

Roofing cement

Metal flashing

▶ *Roof valley leaks.*

Valleys are prone to leaking because water rushes into them from different angles and accumulates with great force near the bottom. Sometimes it's easy to locate the source of a leak, such as a hole in the valley flashing. Repair a crack or small hole by cleaning the area with a wire brush, filling the hole with gutter sealant or butyl caulk, and smoothing it with a putty knife moistened with paint thinner. Repair larger holes (2 to 3 inches) by applying a layer of roofing cement around the hole, embedding an aluminum or galvanized metal patch into it, and covering the area with more roofing cement.

For additional protection, paint the repair with aluminum paint.

If the flashing and roofing look sound, the valley may leak due to improper installation. If the leak is near the bottom of the valley, the adjacent shingles may be too close together, trapping water under them. Trim the shingles alongside the valley so they are farther apart at the bottom of the valley than at the top; the distance across the valley should widen ⅛ inch per foot, top to bottom. (This repair applies to roofs with metal valley flashing, not shingles that are woven across the valley.) Next inspect the edges of the shingles along the valley; they should be sealed with roofing cement. Then lift a few shingles to inspect under

them. The top corners should be "dubbed" (cut off at a 45-degree angle) so they don't have sharp edges that could catch water flowing across the valley. Also inspect the flashing itself for holes or rust. Fill small holes with butyl caulk or gutter sealant. If the valley is flashed with roll roofing, repair holes and cracks with roofing cement. Cover larger holes with a temporary metal patch (composition shingle for roll roofing); spread roofing cement over the area, lay the patch in place, and cover the patch with more roofing cement. If the shingles aren't dubbed or the valley is not flashed properly, have the shingles and flashing stripped away and replaced with new materials by a professional roofer.

Trimming valley shingles

Patching valley flashing

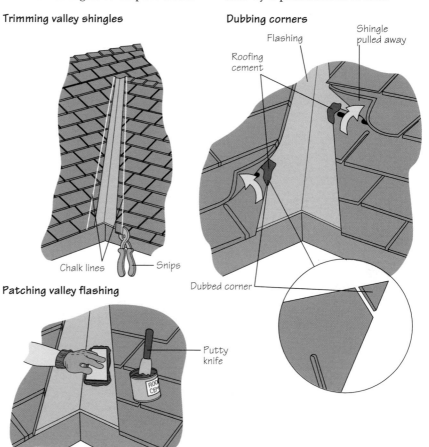

Chalk lines

Snips

Putty knife

Dubbing corners

Flashing

Shingle pulled away

Roofing cement

Dubbed corner

Tip *The most common places for roof leaks are: (1) chimney flashing, (2) vent flashing, (3) valleys, (4) skylight flashing, and (5) eave areas where ice dams form.*

Tip *Inspect your roof every year. Use binoculars if you can't get onto the roof. Look for exposed nail heads; loose, curling, cracked, or missing shingles; loose flashing; dried caulk; and accumulated debris. These problems can be solved with a handful of roofing nails, some roof caulk, a few metal shims, and a broom.*

▶ Composition shingle is damaged or missing.

Repair a crack by spreading roofing cement under it, nailing down both sides of the crack, and covering the repair with more cement.

To replace a damaged shingle, carefully lift the shingle tabs above it far enough to slip a pry bar under the nails holding the damaged shingle in place. Pry out all nails (most composition shingles are 36 inches wide and have four nails) and, if shingles are installed close

Removing old shingles

Tab lifted carefully

Damaged shingle

Pry bar

Nailing new shingle

New shingle

Pry bar placed over nail

Woodblock

together, nails from the two courses above the damaged shingle. With the nails removed, pull the damaged shingle out and slide a new shingle into the same place. If the new shingle is metric (39 inches long), trim it to 36 inches so it will fit. To nail the new shingle, carefully lift the tabs above it and avoid placing the new nails in the old nail holes. If the tabs above the new shingle are too brittle to lift enough to allow for hammering, lift them just high enough to set the new nails in place. Then set one end of a pry bar on the nail head and the other on a woodblock; hammer the bar, not the nail.

▶ Roof leaks around plumbing vent or flue.

Pipes and flues that penetrate the roof require vent flashing around them. When it rusts or comes loose, a leak develops. If the flashing is loose around the top but otherwise sound, seal the top by removing old roofing cement and debris, applying new roofing cement between the top of the flashing and the pipe, and wrapping metallic duct tape around the joint. If the vent has a storm collar above the flashing, apply a bead of silicone caulk between the collar and pipe.

If the flashing itself is rusted or cracked, replace it with new vent flashing. Buy the type with a neoprene gasket that fits around the vent pipe or flue, in a size specified for the diameter of the pipe and the slope of the roof. To remove the old flashing, carefully remove roof shingles above the flashing, starting two courses above and working down until the sides of the flashing are exposed. Remove the nails from the flashing and slide it off the pipe. Slide the new flashing over

the pipe, tuck the top edge under the shingles, and nail down the top corners and middles of both sides with roofing nails. Daub the nail heads with roofing cement, then replace the shingles.

Resealing vent flashing

New caulk

Vent

Vent flashing

Metallic duct tape

Replacing vent flashing

Flexible gasket

Roofing nails

New shingle

Tip *Codes limit the number of times new roofing material can be installed over old without removing the old; most codes allow two layers of roofing, some three.*

Tip *Composition-shingle roofs can last from 10 to 25 years, depending on the quality of shingles and the weather conditions. If many of the shingles are curled, have crumbling edges, are brittle, have lost most of the mineral coating, or have protruding nail heads, it is time for a new roof.*

▶ Wood shingle or shake leaks.

If the shingle is split, slip a flat piece of aluminum or galvanized flashing under it to shed any water that seeps through the crack. If the problem is a protruding nail, pull it out, drive a new one next to the old hole, and cover the head and hole with roofing cement.

▶ Wood shingles or shakes are weathered or stained.

Cleaning cedar shingles and applying a preservative every few years can extend the life of a wood roof, so long as the shingles aren't damaged or cracked. Consult a professional roofing company that offers this service. The process involves having the roof sprayed with a high-pressure washer and then coated with a solvent containing copper naphthenate or a similar preservative.

▶ Wood shingle or shake is damaged or missing.

If a shingle is broken, split the remaining part into lengthwise sections with a hammer and chisel and pull out the pieces. Then slip a hacksaw blade under the overlapping shingle above, cut off the nails, and remove them.

To install a new shingle or shake, cut it to the same width as the old, allowing a ¼-inch gap on each side. Then slide it into place, but leave ¼ to ½ inch of the butt extending below the adjacent shingles. As close as possible to the bottom edge of the overlapping shingle above, drive two 5d HDG box nails into the new shingle (8d for shakes) at an angle. Drive the nail heads snug, but don't embed them in the wood. Then, with a nailing block and hammer, strike the bottom of the new shingle, driving it upward

so it is flush with the adjacent shingles. As the shingle slides upward, the exposed nail heads will move with it, up and under the protection of the overlapping shingle. For added protection tuck a piece of metal flashing between the new shingle and the overlapping one, to cover the nail heads.

Removing a wood shingle or shake

Hacksaw blade   Split pieces

Nailing the new shingle

¼" gaps

Driving shingle upward

¼" drop

▶ New cedar shakes don't match color of old.

To "weather" new cedar shakes or shingles quickly, apply a solution of 1 pound baking soda in ½ gallon water. The new shingles will turn gray in a few hours.

▶ Tile roof leaks.

Because tiles are brittle and have interlocking pieces, most repairs should be done by a professional roofer experienced with tile. If the problem is a broken tile that you can reach from a ladder or open window, slip a piece of aluminum or copper flashing under it to stop the leak. Bend or curve the metal to match the profile of the tile.

▶ Metal roof leaks.

Seal a pinhole leak with roofing cement. If there are extensive pinhole leaks, coat the roof with liquid sealant specified for metal roofs, according to manufacturer's instructions. If leaks occur around fasteners, it is probably because they were installed without allowance for expansion. The same problems will persist unless the roofing is reinstalled correctly.

Repair a larger hole, except in aluminum, by soldering a patch of the same kind of metal over it. Cut a rectangular patch at least 2 inches larger than the hole. Snip off the corners of the patch, fold the edges under ½ inch, and crimp them. Then clean the damaged area of the roof with a wire brush or steel wool, especially where the edges of the patch will touch; polish the edges of the patch with sandpaper. Coat the cleaned edges of the patch and roof surface with flux—acid flux for copper, noncorrosive resin flux for steel or terne metal (steel roofing coated with a tin/lead alloy). Lay the patch over the damaged area and set

Tip *How to measure roof slope: (1) Hold a level so one end rests on the roof. (2) Mark a point on the level 12 inches from the end that is resting on the roof. (3) Hold the level steady and measure the distance between that point and the roof surface, straight down. This distance is the slope of the roof, and is expressed as n in 12—for instance, 3 in 12 or 5 in 12.*

weights on it. Solder by heating the metal with an electric soldering iron and touching the solder to the metal long enough for solder to flow into the joint, working your way around the patch slowly.

To repair a hole in aluminum, spread roofing cement over the damaged area and lay a fiberglass patch over the cement. Then apply a second layer of cement over the patch, lay a second patch over it, and cover the repair with a final coat of cement.

Soldering a patch

Clean surface

Weight

Patch

Soldering iron

Solder

FLUX

Bottom

Edges to be bent

Corner cut off

▶ *Tar-and-gravel roof leaks.*

Because a tar-and-gravel (or built-up) roof is fairly flat, the leak is usually directly above the wet ceiling area. Look for a hole, crack, tear, or blister on the roof surface. Sweep gravel aside to expose the roofing material. If the problem is a blister, slit it with a utility knife to relieve the pressure. With a putty knife apply a generous coating of roofing cement inside the blister, over it, and around it for 2 to 3 inches. Cover the area with a patch of roll roofing, press it into the cement, and nail it around the edges with roofing nails. Apply another layer of cement over the patch, let it partially dry, and spread gravel over the area.

If the problem is a hole or tear, use a utility knife and straightedge to cut a rectangular outline around the damaged section, then remove it. Cut a patch to fit into the cut-out area. Spread a generous layer of roofing cement onto the cutout area, working the cement under all four edges and extending it 2 inches over the surrounding roof surface. Press the patch into place and secure the edges with roofing nails. Apply more roofing cement over the patch and surrounding border. Cover this layer of cement with a new, larger patch; nail it in place, cover it with roofing cement, and spread gravel over it when the cement begins to dry.

Slitting a blister

Putty knife

Utility knife

Cutting out damaged section

Nailing a patch

Covering patch with roofing cement

Tip   *The purpose of gravel on a tar-and-gravel roof is to protect the tar from exposure to direct sunlight. Otherwise, the solvents in the tar would evaporate very quickly, causing the tar to crack and become brittle.*

▶ Roll roofing is worn or damaged and needs replacing.

Repair a hole or blister in the same way as for a tar-and-gravel roof (see opposite page). If the entire roof is worn, replace it with new roll roofing, following manufacturer's directions. Roll roofing is available in "single coverage," which leaves 32 inches of the 36-inch-wide roll exposed, or "double coverage," which has a 17-inch exposure and 19-inch selvage. Double coverage offers better protection.

▶ Snow avalanches off roof.

In areas of heavy snowfall, when snow slides off a roof in one large chunk it can damage gutters, ruin decks, break exposed pipes, collapse lower roofs, imperil pedestrians, and cause other problems. Various types of snow guards, or snow bucks, either hold back the snow or prevent it from sliding off the roof all at once. Some are fabricated from wire, others from bent metal. Depending on the type of guard and slope of the roof, space them 2 to 8 feet apart in staggered rows. Attach them directly to the roof decking, under the shingles, with HDG nails or fasteners supplied by the manufacturer.

▶ Ice dams cause leaks near edge of roof.

When attic heat melts snow near the ridge of the roof, the water runs toward the gutters, encounters colder roof temperatures on the way, and freezes into ice. This ice isn't generally noticed because it's hidden and insulated by the snowpack, but it creates dams that back up more meltwater, forcing it under shingles and causing leaks.

The best solution for this problem is to prevent attic heat from escaping through the roof by adding substantially more ceiling insulation and attic ventilation. Another solution is to install eave flashing when you have a new roof put on. It is a wide, rubberlike membrane that extends up the roof at least 3 feet from the eave. As shingles are nailed over it, the membrane seals around the nails, blocking off potential leaks. Electric heat tapes and cables are partial solutions at best: They only prevent icicles from forming on the gutter.

Controlling ice dams

▶ Moss or fungus is growing on shingles.

Although moss can grow on almost any type of roof, wood roofs are particularly vulnerable to damage from moss and fungus. Moss, usually restricted to shaded areas, acts like a sponge and retains moisture, accelerating decay of the shingles. Fungus, which blackens the shingles and affects the entire roof, also retains moisture and causes decay.

Unchecked it helps to account for wood roofs lasting only 15 years in some climates, instead of 80 years or more in areas where harsh winters control fungus growth.

Fallen leaves, dirt, pine needles, and other debris encourage fungus growth, so sweeping a roof often will discourage (but not prevent) it, as well as removing large clumps of moss. Use a stiff broom that clears the joints between shingles. If the roof has composition shingles, wet it with a hose first so the broom doesn't remove the surface granules. Total fungus control starts with bleaching the roof or washing it with a high-pressure washer, then repairing any loose or broken shingles, and finally applying a nonflammable wood preservative. Because this treatment involves the entire roof, it is an ambitious task for a homeowner. You may prefer to have a professional roof maintenance company provide the service every 5 to 10 years.

If the roofing material is composition shingles, remove fungus by spraying the roof with a solution of ½ ounce sodium arsenate (available from garden centers) in 10 gallons water. A solution of 1 part chlorine bleach to 4 parts water may also work, though not as well. Follow all label instructions about mixing, applying, and storing these products. Spray with a clean garden sprayer. First cover shrubs and plants below the eaves with plastic sheeting; protect the house siding by wetting it thoroughly, and have someone stand by to rinse off areas that get spattered as you work. Wear soft-soled shoes on the roof, gloves, and eye protection. Standing partway up the roof and always

Tip *Several roofing products are available that inhibit fungus growth. One is shingles with zinc granules, available from most manufacturers of composition shingles. Another, common on the West Coast, is a strip of zinc metal that is installed at the ridge of the roof. Rainwater washing over it distributes metallic residue onto the roof. Copper wires installed on the roof every 3 to 4 feet, parallel to the eaves, have the same effect.*

moving up, start spraying at the bottom of the roof and work upward, staying above the slippery, freshly sprayed areas. After applying the solution, rinse it off with a hose, working from top to bottom. Avoid touching or spraying power lines.

Spraying a roof

Plastic

▶ Roof is not fire resistant.

Roofing materials and application techniques are classified by fire-resistance ratings. Class A materials are noncombustible, Class B partially combustible, and Class C combustible. Check with the building-inspection department for local requirements; many communities prohibit certain types of roofing materials. If you have wood shingles or shakes that were not pressure treated with fire retardant prior to installation, there is no reliable way to make the roof fire resistant. You'll have to replace the untreated shingles with Class A materials (or Class B where allowed).

▶ Roof is vulnerable to lightning.

In an area of frequent storms, almost any home is vulnerable to lightning strikes, even if it's surrounded by taller structures. Any building, tree, or structure that is sufficiently ionized (has a certain electric charge) during a storm can attract lightning, no matter how tall it is. Some protection systems neutralize a home so it won't attract lightning; others divert a strike to the earth so it doesn't cause damage to the building. All systems are tailored to the individual home, so take a sketch or photo of yours to a lightning-protection equipment dealer to have an individual system designed for your home. You may be able to install it yourself, depending on the type of system and your skills. You may want to consult your homeowner's insurance agent first to assess the level of risk in your area and to see what kind of rate discount you would be eligible for if your home had a lightning-protection system.

▶ Ridge is sagging.

Most roofs sag slightly over time, but a "swayback" roof sagging more than 2 inches over its length indicates a structural problem. Consult a competent building contractor, structural engineer, or architect to see if the roof can be stabilized by minor reinforcement or if major structural changes are needed.

▶ Roof looks worn and unappealing.

Sooner or later almost every type of roof, with the exception of tile, slate, and some metals, needs replacing. New materials, such as lightweight concrete tiles and spray-on foam, and improved older materials, such as random-thickness fiberglass shingles, offer many attractive

alternatives to just getting a new covering of the same material. Consult knowledgeable roofing professionals about the required roof slope, feasibility of covering the old roofing, weight, durability, fire rating, and cost of each option before you choose replacement materials for your roof.

▶ Gutter is clogged and doesn't drain.

First remove twigs, leaves, and other debris from the gutter, starting at the downspout. Wearing gloves, loosen crusted debris with a stiff brush and scoop out matted debris with a garden trowel. If you notice any problem areas that will need fixing later, mark the location with chalk on the outside of the gutter so it will be easy to find. After cleaning the gutter, flush the downspout with a garden hose. If the pipe is clogged, insert the hose from the bottom of the spout, pack rags around the outlet, and turn on the water full force to loosen the blockage. If that doesn't work, clear the pipe with a drain auger. After clearing the downspout, hose down the gutter. Watch for leaks or sluggish flow, and make repairs.

▶ Gutter overflows but is not clogged.

The gutter doesn't have enough slope for the water to flow properly; it might even slope backward. It should be sloped toward the downspout at a rate of 1/16 inch per foot of run. Do not gauge slope by the roof eave; it may not be level. Instead set a 6-foot level (or a short level on top of a long straightedge) on top of the gutter at several points to check where the gutter is improperly sloped. To adjust it,

Tip *A continuous gutter screen is an excellent way to keep leaves and debris from clogging gutters. Most home centers or building-supply outlets have kits that include a roll of screening material, snap-on fittings to attach the screen, and instructions for installing it. If you can't locate such a kit, buy 1/4-inch hardware cloth (galvanized screening with a wider mesh than ordinary window screen). With metal-cutting snips, cut it into strips just wide enough to wedge between the top edges of the gutter.*

loosen the hangers and reset them at new positions (L brackets can be moved only by removing the gutter first). If you have to adjust the entire gutter, remove it to align the top of the gutter. Use a hydrolevel or a series of measurements with a long level to establish the correct height for each end of the line. First mark points at each end that are level with each other; then, at the downstream end, measure down from the mark enough distance to ensure a slope of 1/16 inch per foot of run. Snap a chalk line along the fascia board or rafter ends to this measurement. When attaching the gutter, slide the backside under the drip edge—the L-shaped roof flashing that bends down over the fascia.

Hanging gutters

Drip edge
Ferrule
Spike
L bracket
Fascia
Strap
Plastic snap bracket

▶ *Seamless gutter leaks at corners.*

Long sections of aluminum gutter expand and contract in length through the seasons, causing stress at the corners. Caulk the open joints with gutter sealant. If the problem recurs every year, buy for each corner a gutter connector that fits the profile of the gutters. Connectors are like sleeves; you slide a section of gutter into each end. To install, cut the long section of gutter near the leaky corner, apply sealant around the inside edges of the sleeve, and slip the connector between the cut ends.

▶ *Gutter leaks.*

Repair tiny holes and hairline cracks with gutter sealant specified for the type of gutter—aluminum, vinyl, or galvanized metal (you may have to buy it through a siding or roofing supplier). First dry the area around the hole or crack thoroughly and buff it with steel wool or a wire brush enough to loosen debris but not remove the zinc coating of galvanized metal. Then apply the sealant and work it into the hole or crack with a putty knife.

If a seam leaks and it wasn't joined with solder, disassemble it by removing the sheet-metal screws or pop rivets used to hold the two gutter pieces together. Clean off the mating surfaces, apply a generous bead of sealant to the lower surface, and press the gutter pieces back together. Secure them with new sheet-metal screws or pop rivets. Seal leaky connector joints in a similar manner, but use screws or rivets only if the repair doesn't work without them.

The best way to patch a large hole or deteriorated area in a metal gutter is to solder a patch over it

(see page 115). If this is not feasible, clean the area with a wire brush or abrasive pad; be sure to remove rust completely. Wipe the area with a rag soaked in paint thinner and let it dry. Then coat the area with a 1/8-inch-thick layer of gutter sealant and press a fiberglass-mesh or metal patch into it. Smooth the sealant where it oozes out around the edges of the patch, then cover the patch with another layer of sealant and smooth it with a putty knife. If a section of gutter has several holes, or the gutter is a modular, snap-together style, replace the section instead of trying to patch it.

Sealing a leaky joint

Loosened gutter section
Sealant
Connector

Patching a hole

Patch
Sealant

Tip *Clean leaves and debris out of gutters at least twice a year (spring and fall) and flush the gutters with a garden hose. Inspect for leaks, excessive rust, broken brackets, and improper alignment, and repair as necessary. If leaves clog downspouts frequently, install leaf strainers above the downspout openings, or, for greater protection, stiff leaf screens over all the gutters. Install leaf screens by curving them and letting friction hold them in place, or by slipping one edge under the roof shingles.*

▶ *Gutter spikes or brackets are bent.*

Bent spikes distort the gutter and force it out of alignment. Straighten a bent spike by prying it up with an improvised "sky hook"—a strong lever with a hook in the middle. For the lever use a short length of angle iron or a crowbar with a notch in the straight end. For the hook use a chain link or a bungee-cord hook. Place one end of the lever over the ferrule (spacer tube that the spike goes through) where it abuts the house. Slip the hook over the bar and attach it to the ferrule where the spike is bent. Lift up on the bar until the ferrule and spike are straight.

Straightening a spike

Gutter
Angle iron
Fascia   Ferrule   Chain link   Gutter spike

▶ *Gutter is loose.*

First remove the spike or hanger that is loose and prop up the gutter so it is straight. Then pour water in the gutter to see if it slopes properly. If it does, reattach the loose hanger, moving it 2 to 3 inches away from the original location. If it's a spike, drill a ¼-inch pilot hole through the face of the gutter first, then slide the ferrule in place and

drive the spike through the hole and ferrule. If the hanger is an L bracket, pull the gutter down and away from the fascia board or rafter tail so you can attach the bracket first, then snap the gutter into it. If the gutter does not slope toward the downspout, see page 118.

▶ *Gutter needs painting.*

To paint new galvanized gutters, etch off residual oils from the manufacturing process by brushing distilled vinegar or other mild acid onto the gutters and rinsing it off; follow label precautions for acid. Then paint the gutters with a coat of zinc chromate green or yellow primer. (This oil-based product is the best choice, but if it's not available, use a latex galvanized-metal primer—etching won't be necessary.) Then paint the gutters with oil-based or latex exterior trim paint. If ungalvanized gutters have weathered and turned a dull gray, they have etched naturally and can be primed and painted after cleaning with a mild solution of TSP and water. Do not sand them or wirebrush them; it removes the zinc coating.

If the gutters were previously painted, scrap off loose or flaking paint and spot-prime bare metal with zinc chromate or latex galvanized-metal primer. Then prime the old painted surfaces according to label directions for the final coat of paint, and complete the painting.

Paint bare aluminum gutters in the same way as galvanized metal. If the gutters have a baked-on enamel finish, prime them with an oil-based exterior primer, then apply the final coat of exterior trim paint.

Vinyl gutters are intended to need no painting, but if you want to change the color and are willing to maintain the paint every few years, you can paint them. Check

with the manufacturer about specific recommendations, or follow these steps: First clean the gutters with rubbing alcohol, following label precautions about wearing gloves and avoiding fumes. Then prime them with vinyl-siding primer and apply a final coat of latex house paint.

▶ *Gutter is missing or needs replacing.*

Replace worn or missing sections of gutter with the same type. If you are installing all new gutters, the choices are vinyl, galvanized steel, and aluminum. Vinyl gutters snap together and come with installation instructions for do-it-yourselfers. Some aluminum gutters are available in modular units that can be snapped together; others are fabricated on-site by professional installers. Galvanized-steel gutters require soldered seams, although if you need to make only a few connections, you could use gutter sealant and sheet-metal screws.

▶ *Downspout deposits water against foundation.*

Water from gutters and downspouts should be diverted away from the foundation at least 8 feet. There are several ways to do this. The easiest is to slip a length of 3- or 4-inch-diameter pipe (nonperforated), at least 8 feet long, over the end of the downspout. Make sure the outlet of the pipe discharges water where it will flow away from the house (but not into a neighbor's yard). A less obtrusive arrangement (although a bigger project) is to bury the pipe, sloping it at least 1 inch per 8 feet of run. You will probably have to make the run much longer to find a discharge point low enough to maintain the slope. If you can't discharge the pipe to daylight, run it into a dry well—a hole in the

Tip   *Gutters have an important job to do in diverting water away from the foundation. The roof surface of a 2,000-square-foot home is approximately 2,500 square feet. In an area with 30 inches of annual rainfall, the gutters of this roof must handle more than 55,000 gallons of water every year, the equivalent of three average-sized swimming pools.*

ground 4 feet in diameter and 6 to 8 feet deep, filled with rocks and gravel. The dry well should be at least 10 feet from the house. Fittings are available for connecting the downspout to the drainage pipe. Also make sure that the soil slopes away from the house all around, at a rate of 1 inch per foot for at least 10 feet. Where this is not possible, slope it at least a foot or two toward a buried drainage pipe, or to a shallow concrete surface gutter installed parallel to the house and sloped toward drainage. If there's no low point to discharge the drainage pipe or gutter, and a dry well is not feasible, have a sump and sump pump installed which discharges water into the backyard or the street (consult municipal codes).

Installing a drain pipe

Adapter

4" drainage pipe

Drain fabric   Topsoil

6'–8'

4'

Dry well

▶ *Chimney flashing leaks.*

Check for loose joints where the flashing attaches to the chimney. Clean out old caulk and debris from around the top of the flashing, especially behind it. Pull the top of the flashing away from the chimney far enough to apply new caulk behind it. Then press the flashing back into the mortar joint and secure it with 1-inch concrete nails driven through the top of the flashing into the mortar. Use a 2- or 3-pound hammer and hold the nails with needle nose pliers. Patch small holes or rusted areas in the flashing by wire-brushing the weak area and painting it with rusty-metal primer. After the paint dries, coat the area with butyl caulk or sealant, press fiberglass mesh into the sealant, and smooth a second layer over the mesh. If flashing is deteriorated or has large holes, replace it with new flashing, making sure that it is overlapped by roofing or other flashing in the same manner as the original piece. Avoid aluminum flashing, as mortar will corrode it. See also page 112.

▶ *Chimney has cracks.*

Seal hairline cracks with butyl caulk. For larger cracks that don't span the width of the chimney, clean out loose and broken mortar and repoint the joints (see left). Long vertical cracks down the center of the chimney result from inadequate air space between the flue and chimney bricks, causing the bricks to heat too much. Although they should remain stable and not pose a threat to the structure of the chimney, they are a fire hazard and should be sealed with fireplace, or refactory, cement. Very large cracks that break bricks, span the chimney horizontally, or distort alignment are dangerous and should be inspected by a brick mason or foundation contractor specializing in chimney repair. It may be necessary to reinforce the chimney with corner brackets, a roof brace, or shoring.

▶ *Chimney mortar joints are crumbling.*

Remove the crumbling mortar with a cold chisel and hammer, to a depth of 1 inch (see page 127), and wire-brush away all debris. Wear safety goggles; mortar dust can irritate eyes. Mix an all-purpose mortar (Type N) according to label directions, slightly stiffer than for laying bricks. Moisten the joints with a fine spray from a garden hose, then pack mortar into the cracks. For horizontal cracks, slide mortar off a hawk (small mortarboard) and into the crack with a pointing trowel or joint filler. For vertical joints, slice some mortar off the hawk with the back of a pointing trowel and force it into the crack. Fill deep joints with two or three layers, letting it stiffen each time. When joints are filled and the mortar is just stiff enough to hold a thumbprint, use a jointing tool with a profile that matches the existing joints (V-shaped or rounded) to compress and smooth the mortar. Remove excess mortar from the bricks with a soft brush.

Tip *Before you have new roofing installed, consult the roofer about removing the old chimney flashing and installing new flashing. Common practice for many roofers is to leave the old flashing in place and simply adhere new flashing over it with mastic. This application will not last long and should not be accepted.*

▶ Chimney brick is loose or damaged.

Individual bricks can be chipped out and replaced quite easily, although structural problems may exist if many bricks are involved. Remove the old brick by chiseling out the mortar around it (or scraping it out with a mortar rake); then chisel out the brick and clean out the cavity with a brush. Obtain premixed mortar or mix a small batch using 1 part cement to 3 parts sand. Wet the cavity, then place mortar on the bottom, back, and sides. Steady the brick by setting it on a board in front of the cavity, then shove it into the cavity so it beds in the new mortar. Pack additional mortar around the brick, as necessary, and tool the joints.

Pushing brick into cavity

Mortar

▶ Chimney lacks spark arrester or weather cap.

Both are required by building and safety codes. A spark arrester keeps embers from flying out of the chimney; a chimney hood, or weather cap, keeps rain from entering the flue and combining with creosote to form acids that eat away the brick and mortar.

Measure the width of the flue (inside dimension) in both directions and buy an arrester, with a hood over it, for that size. Most types can be installed simply by shoving the bottom sleeve part of the arrester into the flue. Some have clamps that are tightened onto the flue walls. If the style of a prefabricated hood doesn't suit your home, have a local sheet-metal shop fabricate a custom one.

▶ Chimney is leaning away from wall.

A chimney and fireplace are on a foundation of their own, independent of the rest of the house, and may settle differently. In some cases settlement occurs early and then stabilizes for many years. In other cases new movement can occur over time. Consult a general contractor, structural engineer, or other professional experienced in foundation and chimney repair to see if reinforcement is necessary.

▶ Concrete chimney cap is cracked or crumbling.

A cracked or crumbling mortar cap should be repaired as soon as possible; otherwise, moisture can soak into it and cause serious damage to the chimney bricks through cycles of freezing and thawing. If the cap is sound and has only a few cracks, widen them with a cold chisel and fill them with butyl or silicone caulk. Smooth the surface with a putty knife moistened with soapy water. If the entire cap is deteriorated, break it up with a brick chisel

and heavy hammer; wear goggles and gloves. Remove the pieces carefully so you don't damage any roof shingles, and clean away all debris. Prepare a sack of ready-mixed concrete to a stiff consistency. Moisten the bricks and flue, and trowel wet concrete onto the bricks, packing it around the flue pipe. Build up the cap in several layers, sloping it away from the flue. Smooth the final layer with a steel trowel. Keep the concrete moist for 4 to 5 days by spraying it daily or covering it with plastic sheeting.

▶ Chimney cap is separating from flue.

The difference in materials between a terra-cotta chimney flue and the concrete cap that surrounds it may cause the two to separate. Seal a thin crack with butyl caulk. For larger cracks, clean the crack thoroughly and brush some latex modified bonding agent into it, then seal the crack with mortar. (*Note:* There should be a 1-inch gap around the flue farther down the chimney and closer to the fireplace to allow the flue to expand with heat.)

▶ Chimney should have a damper.

If the fireplace lacks an operable damper, you can buy a chimney-top damper from a masonry supplier or fireplace store and install it on top of the flue. It is operated from the fireplace by a long chain that hangs down the chimney. Installation varies, but most slide over the flue; others are attached to the flue by forming a new concrete cap (see left) and embedding the anchoring lugs of the damper into the fresh concrete.

Tip *Some experts recommend sealing chimney bricks with a thin coat of liquid silicone. It dries to a clear, dull finish and prevents the brick and mortar from absorbing moisture that can deteriorate the joints.*

▶ *Skylight admits too much sun.*

Install a standard window shade directly beneath the skylight and run a long cord from the bottom of the shade, through an eyehook on the frame or trim at the other end, and down a nearby wall. This type of shade works best on skylights that can be opened to release hot air that builds up above the shade. For more efficient shading, especially for fixed skylights, install a shade screen on the outside. Check with the manufacturer to see if a kit is available. Otherwise, consult a window dealer about weather-resistant shading fabrics.

▶ *Skylight needs cleaning.*

Most people are resigned to waiting for the rain, but if a trip to the roof is worth it, wash glass skylights in the same way as a window. Do not wash plastic skylights, such as acrylic bubbles, with anything that has ammonia in it; use a solution of water and mild dish soap, or special cleaning solutions available from a plastics supplier. If you can't get onto the roof, hose off the skylight from the ground or a ladder, or try reaching the skylight with a mop attached to a long pole. Some skylights pivot and can be cleaned from inside.

▶ *Skylight leaks.*

Wind can drive rain through unsealed cracks, so if the skylight is operable (opening type), check all seals, overhangs, and flanges to be sure that the lid shuts tightly, especially if the roof slope is less than 3 in 12 (3 inches of rise for every 12 inches of horizontal run). The next most likely source of leaks is improper flashing. The top collar flashing should have soldered seams at the corners. There should be no nails in it for 6 inches above the skylight curb; it should lap over the side flashing and extend upward under at least two courses of shingles. The flashing on the sides of the curb should be step flashing, with each L-shaped piece installed over a shingle and covered by the next course of shingles above it. Check the tops of the step flashing to be sure that the skylight flange extends down over them. If not, loosen the tops, apply caulk behind them, and then renail. If the skylight is on a flat roof, have the leak repaired by a professional roofer.

Flashing a skylight

Roof underlayment

Top collar flashing

Curb

Step flashing

Bottom collar flashing

Tip   *A skylight should never have ordinary window glass, which can break into sharp pieces. All skylights must be glazed with safety glass, such as tempered, laminated, or wire glass, or with plastic.*

Tip   *Most plastic skylights are dome-shaped because plastic expands and contracts with temperature changes. The dome allows the material to move without disrupting the watertight seal around the edges.*

▶ *Siding board is cracked or split.*

Prop the lower half of the split piece away from the siding with a chisel. Coat both exposed edges with epoxy resin cement, then slide the chisel out. Nail each half of the split piece to the sheathing or to a stud with HDG casing or finishing nails; predrill holes and countersink the heads. Then use exterior spackling compound or linseed oil putty to fill the nail heads.

For larger holes replace the damaged section of the board. For lap siding drive a wood shim under the siding at one end of the crack; then, while protecting the board below with a scrap of wood, use a backsaw to cut through the exposed part of the cracked siding. To finish the cut, drive two shims under the board above; cut through the rest of the cracked board with a compass saw. Repeat the procedure at the other end. To loosen it, pry out exposed nails with a nail puller; cut off hidden nails with a hacksaw blade. Cut a replacement piece. Prime the front, back, and ends, then tap the piece into place. If the siding is the 3½-inch-wide style, fasten it with HDG nails ½ inch up from the bottom. Wider siding should be nailed 2 inches from the bottom. Predrill before nailing.

To replace a section of flush tongue-and-groove siding, make pocket cuts with a circular saw centered over the studs on each side of the damaged section. Split and pry out the damaged section. Cut a new piece of siding the same length and chisel off the back half of the groove. Prime all edges and faces of the piece. Let dry, then run a bead of acrylic latex caulk along the edges. Predrill the nail holes and nail the piece to the studs with 8d HDG common nails. Countersink the nails and fill with exterior spackling compound.

For vertical siding, follow the same procedures as for repairing a crack or hole, except if you install a new piece, bevel the horizontal cuts in the old board and the new piece 30 degrees so that any water is directed outward and downward.

Cutting out damaged section

Lap siding
Shims
Scrap

Installing replacement piece

Caulk
Chisel
Backside

Tongue-and-groove siding
Studs
Pocket cuts

Repairing vertical siding

30° bevels

▶ *Siding board is warped.*

Warped wood siding can be straightened with screws. Predrill holes through the siding and drive HDG screws, at least 2 inches long, through the holes and into the wood sheathing or wall framing beneath. Drive the screw heads slightly beneath the surface of the siding, then fill with putty or compound and touch up with paint that matches the color of the siding.

▶ *Siding board is missing.*

Missing siding boards should be replaced as soon as possible with a matching type of siding. Cut the new board ⅛ inch shorter than the opening. Prime or seal the front, back, and edges of the new piece. After it dries, apply a bead of paintable caulk to each end, tap it in place, and secure with 8d HDG common nails. Countersink the nails, cover them with linseed oil putty or exterior spackling compound, then paint or stain to match.

▶ *Nails have caused rust stains.*

Sand the rust stains off the siding. Then, wearing rubber gloves and eye protection, brush the nail heads with a phosphoric acid solution to remove the rust and to prevent future rusting. Follow all label directions. Leave the solution on for about 20 minutes, then rinse. For painted siding, repaint the sanded area and the nail heads. Clear siding that's badly rust stained may look better with an opaque stain applied to the sanded areas and nail heads.

Tip *Caulks and sealants come in a bewildering variety of types. When choosing caulk, have your requirements in mind: the type of material the caulk will adhere to (wood, glass, masonry, metal); whether the two surfaces meeting at the joint are the same or different; whether the caulk will be painted; the range of temperatures the caulk will be subjected to; whether it will be exposed to direct sunlight (ultraviolet rays); and the amount of caulking to be done (how important cost is).*

▶ Mildew has formed on siding.

Use a solution of 1 part chlorine bleach to 3 parts water. Spray it on the siding with a hose-end spraying canister. When working with bleach, make sure to wear protective goggles and rubber gloves, and read all directions on the label. For areas with stubborn mildew, a long-handled scrub brush can be helpful. Make sure to clean off all the mildew or it will grow back. Let the bleach solution dry on the siding; don't rinse it off. Mildew often grows in shady areas; if this is the case, consider trimming tree branches that shade the problem surfaces.

▶ Siding has soft, spongy spots, especially near base.

This is a definite sign of rot. Soft sections should be replaced (see opposite page). If the rot is widespread, check the humidity levels inside the house, especially in the rooms where the siding is soft. Constant indoor humidity can result in moisture working its way through walls and condensing on the backside of siding. Rot on siding near the base of a wall may indicate that runoff water from the roof is splashing the siding. Check the gutters for leaks or clogs and provide tubing at the bottom of downspouts to divert water away. If siding is within 6 inches of the ground, the ground should be graded, sloping away from the house, or the foundation wall raised by capping. Consult a general contractor or foundation repair specialist.

▶ Termites are present.

A sure sign of termites is mud shelter tubes that lead from the ground, along a concrete foundation, and up into the siding. Other signs include wings on the ground near the foundation or inside a basement or crawl space. Likely areas of infestation are any place there is wood-to-earth contact or where wood has become soft. Termites can cause expensive structural damage. Hire a licensed pest-control specialist to perform a complete inspection as soon as possible. See also page 67.

▶ Replacement siding is hard to locate.

Always bring along a piece of the old siding when you look for replacement boards. If the local lumberyard or home center doesn't stock the same type, look for a lumberyard that has been in the area for a long time; they may have cutter blades for milling new boards. If not, try an architectural salvage yard that has old siding. You might also ask neighbors with similar siding if they have extra pieces. Or, remove one or two siding boards from the garage, back of your house, or other inconspicuous area and replace them with new boards of the same size, if not pattern. Styles and names may vary according to geographic region and historical period.

▶ Nails have caused rust stains on wood shingles.

See opposite page.

▶ Wood shingles at corners are curled, rotted, or missing.

Replacing a pair of corner shingles is similar to replacing a midwall shingle, with a few exceptions. First remove the damaged shingles; then cut one new shingle to fit, making sure it extends slightly past the corner. Next cut the second shingle so that it butts snugly against the first shingle. Finally, use a block plane to shave down the overhanging edge of the first shingle. If you're repairing more than one course of shingles, alternate the overlapping edges from course to course.

Replacing corner shingles

End of shingle cut to fit

End of shingle planed flush

Alternating corner joints

SOLVING EXTERIOR PROBLEMS

▶ Wood shingles are split, broken, or missing.

Broken or split shingles should be replaced. First split the damaged shingle into a few long pieces with a wood chisel. Then remove the pieces and cut off the hidden nail heads with a hacksaw blade. Cut a new shingle ¼ inch narrower than the opening by scoring the shingle several times with a utility knife, then snapping off the excess. Tap in the shingle ½ inch shy of its final position. Then drive two 6d HDG box nails into the shingle at a slight angle, positioned directly below the butt edge of the shingle above. Snug the heads to the shingle but don't embed them in the wood. Finally, with a hammer and woodblock, tap up the shingle the last ½ inch to hide the nail heads. See page 115.

▶ Cedar shingles look weathered and dull.

Cedar shingles will always turn gray. To slow the process, apply a clear penetrating finish (also called a clear water-repellent preservative) with an ultraviolet protector to the shingles immediately after they are put up. Use a rough-surface bristle brush, not a roller or sprayer. Follow manufacturer's instructions. If the shingles are new, apply two coats; then apply another coat one year later. Shingles that have been up at least two years will need a coat of finish about every two years. To determine if the shingles need a new coat, splash water on them— if it soaks in, it's time to reapply the finish. If the shingles are dirty,

scrub them first with a mild solution of dishwashing detergent followed by a rinse with clear water. Another option that will keep the shingles about the same color as they were originally is to apply a semitransparent stain that matches the cedar color.

Applying finish to shingle siding

Rough-surface paintbrush   Gap toward bottom

Coating shingle edges

Bottom coated by small bristles

▶ Mineral fiber shingles are split, broken, or damaged.

To remove the damaged shingle, loosen the exposed nail heads with a nail puller or pry bar. The shingle should drop out. To install a new one, first cut it to the correct width. For just a few shingles, use a utility knife fitted with a carbide blade; for a lot, rent a shingle breaker. Slip the new shingle in place, then fasten it with 3d HDG nails. Predrill for the nails.

▶ Asbestos replacement shingles are not available.

Shingles made with portland cement and reinforced with fiberglass are a close match for asbestos shingles. Look for them at a local roofing-supply house.

▶ Asbestos shingles are split, broken, or missing.

Repairing asbestos shingles is not a job you should take on yourself. Doing extensive work with asbestos-containing material can create large amounts of dangerous dust. If you are not sure if the shingles contain asbestos, take a small sample of the damaged shingle to a local testing lab or health department to have it evaluated. Then, if asbestos is discovered, hire a local asbestos abatement firm to remove the damaged shingles. You can replace them with a mineral fiber look-alike.

▶ Nails in asbestos shingles have worked loose.

Most likely, the nails are either not driven into solid framing or are corroded. When you are working with asbestos-containing materials, always wear a MSHA-NIOSH– approved respirator for asbestos. These inexpensive face masks are available through building-supply centers. Carefully pull out the nails, then drive in new 4d HDG box nails at a different angle. This avoids using the existing nail hole.

▶ Color of old asbestos shingles is undesirable.

Paint over the shingles with an exterior latex or oil-based paint. First clean the siding with a solution of laundry detergent and chlorine bleach (3 parts soapy water to 1 part

Tip *When caulking: (1) Apply caulk in the spring or fall, when temperatures are between the extremes that cause joints to expand and contract. (2) Clean surfaces and let them dry thoroughly before caulking. (3) If you plan to paint after caulking, prime the surface before caulking. (4) Apply caulk so it adheres to both sides of the crack and the bottom. (5) Clean the tip of the tube often to prevent clogging. (6) At the end of a run, push the caulk into the crack and disengage the tube with a sharp twist. (7) Smooth joints with a plastic spoon or old butter knife.*

bleach). Use a car-washing brush attached to a garden hose to prevent harmful fibers from becoming airborne. When working with asbestos-containing materials, always wear a MSHA-NIOSH–approved respirator for asbestos (available at home centers). Let the shingles dry, then apply the paint.

▶ Hardboard siding panels are coming loose at edges.

If the nails pull out easily, they probably weren't nailed into solid framing. Remove them and fill the holes with exterior spackling compound or linseed oil putty. If the nails are driven in too deep or not deep enough, check the illustration below for the proper course of action. When you replace missing nails, use hardboard panel siding nails. They should be long enough to penetrate the wood framing beneath by at least 1½ inches.

Correcting nailing problems in hardboard siding

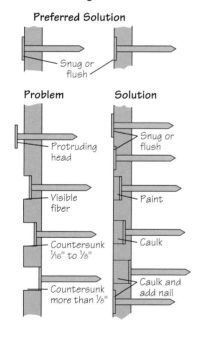

▶ Hardboard siding panels are delaminating.

Water that soaks into unpainted panel edges causes delamination. Either cut away the damaged areas and patch with new siding (see below), or replace the entire damaged panel, making sure to paint all the edges before installing it.

▶ Nails are causing rust stains on panel siding.

Apply a phosphoric acid solution (rust dissolver) to the nail heads. Wait 20 minutes, then rinse it off. Scuff-sand the siding if it has a glossy finish. Then apply a primer/sealer to the stains, followed by a paint that matches the existing color.

▶ Z-bar flashing on hardboard panel siding is rusted or missing.

Use a wire brush to remove any rust. Then sand the area and prime it with an oil-based rusty-metal primer. Finish with an acrylic latex paint that matches the siding color. First apply the primer and paint to a small area and let dry to ensure that the color matches. Adjust the color as necessary and complete the touch-up.

   If the flashing is missing and the panel edges aren't swollen from water damage, prime any gaps less than ½ inch wide and fill with acrylic latex caulk. For wider gaps, install new Z-bar flashing. Carefully remove nails from the bottom edge of the top panel, tuck the Z-bar into place, and nail with new 3d HDG box nails. If the panel edge has water damage, cut away at least 1½ inches of the damaged siding and install new pieces. Paint all edges with a paint recommended for hardboard siding. Install Z-bar above and below the filler piece,

leaving a ½-inch gap between the bottom hardboard edge and bottom Z-bar bend.

Installing Z-bar between hardboard panels

½" gap · Panel siding · Framing or blocking · Z-bar · Panel siding

▶ Brick mortar is crumbling or missing.

Crumbling mortar should be removed and replaced with new mortar, a process called pointing. To remove the old mortar, use a handheld sledgehammer and a tuck pointing chisel. Wear safety goggles and heavy gloves. Chip out the mortar to a depth of about 1 inch, making sure to make the back of the trough flat, not V-shaped. Be careful not to chip the brick. Next, brush out the joints with a stiff-bristled brush, followed by a light misting with water. To fill the joints, mix a small batch (about enough to fill a 1-gallon paint can) of prepackaged mortar mix with water. Place the mix on a hawk. Using a pointing trowel or a joint-filling tool, first pack the vertical (head) joints, then the horizontal (bed) joints. Joints deeper than 1 inch should be filled in two successive passes. Let the mortar dry enough to hold a thumbprint between fillings. When all the mortar

---

Tip *The ideal consistency of brick mortar is moist enough to adhere, dry enough not to slump. Mix it so there is no residual water puddling on the surface. Test it by making a "snowball"—it should hold its shape but water shouldn't drain out of it when you squeeze it.* <u>Caution:</u> *Mortar can irritate skin, so wear gloves.*

is stiff, finish off the joints with a jointing tool. Jointing tools come in different profiles; use a style that matches the existing joints. Spots of mortar that remain on the brick may be removed after a few days with a stiff-bristled brush.

Removing old mortar

Filling head joints and bed joints

Hawk

Small trowel or joint-filling tool

Smoothing the joints

Jointing tool

▶ Brick wall has long, vertical cracks.

If a house foundation doesn't settle evenly, brick veneer siding often cracks in a staircase-shaped pattern. Although the crack itself isn't serious, you should fill it as soon as possible to stop water or insect penetration. Cracks that occur through mortar joints may be repaired with pointing (see page 127). Brick cracks may be filled with masonry crack filler, which is available in tubes and applied with a caulking gun. If the cracking recurs, there may be a foundation problem, which should be examined by a structural engineer.

▶ Bricks above window or door are sagging.

If the lintel that supports the brick over a door or window is badly rusted or rotted, it can weaken and allow the bricks to sag. You can replace a lintel in a one-story building, but consult a professional if there is a second story above it. To replace a lintel, first remove the sagging bricks carefully with a hand-held sledgehammer and a narrow masonry chisel; wear eye protection and gloves. Next cut out the mortar around the lintel and remove it; be sure to remove all metal or wood pieces. The new lintel should be primed and painted steel. Slip it in place and pack mortar around the embedded ends. Next install a strip of galvanized-steel flashing over the lintel. Bend the back of it up against the wall sheathing and lap the front edge over the lintel about ½ inch. Then replace the brick, applying mortar to the top, back, and sides of each brick before slipping it into place. When installing the course of brick that rests

directly on the lintel, omit mortar from every third vertical joint to create weep holes. In these holes, stuff rope made of fiberglass or polypropylene. It will wick decay-causing moisture from the wall cavity while preventing insects from getting in.

Removing sagging bricks

Weak lintel

Installing lintel and flashing

Flashing

New lintel

Replacing bricks

Mortar on 4 sides

Weep holes

Tip   *When laying bricks, wet the bricks before setting them in mortar. Dry bricks absorb moisture from the mortar before it can set up, thus weakening it.*

▶ Brick surface has white powder on it.

The whitish powder found on some brick surfaces, known as efflorescence, is salt that's present in some brick and mortar. When moisture in the brick or mortar migrates to the surface and dries, it leaves behind this white powder. Remove it, with a dry stiff-bristled brush; follow up with either a TSP solution or a heavy-duty hand soap that contains pumice. For stubborn stains, scrub on a mild solution of 1 part muriatic acid to 20 parts water. Be sure to wear eye protection and rubber gloves. When mixing the solution, add the acid to the water, not the water to the acid. Recurring efflorescence may indicate that water is leaking into the wall through defective flashing (see page 91) or cracks in window molding (see page 130).

▶ Brick veneer is leaning away from wall.

This can be caused by a number of things, including poor construction methods or moisture damage. To correctly identify the cause and determine the appropriate repair, contact a structural engineer.

▶ Cracks have opened up between brick and stucco.

First make sure that all surfaces are free of dirt and loose debris. Then fill the cracks with a clear silicone caulk. Cracks wider than ¼ inch should first be filled with foam backer rod, compressible filler material that comes in long strips. The diameter of the rod should be 25 to 50 percent more than the width of the crack.

▶ Bricks above windows on outside wall are cracked.

This is often caused by a deteriorated lintel. See opposite page.

▶ Paint won't stick to galvanized metal.

First, before painting, clean galvanized metal thoroughly, using sandpaper, a wire brush, or a wire wheel mounted on an electric drill. Make sure all rust, corrosion, and flaking metal are removed. Then wipe down the surface with mineral spirits or lacquer thinner. Make sure the surface is clean by wiping it with a white cloth. Finally, use a galvanized-steel primer or a metal etch compound (sold in paint stores), followed by a finish coat.

▶ Paint is chalking, blistering, or peeling.

Wash away chalky paint, blisters, and peeling with a high-pressure washer. Rent a gas-powered model, which creates up to 2,500 psi of pressure. Handle it carefully and wear gloves, eye protection, and rain gear. Do not spray up under lapped shingles or siding. Blisters or peeling that remain after pressure washing may be removed with a hand scraper. Feather the scraped edges before repainting, then prime the bare spots and apply the paint.

If paint problems are caused by moisture coming through the walls from the inside of the house, install ventilating fans in the bathrooms and kitchen. Also paint the interior sides of peeling walls with a vapor-retarder paint, such as oil-based enamel, and seal around window and base moldings with caulk. If peeling and blistering problems

persist, add ventilating plugs to exterior walls to provide a path for moisture inside the walls to escape.

Installing ventilating plug

Spade bit or hole saw

Siding

Ventilating plug

▶ Paint is splotchy and discolored.

This may be the result of mildew growth or because the paint has worn out. First try washing the paint with a mild solution of laundry detergent or a solution of 4 tablespoons bleach to 1 quart warm water. If that doesn't solve the problem, repaint the affected area.

Tip *Many paint problems are caused by poor application techniques. Prepare the surface thoroughly by washing the siding with a solution of 3 parts detergent/water solution and 1 part chlorine bleach, scraping off old paint, eradicating mildew with a bleach solution, sealing knots with pigmented shellac, filling holes and cracks, and priming. When painting: (1) avoid working in direct sunlight, (2) allow paint to dry thoroughly before recoating or adding a second color next to it, (3) apply flat paints before gloss paints, and (4) paint up to visual breakpoints before stopping work.*

▶ Paint won't cover knots.

Knots are probably the densest part of a piece of wood. As such they don't take paint as well as the surrounding surface. To ensure that the paint will hide them, spot-prime knots with a pigmented shellac and then with an oil-based primer/sealer before painting.

▶ Paint on wood shingles is badly cracked and worn.

If there are many layers of paint, take the surface down to bare wood by either sanding or stripping with chemical strippers. Paint applied prior to 1972 probably has lead in it; take special precautions by wearing a dust mask, capturing the residue in plastic sheeting, and disposing of it in an approved landfill. If the paint layer is not exceptionally thick, first wash the shingles with a pressure washer, directing the stream from above or from the side, but not from below. Wear waterproof clothing and eye protection, cover nearby bushes with plastic, and tape plastic over outdoor electrical receptacles and loose-fitting windows and doors. Next scrape away any loose paint and feather the chipped edges with sandpaper. Prime any bare wood. Then repaint the shingles with exterior latex paint, using a rough-surface brush.

▶ Oil-based stain applied with power sprayer is peeling.

Stain can peel if the surface was not sufficiently prepped before the stain was applied. Other possible causes are a low-quality grade of stain or a moisture problem behind the affected area. Once you've determined the problem and corrected it, scrape off all loose stain with a broad putty knife, prepare the wall according to label direc-

tions on the new stain, and apply a fresh coat. If you spray it on, after spraying go over the surface with a brush or roller (backbrushing) to work the stain into the surface.

▶ Paint is peeling off outside trim.

First solve any interior moisture problems (windows that fog frequently are a sign). On a problem wall, painting the interior surface with a vapor-barrier paint and caulking around interior window and base moldings can help. Also make sure that flashing around doors or windows isn't leaking. Then scrape off the loose paint and feather the scraped edges with sandpaper. Pry out all old caulk around the trim and clean off dirt and chalking paint. Prime any bare wood with latex exterior wood primer. Fill all cracks between trim pieces and between the trim and the siding with acrylic latex or butyl rubber caulk. Then apply two coats of exterior trim paint.

▶ Caulk has dried, shrunken, or cracked, or is missing.

First scrape out the old caulk with a molding scraper, thin putty knife, or lever-type can opener. Next remove any dirt or chalking paint from the surfaces to be caulked by sanding or scraping. Fill any gaps wider than ¼ inch with foam backer rod. Finally, refill the gaps with a bead of caulk. Use acrylic latex or butyl rubber caulk over painted surfaces, silicone caulk on clear finished surfaces, and elastomeric terpolymer caulk on masonry surfaces.

▶ Caulk won't adhere.

Most likely the surface has dirt or chalking paint on it. Clean off the dirt or chalk and apply a primer appropriate for the particular surface. Let dry, then apply the caulk. Follow label directions—some caulk won't adhere if applied in cold weather.

▶ Paint doesn't adhere to caulk.

Most types of silicone caulk form a smooth surface that doesn't take paint well. First pull off and scrape out all the caulk. Then refill the gaps with an acrylic latex caulk, butyl rubber caulk, or other caulk specified as paintable. Let dry, then apply the paint.

▶ Weather is too hot or cold to apply caulk.

Different caulks tolerate different temperature ranges. Newer, more expensive caulks may be applied in extremely hot or cold weather. If you must apply caulk now, buy a type tolerant of the extreme temperature.

▶ Stucco has lost color.

If the stucco is painted, first wash the surface, scrape off any loose paint, and patch the cracks. Then apply a new coat of exterior latex paint with a long-nap roller or a rough-surface brush. If you use a roller, follow up with a dry roller or brush to remove drips. An unpainted surface can get a new coat of colored stucco. Apply a mixture of 2 parts white portland cement, 3 parts silica sand, and powdered pigment to create the color of your choice, all mixed to a thick soupy consistency. Use a long-bristled brush. Finish the stucco in your choice of surfaces (see opposite page).

Tip *The main difference in composition between high-quality paint and ordinary paint is that high-quality paint has a higher ratio of vehicle (the oil or latex agent that allows the paint to remain liquid in the can and then harden when applied) to solvent (the thinning agent, either mineral spirits for oil-based paint or water for latex paint). Also, high-quality paint has a lower ratio of fillers and extenders (various materials, such as clay, added for bulk) than ordinary paint.*

▶ *Stucco has cracks.*

If the cracks are very narrow, use a thin bead of elastomeric caulk, such as a terpolymer type, to fill them. Then paint the caulk to match the stucco. If the wall has extensive small cracks and is otherwise sound, coat the entire wall with an elastomeric sealant according to label directions. (Unlike latex paint, these sealants are impermeable to moisture vapor and will blister if moisture migrates from inside the wall toward the outside, so be sure there are no internal sources of moisture.) For wider cracks, scrape the crack with the point of a lever-type can opener, undercutting the edges. Wet the crack, then fill it with stucco mortar mixed to a creamy consistency. Either use a mortar color that matches the existing stucco, or paint the patch when it's dry. If the crack keeps reopening, have the house checked by a structural engineer.

Cleaning the crack

Undercut edges

Reinforcing wire

Applying stucco mortar

▶ *Stucco has holes.*

Fill tiny holes with elastomeric terpolymer caulk. Small holes, up to 1¼ inches in diameter, can be filled with stucco patching material. Slightly larger holes can also be filled with stucco patch, but not quite flush with the surface. Finish filling the hole with a flexible patching compound, spread out around the hole to make a good seal and to give the compound a larger surface to grip.

Larger holes should be filled with new stucco. First determine the type of stucco it is by placing a small piece in a muriatic acid solution. Lime mortar will dissolve; portland cement won't. Next determine to what extent the stucco has to be removed. Tap around the hole, moving progressively farther away from it until you reach stucco that's solid and doesn't move. Remove all cracked and loose stucco from the patch area, down to the building paper or concrete block. Leave the stucco wire (reinforcing mesh known as stucco lath) intact. If it is damaged or missing from the patch area, expose the stucco wire for 3 additional inches around all sides. Cut a new piece of galvanized stucco wire to fit in the hole, overlapping the old wire, and nail it with stucco nails that have fiber spacers to hold the mesh away from the sheathing. Concrete-block walls should be brushed off, sprayed with water, allowed to dry, then coated with a masonry bonding agent.

Next moisten the hole lightly and spread on a ⅜-inch-thick layer of the appropriate type of stucco. Let it firm up, then score deep scratches in it with a nail. Allow it to dry overnight, then apply the

second coat to within ⅛ inch of the surface. Finally, apply a finish coat that matches the texture and color of the existing wall.

Patching a hole in stucco

Applying scratch coat

Building paper

Applying second coat

Stucco wire

Applying final coat

Scratched surface of previous coat

Applying different finishes

Modern American finish

Spatter finish

Snap brush against stick

2x4

Standard smooth finish

Old English finish

Wood float

Round-nose trowel

Tip   *Most older stucco has permanent color added to the final coat. If you want to paint over stucco, wash the wall thoroughly to remove dirt and any loose or flaking material. Then coat the wall with a primer specified for stucco surfaces, and topcoat it with latex paint. Apply the paint with a thick-nap roller (½ inch). Look for missed spots and touch them up with a brush.*

▶ Stucco surface extends into ground.

Building codes now require that stucco applied over a wood-frame wall terminate at least 4 inches above the ground. Otherwise, moisture can get trapped behind it against the foundation sill. If you have an older home with walls stuccoed to the ground, make sure that the gutters and downspouts are not leaking and are successfully channeling water away from the house. Also check nearby drains to ensure that they aren't clogged. Seal all cracks in the wall, especially around door and window trim, and be sure that the stucco is sound. Finally, make sure that the ground against the foundation slopes away from the house.

If you're having new stucco applied, make sure it ends at least 4 inches above the ground and has a metal stop bead along the bottom.

▶ Stucco around windows and doors is cracked.

First wipe away any dust and dirt from the crack edges. Then, for cracks that are wider than ¼ inch, stuff a length of foam backer rod into the crack. Then fill the cracks with either an acrylic/silicone caulk that matches the stucco or trim color, or a clear solvent-based caulk. Acrylic caulk cleans up with water; solvent-based caulk requires something other than water, such as mineral spirits or paint thinner.

▶ Stucco isn't sealed.

Stucco siding should not be sealed. By design it's supposed to allow some moisture in and out, and if it needs to be recoated, any sealer on it would first have to be sandblasted off. If you paint the stucco, use a latex-based paint, which is porous and will allow water to pass through.

▶ Vinyl siding needs cleaning.

The best tool for washing vinyl siding is a power washer. You can rent or purchase one. Homeowner-grade models that produce up to 1,200 psi, useful for many outdoor cleaning projects, are now available. When renting a power washer, choose a small unit for general washing, a large unit for extensive paint scraping. Choose a model with interchangeable nozzles that alter the spray patterns and pressure. To use the sprayer, first seal off any electrical receptacles, vent openings, and light fixtures with plastic and duct tape. Cover nearby shrubs. Then spray the siding with a mild solution of laundry detergent and water. Use a low-pressure nozzle and work from bottom to top to prevent staining and dirt buildup. Shoot the water across the siding, not up into it. Then use a medium-pressure nozzle and plain water to rinse off the solution, working from top to bottom. Whenever possible, work on a shady side of the house—warm, sunny surfaces can dry before you have time to rinse off the dirt and soap.

Power washers produce a high-pressure jet of water that can be dangerous. Observe all manufacturer's warnings and cautions. Do not point the nozzle at unprotected skin, as it can cause a puncture wound. Wear eye protection. Be careful when working from a ladder—the spray wand starts and stops with a bit of a kick.

Cleaning vinyl siding

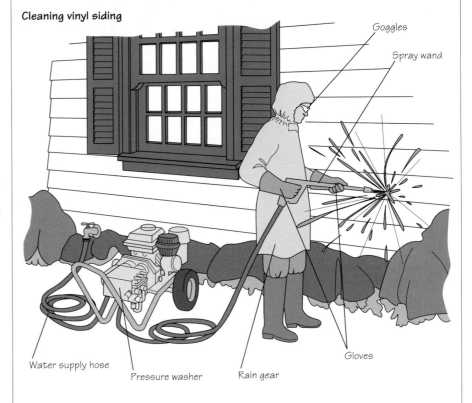

Goggles

Spray wand

Gloves

Water supply hose

Pressure washer

Rain gear

Tip To apply stucco, place a small amount on a hawk (mortarboard). Holding the hawk in one hand and a trowel upside down in the other, scoop some of the stucco onto the bottom of the trowel and then onto the wall in a continuous, upward-pushing motion. Regulate the depth of stucco by varying the pressure. Plan on having much of the stucco end up on the ground as you learn to scoop it off the hawk and onto the wall.

▶ Vinyl siding has faded.

You can paint vinyl siding just like aluminum or wood siding. First clean the siding (see opposite page). Then lightly sand the surface and remove the dust. Next apply an oil-based primer with a brush. Let dry, then apply two coats of a high-quality (high solid content) acrylic latex paint. Be sure to use a color as light as or lighter than that of the siding; darker colors can cause the siding to overheat and warp.

▶ Vinyl siding is difficult for one person to install.

Long pieces of siding can be un-wieldy to handle, especially when a small gust of wind kicks up. If you don't have a helper, position one end of the siding in place and hold it there with strips of duct tape while you work toward it from the other end.

▶ Vinyl siding is damaged.

You can replace an entire piece of vinyl siding or, if seams won't be objectionable, just the damaged section. First choose a time when it's not too cold (below 50° F) or you'll crack the vinyl. To remove a damaged section, make vertical cuts on either side of the damaged area with a utility knife. Then, for the damaged section or a full piece, unsnap the siding by pushing up on the cut piece and pulling down on the piece above it. If that does not work, use a zip tool (available at a siding supplier or home center) to unlock the siding. Hook the end of

the tool into the locking strip of the upper piece of siding and, while maintaining firm downward pressure on the tool, slide it the length of the lower piece. Then lift the upper piece, prop it in place with woodblocks, pull out the nails with a pry bar, and remove the damaged section or full piece. Cut a new piece so it will overlap 1¼ inches at each end. Snap the bottom edge in place and nail in the top. Then press the upper piece down, or use the zip tool to relock it in place.

Unsnapping vinyl siding

Vertical cut
Damaged section
Locked joint
Zip tool
Nail strip

▶ Vinyl siding has crack.

Using a zip tool (available at a siding supplier or home center), carefully unlock the bottom edge of the siding immediately above the damaged piece. Then use a nail puller to remove the nails from the top of the damaged piece. Remove the piece and lay it facedown. Cut a patch out of scrap vinyl siding to fit

over the crack. Clean around the crack with PVC cleaner, then coat around the crack with PVC cement. Attach the patch, good side down. When the cement dries, reinstall the piece.

Adhering patch behind crack

PVC cement
Backside
Patch

▶ Corner of vinyl siding is damaged.

See page 134.

▶ Aluminum siding needs cleaning.

Clean as for vinyl; see opposite page.

▶ Aluminum siding has faded.

Aluminum siding can be painted to give it a fresh, new color. First scrape off any loose flakes, then lightly sand the surface to provide adequate adhesion for the new paint. Wash the siding (see opposite page). Prime any patches of bare metal with an oil- or water-based primer made for metal. Finish

Tip   *There are several ways to cut vinyl siding. If you use a utility knife, use medium pressure to score the vinyl on the face side, then snap the vinyl in half. If you use tin snips or aviation snips, you'll get a cleaner cut if you avoid closing the blades at the end of each stroke. If you use a power saw, install the blade backward for a cleaner cut (this works especially well in cold weather). Be sure to turn the blade around before cutting any other material.*

by applying a coat of high-quality (high solid content) acrylic latex paint. If you use a sprayer or roller, go back over the surface with a brush (backbrushing).

▶ Aluminum surface is corroded.

If a small area is corroded, sand or wire-brush the area to bring it down to bare metal. Then mask off the area, spray on a metal primer, let dry, and brush on two coats of matching paint. For larger areas, see page 133.

▶ Aluminum siding is damaged.

To pull out small, round dents, fit a rubber grommet or several washers on the end of a small sheet-metal screw and drive the screw into the center of the dent. Using a pair of pliers, grasp the head of the screw and pull outward until the dent has popped or flattened out. Remove the screw from the panel and fill the hole with plastic aluminum, available in hardware stores. Apply it as neatly as possible, then let the material harden. Sand and touch up with matching paint.

For larger dents use the sheet-metal screw and washer procedure over a few areas of the dent. Then roughen the dented surface with sandpaper and apply auto-body filler over the area. Before the filler dries, smooth it flush with the siding. Finish by masking off the area, spraying on a metal primer, then brushing on two coats of matching paint.

If the panel has a large hole or gash, first get a new piece of matching siding that's at least 2 inches longer than the damaged area. To cut away the damage, mark two vertical lines, one on each side of the hole. Mark a horizontal line above the hole, 1 inch beneath the butt edge of the panel above. Drill

pilot holes where the lines meet, cut along the marks with tin snips, and remove the cutout. Next remove enough of the top of the new piece so that when locked in place, its top edge will touch the butt edge of the panel above. For a straight edge, score it with a sharp utility knife, then bend it back and forth until it breaks off. Run a bead of butyl rubber caulk along the back of the new piece, then lock it in place so the ends overlap the cutout 1 inch on each side and the top abuts the piece above it.

Repairing a dent

Washer

Repairing a large dent

Auto-body filler

Patching aluminum siding

1"

Caulk on back

Patch

1" overlap at each end

Damaged area cut out

▶ Corner post of aluminum siding is damaged.

First make a vertical cut along one side of the corner post with a sharp utility knife. It may require a few strokes to cut through completely.

Then score the other side of the post and bend the piece back and forth until it breaks off. Cut the nailing flanges off a new corner post by scoring and bending. Apply a bead of butyl rubber caulk to each of the existing nailing flanges and to the replacement post (as shown below), and set the post in place. Secure both ends of the new corner with pop rivets.

Cutting off old corner post

Preparing new corner post

Nailing strip

Flanges

Applying caulk

Flanges

Attaching new post

Flange

Pop rivet

Replacement post

Tip When placing a ladder against a wall, a quick way to test if it's leaning at a safe angle is to stand on the ground with your toes against the ladder feet and your arms outstretched to the front. The ladder is at the safest angle if your fingertips comfortably touch the ladder sides.

▶ Floorboards are rotted.

Rotted floorboards should be replaced with new boards, but first the condition that caused the rot should be corrected. Causes include inadequate ventilation under a porch floor, floorboards with exposed end grain that hasn't been sealed, and settlement (porches that were once sloped to shed water may level over time, allowing puddles to collect).

To increase ventilation, replace solid siding under the floor with lattice, or add screened vents to allow cross-ventilation, especially near corners. If the porch floor does not slope away from the house at least ⅛ inch per foot, consult a contractor experienced with porch restoration about the best technique for restoring proper slope. If the slope and ventilation are adequate and only a few boards need to be replaced, use the same techniques as for replacing interior floorboards (see page 42). Prime or seal each board, including ends, before installing, and use HDG nails.

▶ Wood floor needs painting.

Specialized paints are available for porches and decks that are highly resistant to abrasion and high traffic. Unfortunately, they're available in only a limited range of colors. If the floor is bare wood, coat the boards with a water repellent/ preservative before applying a primer. A previously painted floor should be scraped and sanded first to provide a solid base and tooth for the new coating.

▶ Concrete porch floor is settling.

See page 145.

▶ Porch roof post is rotted and needs replacing.

Shore up the porch roof with a temporary 4x4 brace. First nail a temporary 2x4 cleat to the underside of the roof header immediately next to the rotted post. Cut the 4x4 brace about 6 inches longer than the distance between the cleat and the ground; it should rest on a 2-foot-long pad of 2x8 scrap. Set up the brace with the top under the cleat and the bottom on the pad. Then tap the bottom of the brace with a sledgehammer until the header is raised about ¼ inch. Secure the brace in place by driving a wedge under it and toenailing it to the scrap. Then remove the old post.

The new post should be the same size as the old one. Most lumberyards and home centers stock decorative posts in many styles. If you have difficulty matching the post, try an architectural salvage yard. Prime or seal the new post, and attach an aluminum pedestal bracket to the bottom to prevent trapped moisture from rotting the base. Set the new post in place. Secure the top by toenailing it with two 8d HDG common nails on each side (predrill, and countersink the heads with a nail set). Attach the bottom bracket with 3-inch HDG decking screws. Remove the brace.

Replacing porch roof post

Porch roof

2x4 cleat

4x4 brace

Old post

Direction for tapping wedge

2x8 scrap

Wedge

Direction for hitting post with sledgehammer

Aluminum pedestal bracket

Tip *If your porch feels dark and uninviting, paint the ceiling white. If it's still too dark, paint the floor white with latex deck paint specified for floors, or have the floor whitewashed.*

Tip *Recessed ceiling fixtures are an excellent lighting choice for porches, provided there is some attic space (because it's not insulated, even a low attic usually has enough access). The lights are unobtrusive to neighbors, provide plenty of useful illumination, and maintain privacy by directing light downward into focused pools instead of bouncing it off walls and occupants. Space lights 8 feet apart.*

▶ *Wood tread is cracked or rotting.*

Weak treads are dangerous and should be replaced immediately. First loosen the tread from the cleat or stair stringer by tapping it from below with a sledgehammer. Then pull out the nails with a claw hammer or pry bar. If the stairs have a closed stringer and there's no access from below, dig out the nails with a nail puller. Using the old tread for a pattern, cut a new tread from pressure-treated lumber; brush wood preservative on the cut ends. Then install the new tread with HDG nails, using two nails on each end of the tread. Paint or stain to match.

Replacing tread

Stringer

Tread

5-lb sledgehammer

▶ *Stringer is splitting.*

Support the stringer with a temporary brace. Then add a cleat to the inside of the stringer; it should be 6 inches longer than the split. Bore pilot holes in the cleat and use HDG wood screws every 4 to 6 inches. Then remove the brace.

Bracing the stringer

Stringer

Brace

Attaching cleat

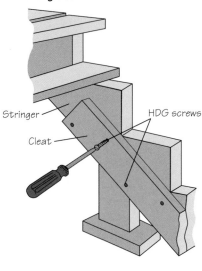

Stringer

Cleat

HDG screws

▶ *Stair treads are slippery.*

If water puddles on the treads, drill ⅜-inch-diameter holes for drainage. If moss makes the treads slippery, scrub it off with bleach diluted in water, according to label directions. If the treads are painted with a high-gloss paint, redo them with a latex paint specified for porches and decks. Follow all directions on the paint label. To make the treads even more skidproof, add a small amount of silica sand to the paint—enough to produce a slightly abrasive surface.

▶ *Treads lean to one side.*

Either the base of the stringer is decayed or the footing has settled. If the stringer is decayed, install a temporary brace to support it near its base. The brace should raise the staircase back to the level position. Draw a level line on the stringer above the rotted area, then use a saber saw or circular saw to cut off the damaged section. Measure a new piece of pressure-treated lumber to fit under the stringer by holding it against the stringer and marking the level cut line on it. Then, with a straightedge held along each stringer edge, mark cut lines parallel to the stringer on the front and back edges of the block. Cut the block to fit, and brush wood preservative on the cut ends. Slip the block under the stringer; then use at least two HDG nails to hold it in place, dulling the nail heads to prevent splitting the piece. To strengthen the repair, attach a short piece of lumber (a cleat) on the inside of the stringer and block (see left). Drill pilot holes in the cleat and attach it with HDG screws.

If the footing has settled but is still sound (neither cracked nor below grade), raise the stringer with a temporary brace, and shim the gap below the stringer with a block of pressure-treated wood cut to fit.

Tip *The best way to keep moths, mosquitoes, and other insects away from porches is with screens. Using 1x2s, build frames that fit snugly into all of the openings of the porch. Prime and paint the frames. Then stretch insect screening over them, staple it to the faces of the frames, and nail primed and painted decorative molding around the frame to conceal the edges. Drill pilot holes for screws into the frame sides every 3 or 4 feet for attaching the screens to the porch posts.*

Tip *Black screening fabric provides daytime privacy, is easiest to see through from the inside, and gives the house a strong design accent.*

If the footing has deteriorated or has sunk below grade, raise the stringer with a temporary brace and remove the footing. Build forms and pour a new concrete footing as described on page 145.

Cutting off the rotted section

Stringer

Footing   Saber saw

Brace

Attaching the new block

HDG nail

New block

▶ *Railing is loose.*

If the staircase is made of wood, use two galvanized-steel strap brackets for each railing post. Slip the brackets around the post base and bolt them to the stringer with ⁵⁄₁₆-inch by 1½-inch lag screws; then drive 1½-inch HDG wood screws through the bracket and into the post.

If you are unable to locate brackets, use carriage bolts. Bore 2⅜-inch-diameter holes through the stringer and post, spacing the holes 4 inches apart with one near the top edge of the stringer. Then install the bolts with malleable washers, which are large washers designed to distribute the bolt tension over a wider area. The bolts should not be so tight that the washers crush the wood fibers of the post.

Reinforcing a wood post

If the railing is metal and embedded in concrete steps, the attachment may have worked its way loose. Remove the damaged concrete around the metal post base, then refill around the post with a soupy mixture of quick-drying concrete patching material. This patch, which is mixed with water, comes in a small tub or cardboard box and is sold at most home centers. If the hole is too close to the edge of the stairs to hold the patching material, anchor the bottom of the railing laterally by drilling a ½-inch-diameter horizontal hole through the metal post, then extending the hole into the concrete with a rotary hammer and ½-inch bit. Blow dust out of the hole with a tire pump, insert an expansion bolt, and tighten the nut against the metal post.

Bolting a metal post

Strap bracket

HDG wood screw

Lag screw

Metal post

Hole drilled through metal first

Expansion bolt

Tip   *Make sure your railings are safe. For porches higher than 18 inches from the ground, most building codes require that railings be at least 36 inches high, that the area between floor and railing have no openings wide enough for a 4-inch sphere to pass through, and that the railing be able to resist a 200-pound lateral force anywhere along its length.*

▶ Garage doesn't have enough storage space.

If you have basic carpentry skills, you can build a storage system on any length wall using the basic modules illustrated below. The dimensions and arrangement shown maximize the use of 4x8 sheets of plywood, but you can adjust the dimensions as desired. If you space the modules more than 4 feet apart, you will have to reinforce the shelves between them. Cut the sides, tops, and shelves from ¾-inch plywood, mark shelf locations on the inside faces of the two sides, and scribe corresponding nailing lines on the outside faces. Assemble each module with glue and 8d box nails. Cut back pieces out of ¼-inch plywood or hard-

board and attach them with glue and 4d box nails. Attach the modules to the wall studs with 2-inch screws, using a level and shims to make them square and plumb. Cut shelves as desired for the spaces between cabinets. If you use plywood, cut the shelves so that the long dimension runs the same direction as the long edge of the plywood (with the grain, not across it). Attach them with glue and 8d box nails, or install shelf track to make them adjustable. Install sliding-door track as shown, and attach roller brackets to the tops of full sheets of ¾-inch lumbercore plywood, which will stay flat, to make the doors.

Building modules

¼" plywood

¾" plywood

2'   4'

Spacing modules

Modules

Wall

4' 4' 4' 4' 4'
20'

Installing modules and doors

1x6
Sliding door
Cabinet   2x4s

▶ Garage roof has too many cross members for storage.

The roof is probably framed with prefabricated trusses. All of the parts of a truss work together to hold up the roof; each truss is rated to carry a certain amount of weight. Storing items on a truss can over-stress it and may permanently damage the roof. Under no circumstances should any member be cut or removed.

▶ Perfboard hooks fall off board.

Perforated board is sold in ⅛-inch and ¼-inch thicknesses; the ¼-inch type has larger holes. Make sure you have the correct pegs for the thickness of the board. Regular steel hooks loosen from everyday use; check a local home center for locking pegs. Two common types of locking pegs are steel pegs with a locking plate and heavy plastic pegs that lock in place when installed.

▶ Large garden tools have no storage area.

If wall space is limited, make a narrow rack that will store several tools. Use two pieces of ½-inch plywood attached to either side of an exposed wall stud. Cut them 16 inches long and graduate the width from 12 to 16 inches. Attach the 12-inch width to the stud sides with four 2-inch wood screws each.

If you have more wall space (3 to 5 feet), hang garden tools from nails driven into a scrap of ¾-inch plywood. First lay the plywood on the floor and arrange the tools with their heads on the plywood and all handles hanging in the same direction. Stagger tools to maximize the space. With the tools in place, drive two nails below each head. Remove

Tip   *Garages are often a weak link in a home's security system. Be sure all entrances to the garage are locked and that the door between the garage and house is locked. Don't leave the garage door open for long periods of time, allowing passersby to notice what's stored in there. Don't leave keys to the house in a conspicuous place in the garage; hide them where only you can find them.*

the tools, attach the plywood securely to the wall with lag screws and washers, and hang each tool from its pair of nails.

Building a narrow rack for garden tools

Top angled to hold tools

Stud

2" screws

16"

16" θ 12"

½" plywood

▶ Long objects, such as molding, pipe, and some tools, are awkward to store.

Organize and store such objects in sections of vinyl rain gutter. Attach the gutter support brackets to the studs, then snap the sections in place.

Storing long objects

Vinyl rain gutters

Support brackets attached to studs

▶ Garden hose is awkward to store.

Do not hang the hose from a peg or narrow hanger; instead, make a sturdy hose hanger from a large cylinder, such as a plastic plant liner. Secure it to the wall with 1½-inch wood screws and fender washers. Or check a home center for a hook-and-loop hose-carrying handle that can easily be hung on the wall.

▶ Garage lighting is inadequate.

One or more pairs of 4-foot fluorescent lights provide adequate lighting for most garage needs. If you have a workbench, position one pair directly over it. As a safety measure, slip clear plastic tubes over the bulbs; these will contain the glass if the lights are accidentally broken. Plastic tubes are available at lighting stores.

▶ Garage is too cold.

First check the garage door. Make sure the weather stripping on the bottom of the door is in good shape and that there isn't any debris preventing it from sealing completely. If the garage has windows, they should be shut tightly and not have any cracked or missing panes. Insulating the walls and ceiling will also help. Finally, if the floor is cold, bury insulation around the foundation. Dig a narrow 2-foot-deep trench around the foundation and place beadboard insulation (rigid foam panels specified for ground contact or burial) against the footings.

▶ Garage access to attic lacks solid door.

Garages without ceilings often have an access opening to the attic, located high up on the common wall with the house. This opening must have a solid door rated at one-hour fire resistance to prevent a fire in the garage from being sucked up into the attic. To make such a door, buy a damaged solid-core door and cut it to size, or attach ⅝-inch wallboard to a piece of ¾-inch plywood.

If the garage has a ceiling with a pull-down staircase, there should be a fireproof cover over the hatch. Cover kits are available from home centers and ladder manufacturers. There are two kinds: premolded fiberglass or an assemble-it-yourself foam cover that fits over the ladder when it's in the closed position.

▶ Concrete floor is stained.

Remove oil, rust, and other stains from concrete with a solution of 1 part muriatic acid to 10 parts water. You can mix a small batch in a plastic watering can. Add the acid to the water, not the water to the acid. Wear rubber gloves, eye protection, a long-sleeved shirt, long pants, and work shoes. Sprinkle the solution on the stain and work it in with a long-handled scrub brush. Wait five minutes, then rinse the surface thoroughly with water. You can also purchase a premixed concrete cleaning solution from a home center or hardware store.

▶ Concrete floor is cracked.

See page 144.

Tip　*All electrical receptacles in a garage should be protected by ground fault circuit interrupters (GFCIs). An exception is the overhead outlet for an automatic garage-door opener (check local codes).*

Tip　*To help you navigate your car into the garage, paint markers on the back wall to aim headlights at, and hang a tennis ball or other harmless object where the windshield will touch it when you've pulled in far enough.*

▶ *Garage floor is slippery from melting snow and ice.*

If snow and ice melting from the car spread out over the garage floor, confine the mess to the area under the car by gluing two continuous strips of garage-door weather stripping to the floor, about 1 foot away from each side of the car. Attach each strip with a bead of outdoor construction adhesive. If you're planning to build a garage, install a concrete floor that's sloped slightly toward a central drain.

Controlling meltwater

Garage-door weather stripping

▶ *Manual door gets stuck.*

Check for objects stored overhead that may be interfering with the door, then make sure that all hinges are securely fastened to the door. If that doesn't help, see right.

▶ *Garage-door locking bar doesn't catch in side latches.*

An object or debris under the bottom of the door, such as a small stone or some leaves, can prevent the door from closing fully. Check along the garage floor and on the door bottom. Also make sure that the locking bars aren't bent and that the locking-bar guides are

properly positioned. Straighten the bars or realign the guides as needed.

Realigning locking-bar guide

Locking bar   Guide

Slot for bar   Track

▶ *Sectional door doesn't open easily.*

The hardware may be out of alignment, broken, or in need of cleaning and lubrication. If the rollers bind in the tracks, the tracks may be out of alignment—either not straight, not perfectly parallel to each other, or not perpendicular to the door. To align a track, loosen the mounting bracket and tap it back into alignment with a hammer and woodblock. If only one roller drags or jams, try shimming or remounting the roller bracket. If the door is still difficult to lift, try cleaning and lubricating all of the door hardware. Start with the rollers and hinges. Remove one at a time and soak it in kerosene; use a paintbrush to work the kerosene into cracks. Take off rust with steel wool or a liquid rust-removing paste. Then wipe off the parts and apply a light lubricating oil, especially on the hinge knuckles and where the rollers and shafts make contact. If you've installed weather

stripping around the sides of the door, it should seal against the door without jamming tightly against it; adjust the strip if necessary. Finally, check the springs for breaks or looseness; there should be slight tension when the door is fully open. See opposite page.

Realigning track bracket

Shim   Door jamb   Track
Bracket
Wood block

Adjusting roller-hinge bracket

Shim
Roller-hinge bracket

Lubricating roller

Track
Roller shaft
OIL
Roller

Tip   *If your garage is cluttered with tricycles, wagons, and similar children's toys that are constantly on the move, designate a parking space for each one by outlining boxes on the floor with colorful floor and deck paint. While you're at it, do the same for lawnmowers, wheelbarrows, and similar equipment that competes for space.*

▶ Springs need adjustment.

Don't attempt to adjust torsion springs, which are mounted crossways above the opening of a roll-up door. They are extremely dangerous to work on. Contact a professional garage-door mechanic.

Springs located along the door track that operate by stretching, which are called tension springs or extension springs, can be adjusted. First raise the door fully and hold it in position by attaching a clamp or locking pliers to one of the tracks, below the last wheel. Make sure that the spring has a safety cable or chain strung through it. Then release the end of each lifting cable from its mounting bracket at the top of the track or the bottom door panel, tighten the slack, tie a new knot in the cable, and reattach it.

Tightening slack in lifting cable

Mounting bracket

Safety cable

Locking pliers

Extension spring

Door in open position

▶ One-piece door sags in middle when open.

Purchase a bracing kit from a garage-door company; it consists of two threaded steel rods and six mounting brackets. To install it, use carriage bolts to attach the brackets to the back of the garage door, three brackets along the top of the door and three at the bottom. Position the threaded rods in the brackets, secure them with washers and nuts, and tighten the tension until the door straightens.

Straightening a garage door

Back of door

Washer   Bracket

Nut

Rod

▶ Automatic door opener doesn't turn on.

First check the transmitter battery. If it's cold, warm it up. Then make sure that the opener is plugged in and that there's power going to the plug. Next check that the wall button operates the opener; if it does not, replace the opener button and wiring with a standard doorbell button and wire. If the transmitter still doesn't open the door, check for objects, such as boxes or lumber, that are blocking the path of the transmitter signal. Replace a broken or missing receiver antenna with a new one from the opener manufacturer. Finally, make sure that the code settings on the transmitter and receiver match.

▶ Automatic door opener works but door doesn't open.

Most likely, the problem is with the door. First pull the emergency disconnect cord and try to open the door manually. If it's difficult to open, see opposite page.

▶ Automatic door doesn't reverse soon enough or reverses as soon as it shuts.

Test the safety reverse by placing a scrap of 2x4 in the doorway and closing the door on it. If the door reverses upon impact, it is adjusted properly. If the door does not reverse, find the front-limit switch located on the overhead rail near the door opening, or check for a knob to adjust the automatic-reversing switch (see page 142). Move an overhead-rail switch forward in $\frac{1}{16}$-inch increments until the door reverses upon impact. If it reverses too soon, move the switch back. If the door closes fully but reverses after a few seconds, adjust the down-limit screw or knob, located on the motor, to relieve

Tip *If your garage door has an automatic opener and the power fails, you can get your car out of the garage simply by pulling the emergency disconnect cord and then lifting the garage door manually.*

Tip *The Consumer Product Safety Act of 1990 requires that all automatic door openers manufactured after January 1, 1993, meet certain safety standards. Among other things, the standards require that a door have a safety reversing mechanism that reopens it automatically if it hits any obstruction higher than 1 inch above the floor.*

pressure. Some turn by hand; others require a screwdriver or wrench.

▶ Automatic door reverses before cycle ends.

Remove any ice, snow, or debris buildup under the door. Also check the door opener rail; if it bows when the door is closed, decrease the down limit. Look for a down-limit adjusting screw or knob on the power unit and adjust it so the door opener doesn't try to force the door down quite so far. If there's no down-limit adjustment on the power unit, look for a front-limit switch along the rail that gets triggered when the traveler arm reaches it. Slide it back toward the power unit slightly so the opener will shut off sooner.

Checking for a bowed rail

Down-limit adjusting knob

Bow in rail when door is closed

Drive chain

Front-limit switch

Travel arm

▶ Automatic door opens for no reason.

Check the transmitter button to see that it's not stuck. If it is, either unstick the button or replace the transmitter. If that doesn't work, try changing your code. An intermittent short in the button wire can also cause the door to open. Check the wire for continuity and, if it's broken, replace it. If the problem persists, purchase a new transmitter and receiver set. Get one that uses two codes simultaneously.

▶ Automatic door lacks autoreverse.

Recent updates in the safety code mandate that new openers have a number of built-in sensing devices to protect against entrapment. First check with the manufacturer to see if an upgrade kit is available. If not, replace the unit with a new, safer one that complies with UL standard number 325. It will include a photoelectric sensor to be mounted on the door jambs, or a sensing edge to be attached to the door bottom.

▶ Garage ceiling is too low for an automatic door opener.

Most standard openers need about 12 inches of clearance between the top of the door and the garage ceiling. There are low-clearance kits that need about 3 inches of headroom. If you have less than 3 inches of clearance and have a wood door, you can cut off some of the top of the door. Just don't trim too much, or when the door is closed, there will be a gap between the top of the door and the stop molding.

There are openers that require no clearance; they utilize a motor that mounts on the back of the door and a drive wheel that runs in

the door track. A power cord connects the motor to a control panel mounted on the garage wall. A specialty item, this may not be available in home centers. Contact local garage-door companies to find one.

Installing an opener that attaches to the door

Motor

Track

Door

Power cord

Control panel

▶ Water and drafts leak in around door.

First make sure that no debris, snow, or ice is preventing the door from closing completely. If that's not the problem, add or replace the weather stripping at the door bottom. Rubber weather stripping specially made for this purpose is sold in most home centers. If the floor under the door is uneven, nail on a strip of ¾-inch-diameter pipe insulation with the slit facing downward. Attach the strip near the back edge of the door, using 4d HDG box nails.

Attaching foam pipe insulation

½" Slit ¾" pipe insulation

Tip *Occasionally, a garage door with an automatic opener may open when the transmitter has not been activated, even when nobody is home. The cause may be a neighbor or a passing car with a transmitter coded the same as the opener. This problem can be solved by recoding the transmitter; check the manufacturer's directions. Another cause might be a short in the wire between the door opener and wall button, which can activate the opener at the slightest jiggle. Replace the wire.*

▶ Automatic-door drive mechanism binds or slips.

If you have a chain-drive system, open the door halfway and measure the chain sag at the carrier; it shouldn't exceed ½ inch. If it does, tighten the chain-tension adjusting screw on the power unit. If you have a screw-drive system and live in a cold area, the grease on the drive may not be made for low temperatures. Spray a penetrating solvent on the carrier and screw shaft to remove the grease. Then lubricate them, using a lightweight oil or silicone spray. For track-drive systems, make sure that the track is clean and that the sections aren't bent. Replace any plastic guides that are broken.

Measuring chain tension

Rail   Carrier   Chain

Door open halfway

Removing built-up grease from drive screw

Penetrating solvent

Cleaning grease from a drive track

Rag with solvent

▶ Light doesn't go on when automatic door opens.

Check the bulb to see if it's burned out. If it is, purchase a bulb that's recommended by the opener manufacturer; often it's one made for heavy-duty use, such as in a car repair drop light. If the problem is not the bulb, consult a professional garage-door specialist.

▶ Bottom of sectional wood door gets wet.

First make sure that the bottom of the door has been sealed or painted, has weather stripping, and is not cracked. Add or replace as needed. Then seal the long joints between the bottom rail and the panels, running a bead of clear caulk along the joint according to label directions.

▶ Varnish on outside of garage door fades quickly.

Clear finishes won't last on outdoor surfaces. Resign yourself to a yearly job of scraping and sanding, followed by another coat of finish. Use marine-grade spar varnish, or refinish the door with a heavy-bodied stain or paint.

▶ Asphalt driveway is cracked or damaged.

Seal cracks as quickly as possible to prevent further damage from moisture or freezing-and-thawing cycles. Fill large cracks with a premixed asphalt crack filler, which comes in squeeze bottles, 1-gallon containers, and caulking-gun tubes; it's available at home centers and hardware stores. First remove any vegetation growing in the cracks and, if you

have a compressor or shop vac, blow out or vacuum the debris. Then fill the crack according to label directions. Next spread a liquid sealer over the asphalt. (You should apply sealer every three to four years, according to label directions.) Use a high-quality sealer with a high solid content. Note that the average life of an asphalt driveway is 20 years; if it's older, it may need to be replaced.

▶ Asphalt driveway has holes.

First remove all loose asphalt and other debris. Then scrape around the hole with a trowel until you reach solid material. Fill the hole to within 1 inch of the surface with cold-mix asphalt patch, which comes in 60-pound bags. Tamp the patch with the butt end of a 4x4, then overfill the hole with more patch and tamp it flush with the driveway surface.

▶ Driveway has oil spots.

First soak up any standing oil with an absorbent clay, such as cat litter. Work the clay into the stain with a stiff-bristled brush, sweep clean, then scrub the stain with scouring powder and water. If the stain has penetrated deeply, mix a paste of talc and kerosene and smear it on the stain. When it dries, scrub with scouring powder and water, then rinse.

▶ Concrete driveway has rust and other dark stains on it.

See page 139.

▶ Concrete driveway has hole.

Follow the procedure for cracks wider than ⅛ inch, described on page 144.

Tip If a water heater or other appliance with a pilot light is located in the garage, it should be on a platform that raises the pilot light 18 inches above the floor. Gas vapors from the car gravitate to the floor and, if they come in contact with a flame before dissipating, may explode.

▶ Brick is broken.

If the brick is laid in mortar, use a brick chisel to break up the surrounding mortar joints and the brick. Use a pry bar to remove loose pieces, then chip any loose mortar from the cavity and brush out the particles. Wet the cavity and the new brick. Mix mortar according to label instructions, then line the base and sides of the cavity with mortar. Press the new brick in place, smooth the joints to match the rest, and clean off any excess mortar.

To replace a broken sand-laid brick, remove the broken pieces with a flat pry bar. Then refill the base with sand, dampen it, and tamp it down with the butt end of a 2x4. Use a paving-grade brick for a replacement. Sweep sand in around the crack.

Removing damaged brick

Brick chisel

Pry bar

Setting new brick

Cavity lined with fresh mortar

▶ Bricks are uneven.

If the bricks are laid in sand, remove the tilted brick and relevel the sand or tamp in new sand to bring the base back up to level. Then replace the brick and sweep sand into the surrounding joints. Poor drainage around laid brick, such as from a badly situated downspout, can cause a sand base to wash away. Relocate the downspout or install diversion drainage, if necessary. Bricks can also settle unevenly if they do not have a firm border, such as a concrete curb or 2x4s held in place with stakes. To make a simple but effective border, excavate a shallow trench around the bricks and lay pressure-treated 2x4s on edge against the bricks. Hold the boards in place with 1x2 stakes, 12 to 18 inches long, driven 1 inch below the tops of the boards. Nail the stakes to the boards with 8d HDG common nails.

▶ Bricks have moss.

Scrape off the moss with a trowel, then scrub the bricks with a solution of 1 part household bleach to 3 parts water. Use a stiff-bristled brush and wear eye protection and rubber gloves. Let the solution dry on the bricks. To prevent a return of the moss, make sure the area has proper drainage and that it isn't shaded by tree branches.

▶ Brick has fresh mortar glops.

Avoid smearing them by waiting until the mortar is almost dry, then remove them with a trowel. Mix a solution of 1 part muriatic acid to 15 parts water, making sure to add the acid to the water, not the water to the acid. Wear rubber gloves, eye protection, a long-sleeved shirt, and long pants when working with acid. Wipe the solution on the brick(s), wait three to four minutes, then flush it away with clear water.

▶ Brick has dried mortar on the surface.

Chip off the dried mortar with a trowel or putty knife. Then mix a solution of 1 part muriatic acid solution to 10 parts water; add the acid to the water, not the water to the acid. Wet the brick, then apply the solution with a stiff-bristled brush, scrubbing it until the mortar is gone. Immediately rinse the bricks with clear water. Remember to wear eye protection, a long-sleeved shirt, rubber gloves, and long pants.

▶ Bricks to be laid on sand need to be evenly spaced.

Set the bricks in plastic grids, available in many home centers; they ensure uniform spacing and stabilize the bricks. Set them on a packed sand base, snapping their edges together to create the layout you want. They come in various sizes to accommodate modular bricks, standard bricks, and patio blocks.

▶ Concrete is cracked.

Scrape out and vacuum away any debris. Lightly mist the crack with a garden hose so that it's damp but not dripping wet. If the crack is ⅛ inch wide or less, fill it with either a soupy mixture of 1 part portland cement to 3 parts concrete bonding liquid, or a masonry crack filler that comes in a tube and is applied with a caulking gun. If the crack is wider, use a cold chisel and a hand sledgehammer to chip away any loose material. To keep the patch locked in, chisel the crack so that edges are undercut. Remember to wear eye

Tip *Ordinary bricks, called common bricks, are sufficient for most garden projects, but for patios, walks, and especially driveways, use paver bricks. They are more durable than common bricks.*

Tip *The most common width for brick joints is ⅜ inch. When estimating the number of bricks needed for a project, allow for the joint space between bricks. Also keep in mind that brick sizes are irregular and vary from the nominal brick size (2x4x8 inches) by as much as ⅜ inch.*

protection. Mix 1 part portland cement to 3 parts sand, then add enough concrete bonding liquid to make a stiff mixture. Set aside a small part of the mixture and add more liquid to it until it's soupy. Brush the soupy mixture into the crack, then pack in the stiff mixture and trowel it smooth. Over the next week lightly spray the crack with water twice a day to help cure the patch.

Undercutting the edges of a wide crack

Crack

Undercut edges

▶ *Concrete is spalling.*

Spalling is chipping or breaking up beneath the surface that causes pieces of the surface to lift. Symptoms of spalling include circular or oval depressions. To repair the concrete, use a cold chisel and hand sledgehammer to chip out the damaged area to a depth of 1 inch, undercutting the sides of the hole. Then clean out the hole and patch it as you would a crack (see page 144).

▶ *Corner of concrete slab has settled.*

Concrete slabs list from settling or washing away of the underlying soil. You can build the slab back up to level with a topping compound. It mixes like tile grout and can be built up to a thickness of 1 to 1½ inches.

If the concrete is severely settled, the slab can be "pumped" back up to level by a process known as mudjacking or slabjacking. A contractor first bores holes in the concrete slab, then pumps a cementious grout into the holes. Slowly, the slab begins to rise until it's level again. When the grout sets, it creates a solid support base. Companies that specialize in mudjacking can be found in the Yellow Pages under "Concrete, Repairs" or through a local building inspector or engineer.

Raising a slab by mudjacking

Original top of slab

Settlement

Grout

Raising hole

Raising holes

▶ *Section of concrete walkway needs replacing.*

First use a sledgehammer to break up the damaged section. Remove all debris and gravel to 4 inches below the walkway surface. In freezing climates, make sure there is at least 4 inches of gravel subsurface below the cavity. Dig a shallow trench along each side of the section and install forms flush with the top of the walkway. Then mix and pour new concrete. Strike off the concrete so it's level with the surrounding surface by dragging a 2x4 across the tops of the forms with a back-and-forth motion. Wait one or two hours for it to set up—when all float water has evaporated and the concrete holds its shape. Then finish the surface: Use a wood or magnesium float for a rough surface, a steel trowel for a smooth surface, or a push broom for a textured surface. To help the concrete cure, cover it with a plastic sheet for about a week. Spray the section once a day to keep it moist.

Pouring concrete

Concrete

Form

2x4

Form

Tip *An alternative paving material to bricks is interlocking pavers. Unlike bricks, which are made from clay, pavers are usually made from cast concrete. They have shapes (usually based on a hexagonal design) that allow them to lock into place for more stability than rectangular units.*

Tip *When working with muriatic acid, as with any acid, follow all label cautions carefully. To dilute, always add acid to water; never add water to acid, as it may cause the acid to spatter. Wear rubber gloves, eye protection, and clothing that protects all of your skin.*

▶ Deck needs more seating.

The easiest way to build new deck benches is to attach them to the railing posts. First make sure that the railing posts are solid. Then use three ⅜-inch by 7-inch carriage bolts to attach a pair of 2x12 seat supports to each post. Cut the 2x12 pieces 18 to 20 inches long (longer at a corner; measure first) and taper them for leg clearance. If the posts are spaced farther than 3 feet apart, bolt an intermediate 4x4 support post to the outside of the rim (end) joist, positioned halfway between the railing posts. Attach 1x4s across the tops of the seat supports for the bench seat; space them ¼ inch apart and secure them with 1½-inch HDG decking screws. Trim the front edge with a 1x2, 1x3, or 1x4 attached to the ends of the supports.

Attaching bench supports

4x4 post

18"–20"

15"–17"

2"

2x12

End joist

Attaching seat boards

Edge trim

Longer seat support under corner

▶ Post bottom is rotted and footing is too low.

You'll need to remove the rotten post section and build up the footing. First install a temporary 4x4 post to shore up the deck. Find the beam that is supported by the rotted deck post, then drop a plumb line from this beam to the ground, as close as possible to the footing. Measure the distance between the underside of the beam and the ground; cut the temporary post 1 inch shorter than this distance. Place this temporary post in position, resting it on a scrap of 2x8. Toenail its top to the underside of the beam; then, using a sledgehammer, drive the post vertical. It should be plumb. Toenail its bottom to the 2x8 scrap.

Next mark a level line on the rotted post immediately above the rotted section. Cut on the line with a handsaw or circular saw. Drive several concrete nails into the top of the footing, spaced 3 inches apart. Build a form around the footing high enough to bring the top of the footing up to the bottom of the dangling post, then nail a post anchor to the bottom of the post. Coat the old concrete with a liquid concrete bonding agent, then pour new concrete in the form. Use a trowel to slope the top of the new concrete slightly away from the post. Let the concrete cure for a week before removing the shoring and forms.

▶ Deck boards are sagging or bouncy.

The joists are spaced too far apart. Add additional joists, spaced halfway between the existing ones. Toenail them in place with 12d HDG common nails where they rest on a beam; use galvanized joist-hanger brackets to support the ends where they abut a header.

▶ Pier is tipping or sliding away.

Shore up the deck with temporary posts (see left). Remove the existing post and pier, then drop a plumb line to locate the center of the new pier location, which will most likely be where the old pier was. Dig a hole for a new pier footing, 18 inches square and 12 to 24 inches deep (or below the frost line, depending on the soil conditions and local building code). Fill the hole with concrete up to ground level, then insert four 1-foot-long pieces of rebar 6 inches into the concrete. When the concrete dries, on top of the footing and around the rebar build a pier form that's 6 inches high and 12 inches square. Fill the form with concrete, sloping the top slightly to shed water. When the concrete starts to stiffen, embed a galvanized post-anchor bracket in it, located directly under the plumb line. Allow two to five days for the concrete to cure; then install a new post, soaking the bottom with preservative first. Stay off the deck until the repair is complete.

▶ Deck fasteners rust or stain the deck.

When building or repairing outdoor structures, always use corrosion-resistant fasteners. For nails, avoid electrogalvanized (EG) and "bright" nails; hot-dipped galvanized (HDG), aluminum, and stainless steel are the best choices. Galvanized nails are the most economical, but the coating on the head can sometimes chip off when hit with a hammer. Recoat chipped heads with a dab of galvanized paint. Screws are available in HDG or stainless steel. Stainless steel screws are much more

Tip *Keep your deck clean. Sweep (even vacuum) it regularly to eliminate dust and grit that can get ground into the finish, causing it to break down faster and destroying the coating that protects the wood.*

Tip *When applying a stain or sealer to a deck, avoid spraying it on. Brush it instead, to ensure better penetration and buildup for longer-lasting results.*

expensive than HDG, but they are more durable and weather-resistant. Screws are more reliable than nails, but take more time to install because pilot holes must be drilled at the board ends to prevent splitting. Stainless steel nailing strips and nailing clips are also available for attaching deck boards. Both types are attached to the deck before the deck boards are placed. If you can't find them in a local hardware store or home center, ask a local deck-building professional for the name of a supplier. Bolts, brackets, hangers, and other framing devices all should be galvanized.

▶ Gaps appear between pieces of wood as deck ages.

It's normal for boards to shrink across their width, creating gaps. For most deck joints this is not a structural problem, but it may be unsightly and, in the case of decking, dangerous for people wearing high-heeled shoes. The only solution to this problem is to pull up the boards and reinstall them closer together. Wood that was not dried sufficiently can also shrink lengthwise. Gaps most often open up at the ends of very long deck boards; sometimes they are wide enough that the boards creep off the joists. To close a gap, remove the long deck board and replace it with two shorter boards.

▶ Parts of the deck are rotting.

Trapped moisture will cause a deck to rot. Probe any suspicious areas with an ice pick or awl. The best remedy is to replace the rotted board, especially if it's load-bearing. To replace the ledger board, post, or joist you will have to shore up the deck temporarily (see opposite page). A

new ledger board should have a ¾-inch to 1½-inch space behind it to allow air to circulate between it and the house siding. Replace rotted sections of decking by removing the entire board or cutting out the rotted section. Any individual board should span at least 2 joist bays. Cut along the inside face of joists. To support the new piece, attach pressure-treated nailers to the faces of the joists with 3-inch HDG nails, then cut and nail the new decking in place. At nonstructural points, such as the cantilevered (overhanging) joist ends, solidify the rotted area with an epoxy-based wood-hardening compound. Depending on the brand, it can be brushed on, injected into ⅛-inch-diameter holes bored in the rotted area, or formed as a putty that will rebuild a missing piece. The compound is expensive and appropriate only for small areas. See also page 100.

▶ Clear wood finish is damaged by sunlight.

Most clear finishes allow UV (ultraviolet) rays from the sun to pass through and damage the wood. Film-forming finishes such as polyurethane eventually lose their bond to the wood, become brittle, crack, and peel. To remove them, scraping and sanding is the solution. (Rent a floor sander to do the deck surface.) A better finish for a deck is a penetrating clear finish that has a built-in UV blocker and mildewcide. For the best penetration, apply it with a bristle brush. To maintain the natural color of the wood, expect to apply the finish every year or two.

▶ Deck needs cleaning.

A high-pressure washer with an output of 750 to 1,000 psi can clean a deck with plain water. A washer with this capacity can be rented or purchased and is also handy for other chores, such as cleaning siding, patios, and walkways, and washing the car. Another way to scrub a deck is to rent an electric floor cleaner/polisher fitted with stiff-bristled brushes. Use a deck-cleaning solution and follow label directions. Make sure that the polisher is plugged into a GFCI-protected receptacle.

▶ Deck has mildew.

Scrub the deck with a solution of 1 part bleach to 3 parts water; a long-handled scrub brush is helpful for working the solution into the wood. Let the solution dry on the deck surface. For stubborn stains, apply a solution of 1 pound oxalic acid mixed with 1 gallon of water. To prevent further mildew growth, make sure the protective coating that you apply to the deck, such as a clear water repellent or semitransparent or opaque stain, contains a mildewcide. Mildewcide additives are also sold in paint stores. Mildew has a tendency to grow in heavily shaded areas, so consider trimming overhanging branches or bushes.

▶ Nails are popping up from deck boards.

Carefully remove the old nails. Replace them with 3-inch HDG decking screws, or drive new 16d HDG nails in the original holes, but at a new angle to avoid the old holes in the joists below.

Tip   *Whenever building an outdoor structure, such as a deck or overhead, observe these tips to ensure long-lasting results: (1) Use pressure-treated lumber or heart lumber of a durable species such as redwood, cedar, or cypress. (2) Use corrosion-resistant fasteners, such as HDG, stainless steel, or aluminum. (3) Apply preservative to the cut ends of boards. (4) Do not nail boards together lengthwise, as this creates a moisture trap—space members at least ½ inch apart to allow air circulation. (5) Cut the tops of vertical members at an angle to facilitate water runoff, or cover them with horizontal boards. (6) Drill pilot holes for nails at the ends of boards to prevent splitting. (7) Stagger nails along the grain of the wood to keep it from splitting.*

▶ Gate won't shut.

First check the latch. Spray silicone lubricant on all moving parts that don't operate smoothly. Next make sure that the strike and latch are properly aligned; if they aren't, re-position them. A sagging gate that won't close should be resquared with a turnbuckle.

Adjusting a turnbuckle

Nail
Turnbuckle

▶ Fence is sagging or falling.

First straighten and brace the fence with 2x4s and stakes. Then, if the sagging post is set in soil, install sister posts. Use a pressure-treated 2x4 half as long as the fence post, with one end bevel-cut. Position it next to the post with the bevel end down, facing out. Drive the post halfway into the ground with a sledgehammer. Leaving 18 inches exposed, bevel-cut the top of the post. Repeat this procedure on the other side of the post. Then bore holes through all three posts

and join them with HDG carriage bolts. Remove the bracing. If the fence posts are set in concrete, drive pressure-treated shims into the gaps between the post base and the concrete. Replace broken concrete footings.

Bracing the fence

Brace

Stake

Installing a sister post

Sledgehammer

Bevel

Pressure-treated 2x4

▶ Post is rotted.

First support the adjacent fence sections and detach them from the rotted post by pulling or cutting the nails. If the rotted area is within 3 feet of the ground, replace the post. If the rotted area is 3 feet or more aboveground, cut away the rotted section. Splice a new post to the remaining section of post with a lap joint. On the remainder of the post, cut away a vertical half for 2 feet. On the new post, remove half of the bottom 2 feet. Angle the ends of the cuts downward to repel water. Mate the pieces together, drill holes, and bolt them with three $\frac{3}{8}$-inch by 4-inch carriage bolts.

Splicing a post

New post

Carriage bolts

Old post

Tip Be sure to verify the property line location before building a new fence. Property lines are defined on a survey that should be attached to the deed for the property. If you can't find the deed, check with the local county clerk's office. To determine exactly where the property line is located, hire a surveyor to stake out the property lines.

Tip When buying lumber for fences, choose pressure-treated lumber or heart grades of a durable species for posts and other fence members that will be in contact with the ground. Avoid lumber with sapwood (nonheart grades of lumber) for such members. Use the lesser grades with sapwood for nonstructural parts of the fence, such as the infill panels.

▶ New posts might lean.

Before setting the post and filling the hole with concrete, drive three 3-foot lengths of pipe horizontally into the sides of the hole, leaving a few inches protruding into the hole. Space the pipes evenly and drive them in at a slightly downward angle. Then set the post in place and pour the concrete.

Anchoring the concrete footing

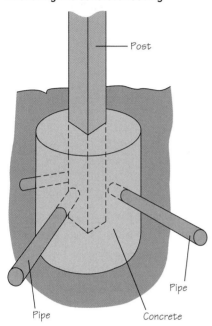

Post

Pipe

Pipe

Concrete

▶ New posts must be perfectly plumb.

To get posts plumb (vertical), use a regular level and alternately check all sides as you secure the post in its final position. Or else use a special post level—the most common type available consists of a pair of level vials mounted on a right-angle bracket, sometimes with an elastic retaining strap. It's sold in home centers and hardware stores, and is often included in packaged deck-building tools.

▶ Tops of fence posts need to be shaped with points.

Use a handheld circular saw and a 2x4 collar that fits snugly around the fence post. Slip the collar over the top of the post and rest it on a C-clamp. Then set the saw blade at 45 degrees. Holding it vertically and resting on the collar, cut each side of the post.

Sawing pointed fence post

Blade set at 45° angle

2x4 collar

▶ Masonry retaining wall has cracks.

This is an indication that the wall doesn't have proper drainage. First make sure that the weep holes at the base of the wall are draining properly. Use a long-handled screwdriver or bent coat hanger to clean out any clogging debris. If the wall does not have weep holes, add a drainage system behind it: Dig a trench along the back of the wall, then lay in perforated PVC pipe bedded in drain rock. Cover the pipe with filter fabric and ¾-inch crushed stone.

▶ Masonry retaining wall is leaning or falling over.

This is most often caused by the force of shifting soil pressing against the back of the wall. It will have to be rebuilt. Masonry supply yards now sell retaining-wall block that solves the problem. These blocks interlock to form a solid, mortar-free wall that sets back automatically. A vertical wall of stone, brick, or block should have drain rock or filter fabric placed between it and the soil behind it, with weep holes or drainage lines installed behind the wall along the base.

Providing proper drainage

Topsoil

¾" crushed stone

Filter fabric

Weep hole

Footing

Drainage pipe

Drain rock

Tip   Garden walls may be made from brick, stone, wood timbers, concrete, concrete block, or adobe. Except for those made of loose-laid stone or wood, all garden walls should be supported by a continuous concrete footing. Most walls lower than 3 feet are within the homeowner's ability to build, so long as there is someone to help with handling the materials.

Tip   When mixing mortar for a stone wall, make it richer than the mortar for a brick wall. Mix 3 parts sand to 1 part portland cement, with ½ part fireclay added for better consistency. The mortar should not contain lime, which might stain the stones, and it should be dry enough that it balls up in your hand but not so dry that it crumbles.

▶ Pool filter motor won't run.

First make sure that the motor is plugged in and the timer is operating and set properly. Also check the electrical panel to ensure that the circuit breaker isn't tripped. If neither is the problem, check the filter to see if it is clogged with debris. If the motor still doesn't run, consult a pool service or repair specialist.

▶ Automatic pool sweep won't run.

Pool sweeps that run on the outflow of the circulation pump or a booster pump, such as a floating-head sweep, an in-floor hose jet sweep, or a vacuum-head roving sweep, won't run properly if the outflow pressure is down. First see if the filter is clogged. If that's not the case, have your filtration and circulation system checked by a professional pool mechanic.

Vacuum sweeps run on suction, either through the filtration pump and skimmer basket or from a self-contained motor. Check the skimmer basket and filter to make sure they're clean. On a motor-driven robot sweep, the power cord should be plugged into a GFCI-protected receptacle; also check the breaker switch—it should be in the *On* position.

▶ Pool sweep is sluggish and follows same pattern.

See above. Also consult the manufacturer's operating manual for instructions on adjusting the drive mechanism, which usually consists of rotating gears or adjusting control knobs to vary the cycles that determine changes of direction.

▶ Bubbles or air pockets appear in pool pump strainer.

Most likely, a gasket in the circulation pump is leaking. Have a professional pool mechanic pressure-test the system to locate and replace it. Air may also be entering through a leak or break in the piping, which is usually underground. Locating and repairing such a leak is very difficult. Consult a professional leak-detection service.

▶ Pool water is murky.

Failure of the filtration system or irregular maintenance can cause this problem. If the filter tank pressure reading is higher than normal, or if there is less water circulating through the system, the filter needs to be cleaned or replaced. Water will also become murky because of a chemical imbalance, sometimes caused by acid rain. Check the water with a test kit and adjust it accordingly by adding the proper chemicals.

▶ Brown or black spots appear on pool sides or bottom.

Algae or iron stains will cause these spots. Increase the chlorine in the water to remove them, monitoring the levels carefully for safe concentrations. Scrub algae spots with a stainless steel brush, then spot-treat immediately with an algaecide specified for swimming pools to prevent dislodged spores from attaching to the pool side or bottom.

▶ Water level of in-ground pool goes down rapidly.

A cement or gunite pool can leak through cracks caused by slight shifts in the surrounding soil. If the crack is thin, lower the water level to below the crack, then fill the crack with plaster, caulk, or epoxy putty. Large cracks may indicate a major soil shift or a drainage problem and should be diagnosed and corrected by a pool professional.

Tears of less than 3 inches or punctures in a vinyl-lined pool can be repaired with a kit from the pool manufacturer. Some kits allow you to work underwater, so check before you drain the pool. Large tears may be difficult to fix properly. Call a pool professional for help.

Another cause of rapid water loss is leaks in the circulation system. Ask a pool professional to perform a pressure check on the system. There are also companies that specialize in locating leaks in underground pipes.

▶ Pool is expensive to maintain.

First make sure you regularly filter, backwash, and chemically balance the pool, according to the maintenance instructions. Keep the pool covered when it's not in use; a solar cover cuts down substantially on heating costs as well as evaporation. A wind barrier may help somewhat as well. You can also discourage splashing caused by water fights and diving. Maintain the pool at 78° F, which, according to the National Spa and Pool Institute and the American Red Cross, is the most healthful temperature. An increase in temperature by 1 degree can add 10 percent to your fuel costs. Also make sure you have an accurate thermometer to check it. On days

Tip *If you live in an area where weather doesn't allow you to use and maintain your pool all year, winterize your pool to make it easier to start up in the spring. Begin by cleaning out leaves and debris, scrubbing the pool walls and bottom, and vacuuming the pool. Then add winterizing chemicals, according to label directions (most suggest running the filter for 24 hours). If you live in a cold climate where temperatures drop below freezing for extended periods, lower the water level so ice has room to expand. Completely drain the pump, filter, heater, exposed pipes, and other equipment by blowing out the water; add antifreeze specified for swimming pools where any water may remain.*

when you aren't using the pool, lower the thermostat by 10 degrees.

You can save money on electricity by operating the filter during off-peak hours and only as long as necessary. Usually, electric rates are cheapest between 6:00 a.m. and noon. To determine the optimum run time for the filter, lessen the duration it runs in half-hour increments until the clarity and chemical balance of the water begin to deteriorate. Then increase the run time until the water normalizes. Switch the automatic run cycle to manual during periods of high use.

To save on chemicals, add disinfectant during the evening; or consider adding an ionizer or ozone generator, each of which can pay for itself in just a few years. Also trim back excess foliage around the pool to minimize debris and organic materials that require stabilizing.

▶ *Pool cover is not childproof.*

Use a safety cover that passes ASTM (American Society for Testing and Materials) standards and is labeled accordingly. It will be strong enough to walk on. Safety covers, which are different from pool covers intended only for retaining heat, are heavy plastic and run on a motorized system with rails, or are manual systems that attach to concrete-embedded anchors with heavy springs. Consult local codes for specific requirements.

▶ *Acrylic or Centrex® (Rovel®) spa surface is scratched, nicked, or damaged.*

Both of these types of surfaces are made from a single sheet of plastic. Extremely durable, they rarely need repair. However, if they do, check the owner's manual that came with the spa or contact the manufacturer for a touch-up kit made specifically for your spa.

▶ *Pool filter hasn't been cleaned for a year.*

Procedures for cleaning a filter vary, depending on its type. A diatomaceous earth (DE) filter will have to be backwashed, the filter elements cleaned with an acid wash, and the spent DE replaced. A sand filter should be backwashed and the sand replenished. Make sure you use the type of sand recommended by the filter manufacturer. You may be able to reuse a cartridge filter; soak it in an appropriate filter-cleaning solution and clean the filter housing. If it still doesn't work adequately, replace the filter.

Identifying pool filters

Cartridge type

Sand type

Diatomaceous earth type

▶ *Gelcoat or fiberglass spa surface is scratched, nicked, or damaged.*

Small blemishes, such as a surface chip, gouge, or crack, you can probably fix yourself. Get a repair kit from a large paint-supply store, boat shop, or the spa manufacturer; it should include some gelcoat that closely matches the color of your spa, and a catalyst. Follow directions carefully, which should include the precise ratio of gelcoat to catalyst as well as the acceptable air temperature and humidity in which to work. You'll also need a razor blade, squeegee, sanding block, sandpaper, wax paper, and polishing compound. If the damage exceeds the gelcoat surface and affects the fiberglass backing, also get some strands of fiberglass. If you prefer to have the repair done by a professional, contact a spa-shell refinisher or boat repair firm.

▶ *Spa pump doesn't run.*

Inspect the electrical panel and switches. Make sure the switch is in the *On* position. If it is, see if the water-pump circuit breaker has tripped; if so, reset it. If it trips again, there is probably a major problem somewhere in that circuit. Don't jam a circuit breaker in the *On* position or bypass it with a pigtail. Deaden the circuit and check all connections and wires for continuity, or call a licensed electrician.

▶ *Spa heater doesn't work.*

Check the shutoff valve and pilot light (for a gas heater); someone may have turned it off by mistake. If this isn't the problem, check for any loose or disconnected electrical wires leading to a thermostat

---

Tip *Local codes have specific provisions for security fences to prevent toddlers from wandering into the pool area. Typically, the fence should be a minimum of 48 inches high, have no horizontal bars that facilitate climbing, and surround the pool on all sides that don't adjoin the house. The gate should be self-closing and self-latching. If you have a patio door that opens directly onto the pool area, install a latch high on the door frame, and consider installing a door alarm.*

or control panel. Or call a licensed electrician to troubleshoot the problem.

▶ Spa lacks rigid cover.

You can purchase a rigid spa cover that provides insulation, prevents water and chemical evaporation, keeps small children and pets from falling in, and protects outdoor spas from dirt and debris. Some of the better rigid covers can be locked in place, which provides peace of mind since the spa is childproof when the cover is installed. If well maintained, a rigid cover will last a long time. It must be cleaned inside and out; and if it is made of a hard surface like Centrex® thermoplastic, it must be waxed periodically. If you have just added chemicals to the spa, wait about 30 minutes to an hour before installing the cover to allow some of the vapors to dissipate; if the cover is installed too soon, the inner surface may start to deteriorate.

▶ Spa water level goes down rapidly.

The cause may be a leak in an underground pipe or fitting. Call a leak-detection service, which can trace a water leak without disturbing the ground surface—even under concrete, asphalt, and cement slabs—with its sonar system and ultrasound field tester.

Once the leak is detected, the company will drain the spa and apply a sealant in a flow-coating process that seeks out the leak and seals it off. When the sealant has cured, the spa can be refilled with water.

▶ Backyard pond lacks a circulation system.

Before you build the pond, get a pool skimmer and install it on the inside of a plastic garbage can by cutting a square hole in the can and bolting the skimmer face plate around the opening. Then bury the can next to the pond deep enough that the water level of the pond is about two-thirds of the way up the skimmer opening. Build the pond, draping the liner over the can. Unbolt the skimmer face plate. Insert the liner so that it's sandwiched between the gasket and the can surface. Reattach the skimmer face plate and cut out the liner from the face plate opening. Install a grounded electrical plug near the can. Finally, lower a submersible pump into the can with a return-water line running back to the other end of the pond.

Installing a pond filter

Pool skimmer unit
Decorative lid
Water level
Face plate
Return line to pond
Plastic pond liner
Gasket
Debris basket
Pump
Garbage can

▶ Garden pond has too much algae.

Algae grows where there is abundant sunlight and no competition for nutrients. These conditions are common in early spring, before the water warms up. With warmer weather, however, other plants get established and create shade, stifling algae growth and causing the algae to die and sink to the bottom. If excessive algae persist into the summer, experiment with a balance of surface plants, submerged plants, marginal plants, and fish to keep algae under control. For temporary control use an algaecide. Read labels carefully and choose an algaecide suitable for your pond. Some algaecides are safe for fish but not plants; others are safe for plants but not fish.

▶ Fishpond freezes over.

If a garden pond containing fish is covered by ice for more than a few days, the fish may suffocate. For a quick, emergency fix, clear a breathing hole by boiling water in a pot and setting the pot on the ice until it melts through. Do not try to bash a hole; shock waves may kill the fish.

In mildly cold regions a submerged circulating pump may keep the surface ice-free. The intake port should be close to the bottom, and the discharge outlet 2 to 3 inches below the surface. Another technique for preventing ice is to cover one end of the pond with clear plastic sheeting stretched over a wood frame a few inches above the water.

Where winters are more severe, install a thermostatically controlled deicer or remove fish from the pond and keep them indoors in cool, well-aerated water treated to remove chlorine compounds.

Tip *If you have excess pool chemicals you want to dispose of, there may be local agencies or individuals that could use them. Contact local water treatment or waste treatment plants (for excess chlorine), public swimming pools, apartment or condominium associations, pool services, or pool installers to see if they could use your leftovers.*

Most home repair projects start at a desk rather than a workbench. You have to do your homework—studying instructions, understanding terms, calculating figures, and planning the work. In this section, you'll find the glossary, tables, and background data to help get your project done right.

► *Building Your Tool Kit*

	Basic Kit	Intermediate Kit	Advanced Kit
All-purpose Hand Tools			
Storage	Tool box (19") Tool apron	Bigger tool box (32") Tool belt	Very big tool box Portable workbench
Layout	Tape measure (25') Combination square Torpedo level Pencils	Steel framing square 24" or 30" level Plumb bob Chalk line and chalk Bevel gauge Awl	100' steel tape measure 6'6" level Compass dividers (6") Water level Stair layout buttons
Cutting	Utility knife and blades Compact crosscut saw Hacksaw and blades	Wallboard saw Coping saw Mini hacksaw Miter box	Doweling jig Side cutters
Shaping	Rasping plane Wood chisels (½", 1", 1½")	Block plane Whetstone and oil Aviation snips	Jack plane Hatchet Cold chisels Brick chisel
Hammering & Prying	Hammer, curved claw (16 oz) Nail sets (½2", ³₃2") Flat pry bar	Framing hammer (20 oz) Nail puller (cat's paw) Crowbar 3-lb maul	10-lb sledgehammer Chipping hammer Rubber mallet
Fastening	Screwdrivers, standard Screwdrivers, Phillips Needle nose pliers (6") Channel lock pliers (1½" jaw) Adjustable wrenches (5", 8") Allen wrench set Adjustable clamps (2)	Socket wrench set Locking pliers (5", 10") Staple gun Nut drivers (³₁6"–½") Center punch	Wrenches, open-end/box Deep sockets for socket wrench Staple hammer Pipe clamps Butt marker Self-centering screw punch or Vix bit
Smoothing & Sealing	Sandpaper (assorted) Four-in-hand file Putty knife (1¼") Taping knife (5" or 6") Caulking gun	Files (flat, round, triangular) Wire brushes (steel, brass) Taping knives (12", 24")	Pole sander Cement trowels Brick trowel
Power Tools	⅜" drill and twist drill set and spade bits (¼"–1½") and countersink pilot bits Jigsaw and blades Extension cord (50' of No. 14 wire)	Circular saw and 3 blades: 20-tooth carbide tip 40-tooth carbide tip metal-cutting Cordless drill and screwdriver bits Pad sander Belt sander 3-pronged plug adapter Extension cord (50' of No. 12 wire)	Router 10" table saw Reciprocating saw Power miter box Power screw gun Orbital sander ½" drill ¾" hammer drill Bench grinder Shop vacuum
Safety Gear	Eye protection Dust mask Latex gloves Flashlight Voltage tester (neon)	Respirator mask Knee pads Ear protection Hard hat Work gloves	First-aid kit (separate from home kit) Portable lights

	Basic Kit	Intermediate Kit	Advanced Kit
Basic Supplies & Fasteners	White PVA glue Electrical tape Masking tape Spackling compound Nails, finishing (3d, 4d, 6d, 8d) Nails, common (8d, 16d) Nails, HDG box (4d, 6d) Brads (assorted) Screws, wallboard (1¼", 2", 3") Screws, sheet-metal (⅜–1") Screws, wood (1" × #6, 1¼" × #8, 1¼" × #12)	Carpenter's wood glue Duct tape Steel wool Graphite powder Silicone lubricant Wire, steel (2–3 sizes)	Nails (roofing, wallboard, duplex, concrete) Screws (full assortment) Hollow-wall fasteners Stove bolts (assorted) Lag screws (assorted) Machine bolts (assorted)
Painting Tools	2" cut-in brush 3" brush Roller and covers Roller tray Extension handle Drop cloths	1½" sash brush Brush spinner Pull scraper	HVLP (high-volume, low-pressure) sprayer
Plumbing Tools	Plunger Drain auger Pipe joint tape Pipe joint compound Plumber's putty Pipe wrenches (12", 14") Pipe solvent cement	Closet auger Basin wrench Tubing cutter Propane or MAPP gas torch Lead-free solder Flux and brush Sand cloth (emery cloth)	Tubing bender Seat wrench Seat dressing tool Spud wrench Bonnet wrench Strainer wrench
Electrical Tools	Voltage tester, neon (2) Multipurpose tool Continuity tester	Circuit analyzer Wire stripper Cable stripper Volt-ohmmeter Very small screwdriver Electrician's pliers	Fish tape Conduit bender Soldering gun
Tile Tools	Notched adhesive trowel Rod saw Rubber float	Tile nippers Snap cutter Rubbing stone	Wet saw

▶ *Tips for Buying Tools*

- Except for a few basic tools, don't buy a tool until you need it.

- Assume that you'll have to buy a tool each time you do a project (if you don't need to, it will seem like a bonus).

- Buy the highest quality tool you can afford.

- Consider used tools and garage sales—many older tools are of high quality.

- Keep a tools "wish list" in your wallet or purse (and give copies to close friends).

- Keep tools sharp. Have saws, blades, and chisels sharpened regularly.

- Obtain extra tools for helpers, especially a tape measure, utility knife, hammer, pry bar, putty knife, screwdrivers, and nail sets.

▶ Nominal Lumber Sizes and Their Actual Equivalents (in inches)

Nominal	Actual	Nominal	Actual	Nominal	Actual
1 × 2	¾ × 1½	1 × 10	¾ × 9¼	2 × 6	1½ × 5½
1 × 3	¾ × 2½	1 × 12	¾ × 11¼	2 × 8	1½ × 7¼
1 × 4	¾ × 3½	2 × 2	1½ × 1½	2 × 10	1½ × 9¼
1 × 6	¾ × 5½	2 × 3	1½ × 2½	2 × 12	1½ × 11¼
1 × 8	¾ × 7¼	2 × 4	1½ × 3½	4 × 4	3½ × 3½

▶ Header Sizes

Most codes do not have tables for sizing headers over doors and windows, but have only formulas for calculating beam sizes. However, the following sizes are generally accepted rules of thumb for headers in various situations.

Location	Size of Header (4 × or built-up 2 ×)	Maximum Span
Single Story or Top Story	4 × 4	4'
	4 × 6	6'
	4 × 8	8'
	4 × 10	10'
	4 × 12	12'
Lower Floor, With Floor Above	4 × 4	3'
	4 × 6	4'
	4 × 8	7'
	4 × 10	8'
	4 × 12	9'

Note: Increase sizes where accumulated loads concentrate on a header.

▶ Insulation Thicknesses

To achieve the listed R-value for a particular type of insulation material, use the thickness specified.

Insulation	R-11	R-19	R-22	R-30	R-38
Fiberglass batts/blankets	3½"	6"	6½"	10"	12½"
Rock wool batts/blankets	3"	5½"	6"	9"	10½"
Fiberglass loose fill	5"	8½"	10"	13½"	17½"
Rock wool loose fill	4"	6½"	7½"	10½"	13½"
Cellulose loose fill	3"	5"	6"	8"	10½"

▶ Lumber Shrinkage

The following lumber sizes (in inches) are established by the American Lumber Standards Committee.

Nominal	Dry	Green
1	¾	2⁵⁄₃₂
2	1½	1⁹⁄₁₆
4	3½	3⁹⁄₁₆
6	5½	5⅝
8	7¼	7½
10	9¼	9½

▶ Plywood Veneer Grades

The following grades are used in descending order of quality:

N. Smooth surface, suitable for natural finishes. Made of select grade wood. Free of open defects.

A. Smooth surface. Natural finish can be used if you are not too demanding.

B. Solid surface with circular repair plugs, shims, and tight knots. Some minor splits are permitted.

C Plugged. Splits cannot be more than ⅛ inch. Some repair and broken grain permitted.

C. Tight knots up to 1½ inches are allowed. Repairs, discoloration, limited splits, sanding defects, and stitching (piecing) are permissible if they do not impair the strength.

D. Knots and knotholes up to 3 inches wide are allowed. Splits and stitching are permitted.

▶ Types of Insulation

Form	R-Value per Inch	Materials	Principal Use	Installation Method	Comments
Blankets or Batts	3.7 3.3	Rock wool Glass fiber	Walls Floors Ceilings Attics Roofs	Fitted between wood-frame studs, joists, and beams	Most common form do-it-your-selfers use; suited for standard stud and joist spacing without obstructions; batts easier to handle than blankets
Loose or Blown Fill	2.9 2.2 3.6 2.4 2.7	Rock wool Glass fiber Cellulose fiber Vermiculite Perlite	Floors Walls Hard-to-reach places Finished areas	Poured between joists or blown into place	Easy to use in irregularly shaped areas; blown fill, the only option for finished areas, should be installed by a professional
Rigid Panels	4.0 5.0 7.4 4.5	Molded polystyrene Extruded polystyrene Isocyanurate board Fiberglass board	Unfinished walls Basement masonry walls Exterior surfaces	Cut to fit and secured in place; must be covered with finish material for fire safety	High insulating value for relatively little thickness; all but fiberglass are highly flammable

▶ Recommended Exposures of Wood Roof Shingles

Shingle Size	3 in 12 Roof	4 in 12 or Steeper Roofs
16"	3¼"	5"
18"	4½"	5½"
24"	5¾"	7½"

▶ Maximum Weather Exposure for Wood Singles and Shakes on Walls

Shingle Length	Single Course	Double Course
16"	7½"	12"
18"	8½"	14"
24"	11½"	16"

▶ Recommended Exposure of Roof Shakes

Shake Length	Roof Slope	
	Less Than 6 in 12	6 in 12 or More
18"	5½"	7½"
24"	7½"	10"

▶ Proportions for 1 Cubic Yard of Concrete (in pounds)

Type of Project	Maximum Size of Aggregate	Cement	Sand	Gravel	Total Aggregate	Water	Air Entrainment
Foundations and Footings	⅜"	565	1,630	1,190	2,820	285	–
	¾"	520	1,310	1,730	3,040	260	–
	1"	490	1,260	1,870	3,130	245	–
Slabs, Patios, and Foundations in Cold Climates	⅜"	580	1,570	1,190	2,760	290	7%
	¾"	580	1,250	1,730	2,980	290	6%
	1"	535	1,170	1,870	3,040	270	6%

Note: 1 sack of cement equals 94 pounds. Water weighs 8 pounds per gallon.

▶ Mixing Your Own Concrete

If you need only a small quantity of concrete—1 yard or less—mix it by hand or in a small cement mixer. To make a 1-cubic-foot batch, divide each of the figures in the proportions chart by 27 (there are 27 cubic feet in 1 cubic yard). For instance, to make 1 cubic foot, the first row of ingredients would become: 22 pounds of cement, 105 pounds of aggregate, and 11 pounds of water. If you need more than 1 cubic foot, weigh the first batch of ingredients in buckets on a bathroom scale. Use a separate container for each ingredient, marking on the side of the container how high it needs to be filled to reach the desired weight. Fill the buckets to the same marks for the remaining batches.

Mix the dry ingredients together first, then add the water. If you are using a machine, have it mix the entire batch for at least three minutes. When you are through with the mixer, clean it out by throwing one or two shovelfuls of gravel and some water in it. Let them scour the inside of the mixer for a while, and then dump them.

▶ Ordering Ready-Mixed Concrete

If you need more than 1 yard, or you want air entrainment in the mix, have the concrete delivered by a ready-mix company. Specify the following when ordering:

Cement Content. Use the proportions chart to calculate the number of sacks of cement you will need in each cubic yard.

Aggregate Size. For most jobs ¾-inch aggregate is suitable, but if you are having the concrete pumped by a small pumper truck that has only a 3-inch hose, you will need to specify ⅜-inch aggregate.

Water/Cement Ratio. Specify .5 or ask for the supplier's recommendation.

Slump. This term is used to describe the consistency of fresh concrete. It refers to the number of inches a 12-inch-high tower of concrete slumps when it is fresh. A 1-inch slump is a very stiff mix, a 10-inch slump very soupy. For residential projects 4 inches is average.

Air Entrainment. Air entrainment is an additive that enhances the durability of concrete in cold climates. Consult the proportions chart for the percentage to be added.

Strength. You may be asked to specify the strength or load-bearing capacity of your concrete. Most residential needs vary from a minimum strength of 2,000 psi to more than 4,000 psi. Be aware that the proper handling and curing of the concrete, not just the correct proportions, are needed to attain the specified strength.

In addition to the per-yard delivery charge, be aware of other fees you may have to pay. A short-load charge is an additional fee for small orders (generally less than 4 yards). A stand-by charge is also customary; this is for any additional time the truck must remain at your site after the allotted per-yard time limit expires (usually about five minutes per yard). The amount can skyrocket if you are not prepared when the truck arrives.

If the truck cannot get close to your forms (for instance, a patio in a backyard), arrange for a pumper truck to arrive shortly before the concrete. You can rent one from the ready-mix supplier or an independent pumping company. Even if you think the concrete truck might reach your forms by backing into the driveway, it is better to have the concrete pumped than to take a chance on having to pay for a broken sidewalk.

► Nail Lengths

Size	Length
2d	1"
3d	1¼"
4d	1½"
6d	2"
8d	2½"
10d	3"
12d	3¼"
16d	3½"
20d	3¾"
30d	4½"
40d	5"
60d	6"

► Nail Finishes

Aluminum. Aluminum throughout.
Blued. Steel, heated to high temperature for light rustproofing.
Bright. Plain steel; rusts.
CC. Cement-coated steel, for light rustproofing.
EG (electrogalvanized). Steel, coated with zinc by electrolysis.
HDG (hot-dipped galvanized). Steel, coated with zinc by dipping.
Stainless Steel. Rustproof steel.
VC. Vinyl-coated steel; vinyl reduces friction and provides adhesion; rusts.

► Nail Uses

Box. Siding; exterior trim; fencing; wood shingles.
Brad. Molding; paneling.
Casing. Molding, where head is not countersunk.
Common. Framing; general construction.
Concrete. Concrete; brick; stucco.
Duplex. Temporary forms and bracing.
Finishing. Trim; cabinetwork.
Paneling. ¼" sheet paneling.
Ringed Shank. Flooring; subflooring.
Roofing. Composition shingles; building paper.
Sinker. Framing; general construction.
Spiral Shank, Aluminum. Redwood and cedar siding.
Spiral Shank, HDG. Decks; fences.
Wallboard. Wallboard.

► Nailing Schedule for Residential Construction

Codes specify the size, number, and placement of nails for framing connections. This table cites specifications typical of most codes. However, check with local officials to be sure these figures are in compliance with applicable codes.

Connection	Number and Size of Common Nails	How Nailed
Joist to sill or girder	3 8d	Toenailed
Built-up girders and beams of 3 members	20d 32" OC at top and bottom, staggered	Facenailed
Bridging to joist, each end	2 8d	Toenailed
Ledger strip (ribbon) at each joist	3 16d	Facenailed
1 × 6 subfloor, to each joist	2 8d	Facenailed
Wider than 1 × 6 subfloor	3 8d	Facenailed
2" subfloor to joist or girder	2 16d	Facenailed
Soleplate to joist or blocking	16d at 16" OC	Facenailed
Soleplate to stud	2 16d	End nailed
	4 8d	Toenailed
Top plate to stud	2 16d	End nailed
Doubled studs	16d at 16" OC	Facenailed
Built-up corner studs	16d at 24" OC	Facenailed
Doubled top plates	16d at 16" OC	Facenailed
Top plates, laps, and intersections	2 16d	Facenailed
Continuous header, 2 pieces	16d at 16" OC along each edge	Facenailed
Continuous header to stud	4 8d	Toenailed
Ceiling joists to plate	3 8d	Toenailed
Ceiling joists, laps over partitions	3 16d	Facenailed
Ceiling joists to parallel rafters	3 16d	Facenailed
Rafter to plate	3 8d	Toenailed
1" brace to each stud and plate	2 8d	Facenailed
1 × 8 sheathing or less, each bearing	2 8d	Facenailed
Wider than 1 × 8 sheathing, each bearing	3 8d	Facenailed

► Nailing Schedule for Wood Flooring

This chart shows the nail sizes and spacing for various wood-flooring materials. For planking wider than 4 inches, #9 or #12 screws should be used for additional fastening.

Flooring	Fastener	Spacing
Tongue-and-Groove Flooring Blind-Nailed (minimum ⅝" subfloor)		
½" × 1½"	1½" machine-driven fastener; 5d screw, cut steel, or wire casing nail	10" apart
⅜" × 1½"	1¼" machine-driven fastener; 4d bright wire casing nail	8" apart
¾"	2" machine-driven fastener; 7d or 8d screw or cut nail	10"–12" apart
¾" × 2¼"	2" machine-driven fastener; 7d or 8d screw or cut nail	10"–12" apart
¾" × 3¼"	2" machine-driven fastener; 7d or 8d screw or cut nail	10"–12" apart
¾" × 3" to 8" plank	2" machine-driven fastener; 7d or 8d screw or cut nail	7"–8" apart into and between joists
Square-Edge Flooring Facenailed		
5⁄16" × 1½"	1" 15-g fully barbed flooring brad	2 nails every 7"
5⁄16" × 2"	1" 15-g fully barbed flooring brad	2 nails every 7"

Source: National Oak Flooring Manufacturers Association.

▶ Wall Fasteners (for hanging or attaching objects to a wall)

Where Fastening	Type of Wall Finish	Light Load	Medium Load	Heavy Load
Into Studs		Picture hanger	Wood screw	Lag screw, or 1 × 2 strip attached at each stud with lag screw
Between Studs	Wallboard	Picture hanger Sheet-metal screw	Expansion bolt Plastic anchor Drive-point hollow-wall fastener Plastic screw-in anchor Toggle bolt	
	Plaster with wood lath	Picture hanger Brad Sheet-metal screw	Sheet-metal screw Expansion bolt Toggle bolt	
Masonry	Brick	Concrete nail Adhesive-backed hanger (for masonry)	Concrete nail Plastic anchor with screw/nail Fluted plastic anchor with screw	Lead shield and lag screw
	Concrete	Concrete nail Adhesive-backed hanger (for masonry)	Concrete nail Plastic anchor with screw/nail Fluted plastic anchor with screw	Lead shield and lag screw Self-anchoring expansion bolt Epoxy bolt system

▶ Wallboard Fasteners

This table shows the spacing required from center to center for each kind of fastener when applying wallboard to walls or ceilings. The table also gives an estimate of the quantity of fasteners needed per 1,000 square feet of wallboard.

Fastener	Spacing		Quantity Needed per 1,000 Square Feet
	Ceilings	Walls	
¼" or 1⅜" annular-ring nail	7"	8"	5¼ lb, 325 nails/lb
6d (1⅞" cement-coated wallboard nail)	7"	8"	6¼ lb, 375 nails/lb
5d (1⅝" cement-coated wallboard nail)	6"	7"	5¼ lb, 365 nails/lb
1¼" Type W wallboard screw	12"	16"	Approx. 1,000 screws
1" Type S wallboard screw	12"	12"	Approx. 875 screws
1⅝" Type S wallboard screw	16"	16"	Approx. 565 screws

▶ Common Wood Screw Options

Length	⅜" to 6"
Gauge	#2 to #16*
Head	Round, flat, bevel
Slot	Standard, Phillips, square-head
Material	Zinc-plated steel, brass-plated steel, solid brass, some stainless steel and chrome-plated steel

*Higher gauge = larger diameter.

Common Lag Screw Options

Length	1" to 12"
Diameter	¼", ⁵⁄₁₆", ⅜", ½"
Head	Square, hex

▶ Size of Screwdriver to Use

Screw Gauge	Standard Driver	Phillips Driver
#1	⅛"	No. 0
2, 3	⅛"	No. 1
4	⁵⁄₃₂"	No. 1
5, 6	³⁄₁₆"	No. 2
7	⁷⁄₃₂"	No. 2
8, 9	¼"	No. 2
10	⁵⁄₁₆"	No. 3
12, 14, 16	⅜"	No. 3
18 & up	½"	No. 4

▶ Bolt Types & Common Sizes

Type	Length	Diameter
Machine	1"–12"	¼"–¾"
Carriage	1"–12"	¼"–¾"
Stove	½"–4"	⅛"–⁵⁄₃₂"

Nuts and usually washers are used with bolts.

▶ Nails per Pound
(common nails)

Nail Size	Quantity	Nail Size	Quantity
2d	845	12d	60
3d	540	16d	45
4d	290	20d	30
6d	165	30d	20
8d	100	40d	17
10d	65	60d	10

▶ Adhesives & Mortars

Type	Description	Uses
Polyvinyl acetate (PVA)	Water-based white glue; inexpensive; sets quickly, dries clear; is not waterproof	Multipurpose; for interior use only
Aliphatic adhesive	Carpenter's wood glue; stronger and slower setting than PVA white glue	Multipurpose; for woodworking
Hide glue	Comes in granules, which must be dissolved in warm water; must be kept warm while using	Woodworking joints and veneers
Powdered casein	Mix 15 minutes before using; somewhat water-resistant	Oily woods such as teak and yew
Resorcinol	Catalyst (two-component) glue	High-moisture situations such as kitchen and bath cabinets; outdoor projects
Epoxy	Catalyst glue	Adhering wood to other materials
Contact cement	Water-resistant glue; solvent-based type is flammable	Bonding veneers and laminates
Construction adhesive	Caulklike adhesive available in cartridges	For reinforcing structural connections: subfloors, sheathing, paneling, decking; interior and exterior types available

For Tile Setting

Type	Description	Uses
Type I mastic	Solvent-based organic tile adhesive; ready to use; flammable	Setting tile in damp areas
Type II mastic	Latex-based organic tile adhesive; easy to clean; nonflammable	Setting tile in dry areas
Dry-set mortar	Portland cement mixed with sand, additives, and water	Setting tile over mortar bed, backer board, or concrete
Latex–portland cement mortar	Portland cement mixed with sand, liquid latex (sometimes diluted with water); water-resistant; high workability	Setting tile in damp areas over mortar or concrete
Epoxy adhesive	Epoxy resin mixed with hardener; works best between 70° and 85° F; expensive	Setting tile over plywood or old resilient floor
Epoxy mortar	Epoxy resin mixed with hardener, sand, and portland cement	Setting tile over uneven surface

▶ Comparison of Caulking Materials

Caulking Material	Life	Application	Remarks
Oil-based	1–2 years	All household surfaces	Least expensive, least durable of all caulks. Oil tends to seep out and may stain unprimed surfaces while drying out caulk itself, leading to shrinking, cracking, and the need for replacement.
Latex-based	3–10 years	Indoors; outside only if painted and not where seal moves or is subject to moisture; only for narrow joints (less than ¼")	Because it is water soluble, should not be used where it will become damp. Insufficiently flexible to withstand frequent expansion and contraction; shouldn't be used on movable joints. May disintegrate on concrete or cement.
Acrylic-based	10 years	All applications, indoors and out; for joints up to ½" × ½"	Durable, fast-curing (about 1 hour), does not stain. Should not be painted.
Butyl rubber	3–10 years	Outdoors, especially on metal and stone; good in places where water may collect, such as eaves and downspouts, since it is water-resistant; only for narrow or moderately narrow joints (less than ½")	Needs no paint. Make take more than a week to cure. Will shrink over time.
Elastomeric (synthetic base: silicone, poly-sulfide, or polyurethane)	20 years +	All applications, but does not adhere to paint; polysulfide doesn't adhere to porous materials	Highly flexible, long-lasting caulk. May be used on large joints. Some types require surface priming before application, and some cannot be painted.
Polyurethane or urea formaldehyde foam	Varies with exposure	Not a true caulking material but excellent for filling large cracks	Available in aerosol cans. Expands tremendously. Must not be exposed to direct sunlight. Excellent as a filler before caulking.

▶ Selecting Exterior Primers

Material	Primer
Painted wood	Oil-based exterior primer
Bare wood (nonstaining)	Latex exterior primer
Bare redwood or cedar	Oil-based exterior primer
Stucco	Latex stucco primer
Vinyl	Latex house paint or oil-based primer
Galvanized steel	Zinc chromate primer
Bright steel	Latex metal primer
Rusted steel	Oil-based rusty-metal primer

▶ Selecting Interior Primers & Sealers

Surface	Product
New wallboard	Latex primer or PVA sealer
New plaster	Latex or alkyd primer
Painted wallboard	Spot-prime stains and repaired patches with white-pigmented shellac; prime old, worn painted surface with latex or alkyd primer
Painted plaster	Same as painted wallboard
Bare wood to be painted	Alkyd enamel sealer or undercoat
Painted wood to be painted	Spot-prime repairs with white-pigmented shellac
Bare wood to be clear-finished	Sanding sealer
Masonry	Alkyd or latex penetrating sealer
Metal	Alkyd enamel sealer or undercoat, with rust inhibitors if needed

▶ Professional Painting Tips

• Use a beveled paint roller to spread paint in corners without buildup.

• Paint heating-system registers and grilles with aerosol paint.

• Avoid overbrushing enamel paint. Working quickly, apply a generous finish coat and brush lightly. Do not try to touch up areas you've already painted. If you have problems, let the paint dry, degloss, and repaint.

• Wipe paint off your paint shield after each use.

• Reduce paint odor by stirring a few drops of vanilla extract into the paint. There are also commercial paint fragrances. Both override normal paint odor.

• Use painting tape to mark borders and other areas where you don't want paint to bleed under the tape edge. This tape has a unique microbarrier edge that prevents such seepage. It also won't leave a sticky residue or remove the undersurface when pulled up.

▶ Which Paint (Sheen) Should You Use?

Area	Best Choice	Acceptable Choice
Ceiling	Flat	Eggshell
Living room	Flat	Eggshell
Hallway	Flat	Eggshell
Bedroom	Flat	Eggshell
Child's room	Eggshell	Semigloss
Bathroom	Semigloss or Gloss	Eggshell
Kitchen	Semigloss or Gloss	Eggshell
Kitchen cabinets	Semigloss or Gloss	Eggshell
Woodwork, windows	Semigloss or Gloss	Eggshell

▶ Sandpaper Selection Guide

40-grit (extra coarse)	For stripping and extraheavy sanding of painted surfaces
60-grit (coarse)	For stripping and heavy sanding of painted surfaces
100-grit (medium)	For first sanding of wallboard and plaster walls, painted walls, and wood surfaces
120-grit (medium fine)	For first and final sanding of wallboard and plaster walls, painted and varnished walls, and wood surfaces
150-grit (fine)	For final sanding of painted and varnished walls and wood surfaces
Medium wallboard	For first sanding of wallboard and plaster walls, and bare or painted screen
Fine wallboard screen	For final sanding of wallboard and plaster walls, painted or bare

▶ Roller Naps

Finish Texture	Surface to Be Painted	Nap Size
Smooth	Walls, floors, finish work, cabinets	³⁄₁₆", ¼"
Medium smooth	Walls	⅜", ½"
Rough	Textured walls, light stucco walls, masonry floors	¾", 1"
Extrarough	Brick, concrete block, masonry, stucco	1¼"

▶ *Disposal of Hazardous Wastes*

We deal with some hazardous wastes almost daily. The chart below lists common waste products and how to dispose of them. If you live in an older home, you may be living with these hazardous substances:

• Radon is a radioactive gas generated in the bedrock of some regions of the United States. Radon can enter a home through its foundation. Contact your state health department for testing information.

• Asbestos was once used extensively in siding, floor tiles, joint compound, and pipe insulation. It is dangerous only if disturbed. Do not cut, sand, or handle material that might contain it.

• Lead was used in paint, water pipes, and pipe solder. Exposed paint predating 1960 should be painted over, and lead pipes should be replaced. Soldered copper joints present little danger.

• Formaldehyde is a gas emitted by many building products—particularly particleboard. Some people are sensitive to the gas and experience coughing, headaches, dizziness, and nausea. Formaldehyde content is now enforced by federal standards. Fortunately, emissions decrease over time. If you suffer from these symptoms, call your state health department for an air test.

This chart provides general guidelines on how to dispose of common household hazardous wastes. Be aware that waste management guidelines will vary considerably from community to community. Before you dispose of anything that you think might be hazardous, check with a local source, such as your local waste collector or waste management agency, your local or state environmental protection department, or the Country Extension Service.

The items checked in the "Special Disposal Problem" column should not be discarded in common trash. Many communities now sponsor annual or semiannual hazardous waste pickup days for these items or have special hazardous waste drop-off facilities where you can take them.

Waste	OK in Trash	Dilute and Flush	Evaporate and Place in Trash	Recycle or Return	Special Disposal Problem
Aerosol cans, empty	X				
Automobile items					
Antifreeze			X		
Battery				X	
Diesel fuel					X
Gasoline					X
Motor oil				X	
Tires					X
Cleaners and solvents					
Brush cleaner					X
Degreaser solvent					X
Drain cleaner		X			
Dry-cleaning fluid			X		
Mildew remover	X				
Oven cleaner		X			
Paints and finishes					
Latex paint			X		
Oil-based paint					X
Mineral spirits			X		
Paint stripper		X			
Paint thinner			X		
Rust remover		X			
Wood preservative					X
Pesticides					
Insecticide					X
Pet pest collar					X
Rat poison					X
Weed killer					X

► Safety

Any construction site has potentail dangers, but you and your helpers can prevent accidents with a little know-how and good judgment. Here are some tips for working with tools and materials and for keeping the work site safe.

Personal Gear. Your eyes are very vulnerable to contact, dust, and chemical inuuries. Always wear safety glasses or goggles when using power tools or when performing any task that could put your eyes at risk, such as spraying wood finisher. Use a dust mask when sawing pressure-treated wood and applying finishes. Unless you are walking on the joists or laying down decking, wear shoes with hard soles that resist nails and other sharp objects.

Power Tools and Extension Cords. When you use power tools while standing on the ground, you're at risk from electrical shock from a malfunctioning tool or cord. To protect yourself, always plug power tools and extension cords into receptacles that have GFCI (ground fault circuit interrupter) protection. You may already have an outdoor GFCI receptacle; if not, look for one in your bathroom and run a cord from it. Otherwise, buy a portable GFCI outlet; you can plug it into an ordinary electrical receptacle (grounded or ungrounded) and plug cords for power tools into it.

Heavy Loads. Don't lift heavy objects yourself. Always have a helper ready to assist in carrying heavy and bulky materials and in lifting deck components into place. The greatest risk is lifting and twisting at the same time. You may want to wear around your waist a special support belt, available at most home-improvement centers.

Ladders. Because of the danger of electrical shock, pay attention to over head power lines when using a ladder outdoors. never stand on the top platform of a stepladder; it is not designed to accommodate loads at its very top. Never climb a ladder higher than a manufacturer recommends, and don't use a ladder with broken parts.

Work Site. Clean up the site regularly. Remove all debris to prevent falls and slips. Don't leave tools and supplies lying where someone can trip over them. Be especially careful about how you handle boards with nails and where you place them; remove protruding nails or bend them over so no one will put a nail through a shoe. Cover footing holes and other excavations with sheets of plywood when you leave the job site. Don't use plastic or tarp for this purpose—they cannot support a person's weight. If the holes are too large for plywood, barricade and fence off the area, and post a "Keep Out" or "No Trespassing" sign.

Utilites. Contact your local utility to come to the site and mark any underground television cable, power, telephone, water, and sewer lines, as well as gas lines, before you begin any digging, especially close to property lines. In addition, if you have a septic tank and leach field, mark the location before you begin to dig.

Electrical Installations. If you are unfamiliar with electrical wiring, contact a licensed professional to do all installations.

Pressure-treated Lumber. Always wear safety glasses and a dust mask when sawing this lumber. After touching it, wash your hands before eating, drinking, or smoking. Dispose of left-over wood and scraps in regular household trash or according to local requirements. never burn pressure-treated lumber—it produces toxic fumes.

Materials and Supplies. Some building supplies, such as preservatives, finishes, and adhesives, are toxic. Read and follow the manufacturer's labels for safe use, storage, and disposal.

Debris. To help protect the environment, follow local regulations or the manufacturer's recommendations when disposing of constructions debris, toxic materials, and other trash.

Tool Safety. Use the right tool for the job. Keep blades sharp. Always read the owner's manual and understand the manufacturer's instructions before using any power tools. Never use power tools outdoors when it's raining or let a power cord connection lie on damp or wet ground.

Clothing. Wear comfortable, loose-fitting garments. Don't wear clothing or jewelry that could get caught on tools. If you are waring loose-fitting long sleeves, roll them up so there's no chance they will be caught by power tools. Wear boots or heavy work shoes during excavation and framing to protect your feet from falling objects and boards with protruding nails. You can wear lighter-weight shoes, if you prefer, during installation of the decking and railings.

Helpers. Instruct your helpers about work safety, including procedures for an emergency. Check your homeowner's policy to be sure that you have adequate coverage if a helper or visitor should be injured during construction.

Contractors. An uninsured contractor is a liability. Always ask for proof of insurance, and don't hire a contractor who does not have proof of coverage for workers and subcontractors.

First-aid Kit. Keep a fully stocked kit on the work site.

Acoustical spray Popcornlike texture sprayed onto ceilings for sound-deadening and decorative purposes.

Acoustic tile Ceiling tile made of fibrous material to absorb sound; usually 12 inches square.

Adhesive Any type of glue, but usually refers to high-strength glues used for installing subflooring, wallboard, paneling, carpet, tile, or mirrors.

Aggregate The rock, gravel, and sand used in making concrete.

Aliphatic adhesive A glue (usually yellow but sometimes white) derived from vinyl acetate compounds that are modified with aliphatic polymers; takes longer to dry but is stronger than ordinary white (PVA) glue; generally referred to as carpenter's wood glue.

Allen wrench Hexagonal, rod-shaped tool for turning allen screws, which have hexagon-shaped depressions in the head.

Anchor bolt A device used to secure a wood mudsill to a concrete or masonry foundation wall or slab.

Annular-ring nail Nail with ribs or rings around the shank for better holding.

Astragal A molding for double doors that attaches to the edge of one of the doors to cover the gap between the two doors when they are closed.

Backbrushing Blending fresh paint into a previously painted area so there is no obvious line.

Baluster A vertical member of a railing, on a staircase, for instance.

Balustrade A railing made up of a top rail, balusters, and often a bottom rail.

Band joist A joist nailed across the ends of floor or ceiling joists; also called a rim joist.

Barge rafter The rafter at the outside edge of a roof overhang; also called verge rafter.

Baseboard A trim board placed at the base of a wall next to the floor.

Base molding A strip of wood used to trim the upper edge of a baseboard.

Base shoe A strip of wood used to trim the bottom edge of the baseboard next to the floor. Also called a carpet strip.

Basen wrench Tool for removing or installing nuts or bolts in hard-to-reach places, usually under sinks.

Batt A precut length of fiberglass insulation.

Battens Narrow pieces of wood used over the joints of wider pieces, especially on board-and-batten siding.

Beam A structural member, usually steel or heavy timber, used to support floor or ceiling joists or rafters; also called girder.

Bearings Movable rings placed over the ends of a motor shaft or other arbor (shaft) to eliminate friction as the shaft rotates in its mount.

Bearing wall A wall that supports floor loads or roof loads, with a girder or foundation support underneath it.

Bevel A surface cut at an angle other than 90 degrees across the edge, end, or face of a piece of wood or other material.

Bevel gauge A measuring tool with two arms that can be adjusted and set at any angle, then used for duplicating that angle.

Blanket insulation Fiberglass, mineral wool, or other insulation in the form of mats or blankets that can be rolled out between joists or studs.

Blocking Short pieces of wood nailed between joists or studs for reinforcement; with joists, similar to bridging.

Bob A weight suspended on a string for testing true vertical alignment.

Bonding agent A liquid adhesive used for enhancing the bond between old concrete and fresh concrete.

Bridging Narrow wood or metal members placed on the diagonal between joists to stiffen the joists and spread the weight load; similar to blocking; also called cross-bracing.

Bull nosing A tile or board with a blunt, rounded edge, used for finishing exposed edges or corners.

Bushing A sleeve inserted into a hole or fitting to protect it from contact with the cable, shaft, or other device set in the hole.

Butt hinge A door hinge attached to the edge of a door and the face of the jamb, so only the knuckles of the hinge show when the door is shut.

Butt joint The junction of two pieces of wood where the end of one meets the side of another at a right angle.

Carpenter's wood glue Also called aliphatic adhesive, it is used for woodworking projects.

Carriage _See_ stringer.

Carriage bolt A bolt with a smooth rounded head.

Casement window   A window with hinges attached to the side of the sash, so it can be opened outward like a door.

Casing   Molding used to trim door and window openings between the jambs and walls, like a picture frame.

Cast polymer   A synthetic material used for sinks, countertops, and shower bases. Also called cultured marble.

Caulk   Viscous material used to seal joints and make them water- and airtight.

Cement   A strong adhesive material; or, one of the components of concrete.

Chair rail   A type of molding installed horizontally along a wall, just above the wainscoting at the same height as a chair back.

Chamfer   A small bevel cut along the edge of a piece of wood.

Channel lock pliers   Large pliers with adjustable parallel jaws.

Chase   An enclosed space, such as inside a finished wall, for running duct work or vent pipes between floors.

Chimney cap   The mortar or concrete top of a chimney that surrounds the flue pipe.

Chimney hood   A metal or concrete cap for keeping rain and snow out of a chimney flue; also called weather cap.

Circular saw   A power saw with a circular blade.

Clapboard   An archaic term for horizontal beveled siding with overlapping boards.

Cleat   A strip of wood fastened to a surface and used as a support or to provide a foothold or handhold.

Cold chisel   A solid-steel chisel intended to be struck with a hammer, used for chipping or breaking metal.

Collar tie   A horizontal board nailed between two rafters to keep them from spreading apart; also called a collar beam or tie beam.

Combination square   An adjustable measuring tool that reads both right angles and 45-degree angles.

Common nail   A standard nail, available in a variety of lengths, used for general construction.

Compressor   A machine that compresses air for use with air tools; or the part of a refrigerator or air conditioner that compresses fluid as part of a cycle to create temperature changes in that fluid.

Concrete   A mixture of cement, aggregate, and water that hardens through a chemical process called hydration.

Concrete block   Hollow blocks made of concrete, joined with mortar for constructing walls and foundations.

Construction adhesive   Strong adhesive, usually packaged in tubes for a caulking gun, used for gluing subfloor panels, insulation, paneling, and other building components together.

Coped joint   A junction in which one end of a piece of molding is cut to fit the shaped face of another. Unlike a miter joint, it doesn't develop a gap between the boards if they shrink.

Coping saw   Handsaw with a very thin blade for cutting tight curves; used to follow molding profiles in making coped joints.

Corbel   A recessed area in the surface of a ceiling.

Corner bead   A strip of formed sheet metal that protects the corner of a stucco or plaster wall.

Cornice   The overhang of a roof at the eaves, usually consisting of a fascia board, soffit, and decorative molding. Or, any decorative member placed at or near the top of a wall.

Counterboring   Deepening the hole for a screw or bolt so the head can be covered and concealed with a plug.

Countersinking   Boring the end of a hole for a screw or bolt so the head can be brought flush with or below the surface. Also, sinking or setting a nail or screw so the head is flush with or slightly below the surface.

Courses   Layers or rows of material, such as shakes or shingles on a roof or bricks in a wall.

Crawl space   The area under a house, usually with a dirt floor and not enough headroom for a basement.

Cripple wall   A low wall between the foundation and first floor; also called pony wall.

Crowbar   A 2- to 3-foot steel bar with a curved hook at one end and a flattened chisel shape at the other end, used for prying up boards and pulling nails.

Crown molding   A convex molding used horizontally wherever an interior angle is to be covered (usually at the top of a wall, next to the ceiling).

Curb   A frame for holding a skylight above the roof.

Cushion-back carpet   Carpet with foam backing attached, which allows it to be glued directly to a floor without a separate pad.

d Represents penny, after "denarius," a Roman coin of low value. Used to designate nail size—for example, 8d nail = eight-penny nail.

Damper A movable flap that closes a chimney flue or ventilating duct to prevent outside air from entering the house.

Dead bolt A door lock with a metal bar that slides into a recessed cavity in the door jamb.

Decking screw A hot-dipped galvanized screw, similar to a wallboard screw but usually in longer lengths, that can be driven without drilling a pilot hole; often used for attaching 2-by decking lumber.

Diverter Valve for changing the flow of water from one outlet to another.

Dolly varden siding Bevel siding with a rabbet in the bottom edge to accept the top edge of the piece below it.

Doorjamb The case that surrounds a door; consists of two upright side pieces called side jambs and a top horizontal piece called a head jamb.

Dormer An extension of attic space jutting out from the main roof.

Double-glazed, -ing Describes a double thickness of glass; two panes separated by a sealed space filled with air, an inert gas such as argon, or a solid transparent gel.

Double-hung window A window with an upper sash and lower sash that slide up and down.

Dovetail joint An interlocking joint created by cutting evenly spaced tapered slots into the end of one board, which creates a row of tooth-like projections that slide into corresponding slots cut into the end of the other board. If the teeth are straight and not tapered, the joint is called a finger joint.

Dowel joint A joint created by inserting dowels into the edges of two boards.

Downspout Vertical pipe, metal or plastic, for carrying water down from roof gutters.

Drip cap A wood molding or metal piece placed above a door or window frame. Causes water to fall beyond the outside edge of the frame.

Drip edge A piece of angled metal placed along the edge of a roof. Prevents water from running down the fascia or cornice.

Drywall *See* Wallboard.

Dry well A hole for collecting water and dispersing it into the ground.

Durable species Trees with wood that is naturally resistant to rot, such as redwood, cedar, and cypress. Does not need to be pressure treated for exterior use.

Eave Lowest overhanging part of a sloping roof, or the area under it.

Efflorescence A white powdery substance that forms on concrete or masonry walls, left by water seeping through the wall and leaching out certain salts.

Epoxy A type of adhesive that is extremely strong and durable, made by mixing a catalyst with a hardener at the time of use.

Expansion bolt A bolt with a tapered end or other device that spreads and grips the sides of a hole as the bolt is tightened; usually used in concrete or masonry; also a hollow-wall fastener consisting of a screw inside a sleeve that expands behind the wall as the screw is tightened.

Face frame The frame that forms the front of a cabinet and shows between the doors and drawers.

Face nailing Driving nails perpendicular to the surface of a board or joint of two pieces of wood. Also called direct nailing.

Fascia board A flat board, typically parallel to the ground, that forms the face of the cornice or eave of a roof; the member to which most gutters are attached.

Feather To smooth patching compound or other mastic material so the thickness tapers to nothing at the outside edges of the filled area.

Fiberglass insulation Insulating material made from glass fibers; may be loosely textured blankets, matted boards, or lightweight beads.

Fiberglass-mesh tape Self-sticking fabric of loosely woven fiberglass.

Field nailing Nailing in the interior portions (not edges) of plywood or other panels.

Finishing nail A thin nail with a small, compact head, available in various lengths; leaves very small impression in the wood surface.

Fire stop A solid, tight-fitting piece of wood or other material placed between studs, joists, or stair stringers to prevent the spread of fire and smoke. In a frame wall, usually a piece of 2x4 cross-blocking between studs.

Flange   A rim that allows one object to be attached to another object.

Flashing   Sheet metal, roofing felt, or other material used at the junction of two surfaces on a roof to prevent the entry of water.

Float   To evenly spread a material such as plaster, mortar, or concrete.

Flue   In a chimney or vent, the opening through which smoke and other gases pass.

Flush   A term of relationship in which the surfaces of two or more objects form a smooth plane.

Flux   An acid-bearing substance spread on a metal surface so solder will bond to the metal.

Foam backer rod   Filler material for building up gaps prior to caulking.

Forms   The temporary structure, usually of wood, that shapes poured concrete.

Foundation seal   Insulation or similar material placed between the top of a foundation wall and the wood sill for sealing out drafts, dust, and air infiltration.

Foundation sill   A 2-by board bolted to the top of a foundation wall for supporting the floor joists or a low cripple wall; also called sill plate or mudsill.

Framing   The skeletal structure of a building; usually wood.

Frass   Fine sawdust produced by wood-boring insects.

Frost line   The lowest depth at which the ground can be expected to freeze in a given region. It determines the required minimum depth for foundation footings and basement wall insulation.

Fur   To build out a wall or ceiling by attaching 1-by strips (furring) to the framing members.

Furring   Narrow strips of wood, usually 1-by strips, attached to walls or ceilings; forms a true surface on which to fasten surface materials; also called strapping.

Gable   The triangular part of an exterior wall formed by the slopes of the roof.

Girder   See Beam.

Glazing   Material, usually glass, used for windowpanes.

Glazing compound   Putty used for sealing the gap between a windowpane and the frame.

Grade   The surface of the ground around a building; the process of scraping and filling the ground to slope or level the surface.

Grout   Cement-based material, sometimes with sand added, for filling joints between tiles; thin concrete mix used to fill hollow cavities of concrete-block wall.

Hardboard   A synthetic wood panel made by chemically converting wood chips to fibers and then forming the panels under heat and pressure.

Hardwood   The wood of broad-leafed, often deciduous, trees such as oak or maple; not a reference to the actual hardness of the wood.

Hawk   A board with a handle on the bottom, used for carrying mortar or plaster; also called a mortarboard or a hod.

HDG (hot-dipped galvanized)   Process for coating metal hardware, such as nails and screws, with zinc to protect them from corrosion.

Header   A horizontal member over a door, window, or other opening that supports the framing members above it (also called a lintel); also, a beam used to support the ends of joists.

Heat-bond tape   Glue-impregnated tape used for seaming carpet.

HEPA (high efficiency particulate air) filter   Used for vacuum cleaners or respirators to remove dust with microscopic fibers.

Hinge knuckle   The part of a hinge where the leaves intertwine; the linked knuckles hold the hinge pin.

Hip   The convex angle formed by the meeting of two roof slopes, usually at a 90-degree angle to each other.

Hollow-wall fastener   A device for hanging objects on a wall; fastens to the wall surface between studs.

Hot-melt glue   Adhesive that is ready for bonding when heated.

Incandescent bulb   A bulb that produces light when electricity heats a metal filament to incandescence; a standard household lamp emitting a yellow-white light.

Jack post   A steel column with a screw jack attached to its top for raising and shoring beams.

Jalousie   A type of window with a number of narrow horizontal panes that pivot together.

Jamb   The frame surrounding a door or window, consisting of two vertical pieces called side jambs and a top horizontal piece called a head jamb.

Jigsaw   A portable power saw with a narrow reciprocating blade, usually used for cutting curves; also called saber saw.

Joist   One of a series of parallel members, usually 2-by lumber, that support a floor or ceiling.

King stud   In wall framing, a full-length stud on either side of a door or window that, together with the trimmer stud, frames the opening.

Lag screw   A screw, usually large, with a square or hexagonal head, designed to be driven with a wrench.

Lally column   A steel post filled with concrete, used in basements to support heavy house loads.

Laminate   A thin veneer, often plastic, used as a surfacing material and intended to be bonded to a solid substrate; to build up a board or panel by gluing or fastening several members together.

Laminated glass   Safety glass consisting of two panes adhered to an intermediate layer of tough plastic material.

Lap joint   A woodworking joint in which both pieces lap over each other, usually at right angles, and one or both pieces are notched to accept the mating piece.

Lath   A building material of metal, gypsum, wood, or other material that is used as a base for plaster or stucco; thin strips of wood.

Ledger   A board or strip of wood fastened to the side of a framing member such as a wall, on which other framing members (usually joists) rest or to which they are attached.

Level   Parallel to the surface of a body of still water. Also, a device used to determine when surfaces are level or plumb.

Lintel   See Header.

Louver   One of a series of parallel slats in a window or door arranged to permit ventilation and to limit or exclude light, vision, or weather. Louvers can be stationary or movable.

Low-E (low-emissivity) glass   Used for energy conservation; has a coating on one side, or a film suspended between two panes, of a microscopically thin layer of metal oxides that admits visible light but reflects heat waves.

Masonry   Any construction made of stone, bricks, concrete blocks, poured concrete, and similar materials. Also, the technique of building this kind of construction.

Mastic   A viscous material used as an adhesive for setting tile or resilient flooring.

Media pad   An evaporation pad in a humidifier that wicks moisture from the reservoir and releases it into the air.

Mineral spirits   A petroleum distillate used as a solvent and thinner, primarily with oil-based paints and varnishes.

Miter   Usually a 45-degree cut, but can be a cut at any angle that is matched by a cut of the same angle.

Miter joint   A joint between two boards with matching miter cuts at the ends, used to conceal the end grain of both boards.

Molding   A strip of wood with a decorative profile cut along the edges or face of the wood, used to cover exposed joints or edges, or as a decoration.

Molly bolt   See Expansion bolt.

Mortar   A mixture of sand and portland cement; used for bonding bricks, blocks, tiles, or stones.

Mortise and tenon joint   A woodworking joint made by cutting a mortise, or hole, in one piece and, on the other piece, a tenon, or projection, to fit into the mortise.

Mortise dead bolt   A dead bolt that fits into a mortise bored into the doorjamb, rather than into a surface-mounted metal pocket.

MSHA-NIOSH (Mine Safety and Health Administration–National Institute for Occupational Safety and Health)   A regulatory agency responsible for setting safety standards for certain occupational practices and equipment.

Mudsill   See Foundation sill.

Mullion   The vertical divider between the windows in a unit that is made up of two or more windows.

Muntin   A strip of wood that divides a window sash into separate panes.

Needle nose pliers   Pliers with a long, very slim nose.

Newel   The main post at the foot of a stairway. Also, the central support of a winding or spiral flight of stairs.

Nosing   The part of a stair tread that projects over the riser. Also, the rounded edge on any board.

OC (on center)   Indication that the distance between repetitive structural members, such as studs or joists, is measured from centers, rather than edges, of the members. (The measurement from the edge of one member to the closest edge of the next member is referred to as span.)

Orbital sander   An electric sander that vibrates in a tight oscillating pattern (as opposed to the wider circular pattern of a disk sander).

O-ring A rubber ring used as a gasket and having a circular cross section.

Particleboard A form of composite board or panel made of wood chips bonded with adhesive.

Penny *See* d.

Phillips head Describes a screwdriver with an X-shaped tip or a screw with an X-shaped slot.

Pilaster A vertical structure that protrudes from the face of a wall for structural or decorative purposes; often resembles a column embedded into the facade.

Pilot hole A hole drilled to guide a screw or nail; minimizes splitting and provides the optimum gripping surface for screw threads.

Plate A horizontal framing member at the bottom or top of a stud wall. The soleplate is at the bottom; the top plate is above the studs; and a cap plate is above the top plate.

Plumb Truly vertical; exactly perpendicular to a level surface.

Plumber's putty Putty used when installing plumbing fixtures for sealing drain fittings, gaps around faucets, and similar watertight joints.

Plywood A wood product made up of thin layers, or veneers, of wood bonded together with adhesive, usually at right angles to each other.

Pointing Filling and finishing the mortar joints of brickwork.

Polycarbonate A tough, transparent plastic that, in sheet form, can be used as a shatterproof windowpane.

Post A vertical support member, usually made up of only one piece of lumber or a metal pipe or I beam.

Pressure-treated lumber Lumber that is rot-resistant due to preservatives injected into it under pressure; used in applications—such as outdoor structures or foundation sills—where the wood may be in contact with the ground, the weather, concrete, or masonry.

Primer Paint formulated for coating a surface so it is properly sealed and will provide maximum adhesion for the finish coat, or topcoat, of paint; when applied, it is referred to as the undercoat.

Pry bar A short, flat, curved bar that is used for prying up boards and pulling nails.

PVA (polyvinyl acetate) Used in primers designed to cover bare plaster or wallboard, and in white glue.

Rabbet A square-edged channel cut along the edge of a board, similar to a dado or groove.

Rafters The main framing members that support the roof.

Rebar Reinforcing bars or rods for concrete and concrete-block work.

Reciprocating sander A finish sander in which the pad vibrates back and forth.

Reciprocating saw A heavy-duty handheld power saw with a long slender blade that vibrates back and forth; used for demolition and rough framing.

Resilient flooring Thin floorcovering material, such as vinyl or linoleum, installed as tiles or in large sheets.

Ridge The horizontal line where two roof slopes meet. Usually the highest place on the roof.

Ridge beam A large board, running the length of a roof, that provides support to the upper ends of the rafters when they have no collar ties or ceiling joists to keep them from spreading apart.

Ridge board A 1-by or 2-by board running the length of a roof, against which pairs of rafters abut.

Rim joist A joist nailed across the ends of the floor or ceiling joists; also called band joist.

Rip cut A cut made by a saw along the same direction as the grain.

Rip saw A saw for cutting boards in the same direction as the grain.

Rise In a stairway, the vertical measurement from one tread to the next. In a roof, the vertical measurement from the top of the wall plates to the tip of the ridge.

Rough lumber Lumber as it comes from the saw, before it is surfaced.

Rout To cut grooves, mortises, or rabbets into a board, or to shape the edges, usually with a router.

Router A power tool that uses a variety of interchangeable bits to rout grooves of various sizes and shapes or to cut various shapes into the edges of boards.

Saber saw *See* Jigsaw.

Safety glass Glass, such as tempered or laminated glass, that won't break into sharp shards when shattered.

Sash The frame that holds the glass panes in a window; either movable or fixed.

Screw terminal A means of connecting wiring to electrical devices using a threaded screw.

Scuttle   A hatch for access into an attic.

Setscrew   A screw that is tightened against a blade, bit, shaft, rod, or other component to hold it in place.

Shake   A thick wood shingle, usually edge-grained.

Sheathing   Boards or panels, such as plywood or structural hardboard, fastened to the roof framing or wall framing, to which the roofing or siding is applied; often serves a structural function for earthquake or wind resistance.

Sheet-metal screw   A screw with a sharp point and deep threads that extend from tip to head, used for attaching pieces of sheet metal.

Shim   A thin piece of wood or metal, often wedge-shaped, inserted between parts of a structure to bring them into alignment.

Shiplap siding   Horizontal board siding with V joints and rabbeted bottom edges that allow the boards to lie flush against the sheathing or framing.

Shoring   Temporary support of a floor, ceiling, or roof.

Sill   The bearing member in the structural framing that rests on the foundation wall. Also, the member forming the lowest side of an opening, such as a doorsill or windowsill.

Sill plate   _See_ Foundation sill.

Sister   To reinforce a joist or other framing member by nailing a board of the same size to it.

Sizing   A liquid coating traditionally used to prepare wall surfaces for wallcoverings; usually not necessary when a primer undercoat is used.

Slab   A concrete floor, usually 4 inches thick and reinforced with heavy wire mesh.

Sleepers   Boards, usually pressure-treated 2x4s, that are attached to a concrete slab for supporting a wood subfloor.

Soffit   An overhead, boxlike enclosure. On the exterior of the house, it encloses the area beneath an overhanging roof eave. In interior spaces, it is a dropped section of ceiling that may conceal obstructions.

Softwood   The wood of conifers such as Douglas fir, pine, and redwood; the term has no reference to the actual hardness of the wood.

Soleplate   In a stud wall, the bottom horizontal member, which is nailed to the subfloor; also called a bottom plate.

Solid-surface material   A type of synthetic countertop material that has the same color and texture all the way through, rather than a finish coat applied over a core of a different material.

Spackling compound   Puttylike patching material for plaster walls.

Spade bit   A drill bit for boring wood that has a flat cutting blade with a pointed end, rather than a twisted or drum shape.

Spalling   The spontaneous flaking or popping off of small chips from a concrete surface due to freezing.

Spark arrester   A metal screen for chimney tops that prevents embers from escaping with the smoke.

Square   A term used to describe an angle of exactly 90 degrees. Also, a device used to measure such an angle. Also, a unit of measure equaling 100 square feet used in describing amounts of roofing or siding material.

Square-drive screw   A screw with a square indentation on the head for driving with a square-shanked driver; similar to a hex-head or Phillips-head screw; also called Robertson screw.

Stile   A vertical framing member in a panel door, wainscoting, or a paneled wall.

Stock   Wood or other material that is cut and shaped for joining.

Stool   The horizontal shelf on the interior of the bottom of a window.

Stove bolt   A bolt with a screw head and a threaded shank to which a nut can be attached.

Stringer   In a stairway, the supporting member to which the treads and risers are fastened. Also called a carriage.

Stud   In wood-frame construction, the vertical 2x4 boards in a wall, usually spaced 16 inches apart.

Subfloor   Boards, plywood, or other panels attached to the joists, which provide a base for the finish floor.

Substrate   Backing material used under a tile or laminate countertop installation.

Sump   A pit in the lowest area of a basement floor for collecting water from the surface of the floor.

Sump pump   A pump for removing water from a sump.

Surfaced lumber   Lumber planed smooth, usually on all four sides.

Taping knife/blade   _See_ Wallboard knife.

Thin-set adhesive   Cement-, latex-, or epoxy-based tile-setting adhesive that must be mixed with a liquid; stronger and more heat- and water-resistant than organic adhesives.

Thumb latch   A type of safety window lock.

Toenailing   Driving nails obliquely through the end of one board into another, when the end of the first board abuts the face of the second.

Toggle bolt   A hollow-wall fastener with a device on the end that, when inserted through a small hole in the wall, spreads out like two wings and prevents the bolt from being pulled back through the hole.

Tongue-and-groove boards
Interlocking siding or flooring boards with a narrow projection milled along one edge that fits into a matching groove cut along the edge of the next board.

Tread   In a stairway, the horizontal surface on which a person steps.

Trimhead screw   A wallboard screw with a very small head.

Trimmer stud   A stud that supports a header for an opening in a wall.

Truss   An assembly of wood or metal members that serves as a relatively lightweight but strong framework to take the place of rafters and joists in the support of a roof or floor.

Try square   A small square used to scribe cut lines on boards or to test right angles.

TSP (trisodium phosphate)   A powerful cleaning compound that is mixed with water and used for scrubbing walls and ceilings in preparation for painting.

Twist drill   A conventional screw-like drill bit, intended for boring metal but often used on wood.

Undercoater   A primer specified for preparing wall surfaces for wallcoverings.

Underlayment   The material placed under the finish coverings of roofs or floors to provide waterproofing as well as a smooth, even surface on which to apply finish material.

Underliner   Canvaslike fabric for smoothing walls prior to applying wallcoverings.

Underwriter's knot   A knot used to tie two insulated conductors at the terminals inside an electrical plug or fixture; used to relieve strain on the terminal connection.

Urethane   A chemical compound that adds durability to floor finishes, paints, and other coatings.

Utility knife   A knife with replaceable blades that resemble single-edged razor blades.

Valley   A roof depression formed where two roof slopes converge.

Valve grease   Lubricant for the internal parts of a faucet or valve.

Vapor barrier   Plastic sheeting or similar material used to block moisture; applied to framing before wallboard is installed or over bare ground in the crawl space. When applied under wallboard, it prevents moist air in the living space from penetrating into the wall or ceiling cavity where it may condense and be trapped in cold weather.

Veneer   A thin layer of wood or other material, usually one that has beauty or value, that is applied for economy or appearance on top of an inferior surface.

Wainscoting   Decorative paneling that covers only the lower portion of a wall.

Wallboard   Panels used for finishing interior walls and ceilings, consisting of a core of gypsum plaster covered on both sides by layers of paper. Also called gypsum wallboard, gypboard, drywall, and Sheetrock®, a trade name.

Wallboard knife   A broad, flat putty knife for applying and smoothing wallboard compound; also called taping knife.

Wallboard screw   A type of screw intended to be driven with an electric screwdriver or drill, with a sharp point and deep, sharp threads that extend from point to head; used for many applications.

Wallboard tape   Nonadhesive, perforated paper tape for covering wallboard joints.

Washing soda   A cleaning product for walls and other surfaces, sold as a powder; known by the trade name Spic and Span®.

WD-40®   Trade name for an all-purpose lubricant.

Weather stripping   Strips of metal, plastic foam, or other materials placed around doors and windows to keep out air, moisture, or dust.

Weep holes   Small holes at the bottom of a concrete or masonry retaining wall that allow moisture trapped behind the wall to escape.

Wicking   The process of water being transferred through a porous material by capillary action.

Wood screw   A screw for fastening wood pieces. It has tapered threads and a section of unthreaded shank between the threads and head. The head can be rounded, beveled, or flat.

Wrecking bar   A long steel bar with a point at one end and a flattened chisel shape at the other, for demolition work.

Note: Page numbers in italic type
  refer to illustrations.

U.S./Metric Measure Conversion Chart

		Formulas for Exact Measures			**Rounded Measures for Quick Reference**		
	Symbol	**When you know:**	**Multiply by:**	**To find:**			
Mass	oz	ounces	28.35	grams	1 oz		= 30 g
(weight)	lb	pounds	0.45	kilograms	4 oz		= 115 g
	g	grams	0.035	ounces	8 oz		= 225 g
	kg	kilograms	2.2	pounds	16 oz	= 1 lb	= 450 g
					32 oz	= 2 lb	= 900 g
					36 oz	= 2¼ lb	= 1000 g (1 kg)
Volume	pt	pints	0.47	liters	1 c	= 8 oz	= 250 ml
	qt	quarts	0.95	liters	2 c (1 pt)	= 16 oz	= 500 ml
	gal	gallons	3.785	liters	4 c (1 qt)	= 32 oz	= 1 liter
	ml	milliliters	0.034	fluid ounces	4 qt (1 gal)	= 128 oz	= 3¾ liter
Length	in.	inches	2.54	centimeters	⅜ in.		= 1.0 cm
	ft	feet	30.48	centimeters	1 in.		= 2.5 cm
	yd	yards	0.9144	meters	2 in.		= 5.0 cm
	mi	miles	1.609	kilometers	2½ in.		= 6.5 cm
	km	kilometers	0.621	miles	12 in. (1 ft)		= 30.0 cm
	m	meters	1.094	yards	1 yd		= 90.0 cm
	cm	centimeters	0.39	inches	100 ft		= 30.0 m
					1 mi		= 1.6 km
Temperature	°F	Fahrenheit	⅝ (after subtracting 32)	Celsius	32° F		= 0° C
					68° F		= 20° C
	°C	Celsius	⁹⁄₅ (then add 32)	Fahrenheit	212° F		= 100° C
Area	in.^{2}	square inches	6.452	square centimeters	1 in.^{2}		= 6.5 cm^2
	ft^2	square feet	929.0	square centimeters	1 ft^2		= 930 cm^2
	yd^2	square yards	8361.0	square centimeters	1 yd^2		= 8360 cm^2
	a.	acres	0.4047	hectares	1 a.		= 4050 m^2